THE BANKER'S HANDBOOK OF

LETTERS AND LETTER WRITING

A Complete Collection of Time-Saving Letters that WORK

3RD EDITION

JEFFREY L. SEGLIN

BANKERS PUBLISHING COMPANY
PROBUS PUBLISHING COMPANY
Chicago, Illinois
Cambridge, England

ISBN 1-55738-326-X

Printed in the United States of America

EB

1 2 3 4 5 6 7 8 9 0

To my father, Lester Seglin, and my best friend, Jim Lewis, whose criticism, advice, and compassion have enriched my work and my life.

From quiet homes and first beginning,
Out of the undiscovered ends,
There's nothing worth the wear of winning,
But laughter and the love of friends.

—Hilaire Belloc

Contents

Acknowledgments

Many people have helped complete this book. Without each of these people, the book would not have been possible. Of particular help in supplying letters were Robert Behrens; Wesley K. Blair III, Cambridge Savings Bank, Cambridge, Massachusetts; Gayle Ciaramicoli, Home National Bank, Milford, Massachusetts; Alexander Colby, State Street Bank, Boston; Edward Coleman; Bethany Coleman; Patricia Collins, Home National Bank, Milford, Massachusetts; Susan Comeau, State Street Bank, Boston; Suzanne Conlin, Bank of Boston, Boston; Gordon B. Cooper, Bank of Virginia, Hampton, Virginia; Carl Coordt, Imperial Bank, Los Angeles; John Gallinagh, New England Federal Savings Bank, Wellesley, Massachusetts; W. Loren Gary; Joan van Gorkon, Bank of Wheaton, Wheaton, Illinois; Lane Goss, State Street Bank, Boston; Catherine Hegan, Bank of Boston, Boston; Paul Jannott, Bank of Commerce, Warren, Michigan; Ellen Langley, Dollar Savings Bank, Pittsburgh; Robert Langley, Dollar Savings Bank, Pittsburgh; K. Linford Loesch, Meridian Bancorp, Philadelphia; C. Eugene Looper; Norman Lubin, State Street Bank, Boston; John MacDonald, Home National Bank, Milford, Massachusetts; Michael Mazzocco, Busey First National Bank, Urbana, Illinois; Gerald Mueller, New England Federal Savings Bank, Wellesley, Massachusetts; Howard Palay; Patti Palay; Deborah Robbins, State Street Bank, Boston; William M. Schwab, Bristol Savings Bank, Bristol, Connecticut; Jeffrey Schwartz; Bernard Stock, Home National Bank, Milford, Massachusetts; Mark Stoeckle; John Taylor; Don Wright, Allied Lakewood Bank, Dallas; and Ralph Zelinsky. Mr. Mueller was also kind enough to review the contents of the second edition and provide insightful advice that is reflected in this third, revised edition.

Others who supplied leads and useful information were: Rachel Victoria Berg; Lesley Crabb; Joan Kenney; Melvin Mortimer, owner of Mortimer's Locksmith in Norge, Virginia; Donna Reiss, the director of Tidewater Community College's Writing Center; Mrs. Blanche Roen; and Mary Ann Tierney.

Friends and colleagues who offered support, encouragement, and advice were: Lisa T. Gary; Larry, Carol, and Rebecca Grimes; Peter Kacmarek, who as editor for the third edition of this book, added new life and value to it; Helen Louise McGuffie; David, Brian, and Lauren Palay; Robert Roen, who conceived and developed the first edition of this book; my mother, Beverly Seglin, who ten years ago welcomed me and several hundred letters into her home and gave me the space to meet the deadline for the first edition; and my wife, Nancy Seglin, whose insight as an editor is only surpassed by her patience and love.

Introduction

Bankers know as well as any other businessperson the importance of effective letter writing. You can't have a good banking relationship with customers if they don't know what you're trying to relate to them in a letter. The services of a bank cannot be marketed if a prospective customer is baffled by the service described. How can a lender expect repayment on a loan when, because of a muddled letter, the person who borrowed the money can't even understand the terms of the loan?

Letter writing is crucial to the success of every banker. Without letter writing skills, the banker's effectiveness is stymied.

My objective in *The Banker's Handbook of Letters and Letter Writing* is to help you to write effective letters. Ineffective letters are a waste of time and money. This realization should be enough to convince every banker of the need to be a good letter writer. Letters may not seem like the crux of the banking industry, but if you consider that effectively written letters can increase the quality of working relationships and the quantity of business your bank can attract, and decrease wasted hours and money, you can begin to see the importance of learning to write letters well.

You should be prepared to approach this book with one chief goal in mind—to learn how to write effective letters. You also might approach this book with the idea that although letter writing is not a simple skill, with practice you can become a good letter writer. Once you learn the basics and put them into practice, your letters will get better and begin to flow more easily.

Before you begin to write more effective letters, you must learn what makes up a good letter. The first part of this book takes you step-by-step through the basics of letter writing. A letter is only effective if you know the proper mechanics involved in a letter's structure and appearance. All letters take basic formats; these are explained in the first part of the book. Grammar, punctuation, spelling, and language usage are important to pay attention to if your letter is to be understood and well-received by its reader. You needn't fear an extensive course in grammar here. What you'll receive are the fundamental common-sense rules of grammar which are easily learned and should become natural not only to your letter writing, but also to all of your other writing as well.

There is also a chapter in part one on word processing. While it won't answer all of the technical questions you might have about the uses of computers in a banking environment, it will guide you toward effectively using both the information and the letters in *The Banker's Handbook of Letters and Letter Writing* on your bank's word processing system.

The second part of *The Banker's Handbook of Letters and Letter Writing* consists of 345 sample letters, broken into categories reflecting the various aspects of banking. Each chapter also consists of an analysis of the strong points of the sample letters. All of the sample letters collected here have been written for actual use by professionals in banking. Names of people or corporations have been changed, but the content remains essentially unaltered. The letters have been chosen to serve as models of good letters resembling those you may have to write in your everyday banking business. You can adapt the letters to meet your needs as well as use them as a touchstone to aim toward in your letter writing.

In my research for *The Banker's Handbook of Letters and Letter Writing*, I've pored through hundreds of letters to find those that have the quality and diversity to make this book a useful tool for you when you are writing letters.

Many of the letters in part two can be used as form letters or as prototype letters on a word processing system (see Chapter 6). If names, numbers, and addresses are changed in these letters, they can be used for many different customers.

All of the letters in part two are models of good letters. By reading these letters you will learn how effective letters in various aspects of banking should be written.

The figure legends to each of the sample letters give you a concise description of the letter's purpose. The narrative interspersed among the letters gives you a brief analysis of each letter's strong points.

I don't expect many readers to diligently read through every sample letter in every chapter of part two. Read those sample letters that can best help you improve or increase the scope of your letter writing. Study these letters and, if you apply the basics learned in part one, you'll be well on your way to writing better, more effective letters.

The four appendixes to this book consist of helpful lists and rules for you to refer to in your letter writing. Appendices I, II, III, and IV feature many items which can make your letter writing a bit more pleasant and a less arduous task. All four appendices are arranged alphabetically for easy reference.

The words to watch in Appendix I are by no means all-inclusive of every word ever used incorrectly. The list does, however, include some that are either tricky to use or often are used incorrectly. If you have a question about how a word or phrase should be used, check Appendix I. If it is not included in the appendix, you will find a good reference to consult listed in the bibliography.

Appendix II lists several rules of punctuation which cause confusion or problems in correspondence. Appendix III is divided into two categories. The first gives a list of two-letter state abbreviations. The second lists common abbreviations. Abbreviations should be used sparingly in your correspondence. Occasionally you will receive a letter or memorandum which contains an abbreviation. The list in appendix III will help you decipher some common abbreviations used by bankers.

Appendix IV, the Grammar Hotline Directory, consists of names of colleges and universities across the country which offer help with grammar problems to people who call. The list is categorized alphabetically by state. The information given consists of: the city in which the hotline is located, as well as a zip code for that city; the college or university sponsoring the hotline; the phone number and name of the hotline; the hours of operation; and the contact at the hotline. If you're faced with grammar problems, consider turning to one of these hotlines.

The annotated bibliography directs you to and gives you a brief synopsis of books and publications that may be of use to you in increasing the effectiveness of your letters.

As with all things, perfection can only be reached with practice. If you apply the basics learned in the first part of *The Banker's Handbook of Letters and Letter Writing*, and study the examples presented in the second, your letter writing skills will become more effective. The end result will be the ability to have your readers think that what took much thought and planning on your part flowed smoothly and effortlessly.

Part 1
The Basics

Planning the Letter

1

Planning is a key factor in the accomplishment of any goal. Letter writing is no exception. To successfully construct a clear, effective letter, a good plan is necessary.

The following three steps are essential in planning any letter:

1. Researching the facts
2. Analyzing the subject and reader
3. Knowing your objectives and how to accomplish them

If you follow these steps as you are planning to write any letter, you should find that your letters will be clear, well-received, and successful in achieving your desired goal.

Researching the Facts

Before you write a letter, it makes sense to know what you plan to talk about in that letter. If you wing it and write whatever comes into your head, chances are you will end up with a confused, ineffective letter.

Get the facts together prior to putting together a first draft of a letter. If you have corresponded with this customer before, examine all previous correspondence. Depending upon the volume of this correspondence, and assuming the customer to be a fairly good letter writer, you can learn a good deal about the personality, interests, and values of the person to whom you are writing.

As you examine previous correspondence, jot down a note or two about some key traits you discover about this customer. For example, you have gone through your correspondence file for a customer named Sam Johnson. You note that the following general items appear in letter after letter from him:

commitment to existing business relationships

places importance on personal relationship between banker and customer

often suggests ideas for improving business practices and banker/customer relationship

strong interest in reducing costs

After you have collected some facts on your customer, you should direct your attention to the topic or topics to be covered in the letter. Once again, the simplest and ultimately most effective thing to do is to take a piece of paper and write down those topics you plan to cover in the letter. Under each topic you might write some examples or a few words recalling a discussion you might have had with your customer about one of these topics.

Let's stick with the example of customer Sam Johnson. You have had a business meeting with Mr. Johnson and you want to write a follow-up letter. You already know something about his personality from the earlier research you did. You decide you want to cover the following topics in your letter:

thanks for meeting

his idea for a lock box
    speeds up collections
    cost-effectiveness

appreciate his views on banking
    loyalty to existing banking relationships
    personal relationship

arrange for another meeting

The order in which you write down ideas for topics is unimportant at this point in the planning stage. The main thing is to make sure the letter covers the topics that will let customer Johnson know you are writing to him about issues that are of concern to him.

Timeliness is extremely important in any letter, including the one we are using as an example. You want to get a letter to your customer while the topics being discussed are still fresh in both your and your customer's mind. As you are doing your research, determine how long discussion has been taking place about the topics to be included in your letter and what, if any, action has already been taken.

Analyzing the Subject and Reader

You've completed your research. You know something about the person to whom you are writing. You have a good idea what topics will be covered in the letter. The information you have gathered must now be analyzed so you can logically organize it for the best results.

An outline is a good method of organizing topics and visualizing the order in which you wish to discuss these topics in the letter. You can order the letter chronologically, by order of importance of the topics discussed, or whatever order is most effective. Your choice of order is flexible, but it must be logical and you should not mix thoughts in sentences or drop them before they are completed.

Continuing with the example of the follow-up letter to Sam Johnson, you might decide to outline your letter as follows:

Paragraph 1. a. Thanks for meeting
b. Appreciate view on banking
loyalty to existing banking relationships
importance of personal relationships
Paragraph 2. a. Idea for lock box
speed up collections
cost-effectiveness
Paragraph 3. a. Arrange another meeting

You'll notice that the only difference between this rough outline and the list of topics jotted down earlier is the order of topics. The ordering of topics is an important function of the outline.

With a letter as simple as the follow-up letter to Sam Johnson being written here, it is perfectly acceptable to outline the topics in your head and go directly to the rough draft of your letter. The important thing in writing an effective letter is not writing a good outline, but rather being able to write a letter that is ordered logically and is structured well enough for you to know where it is going. If you can do this in your head, fine. You may have to work out some kinks in the rough draft, but if you can save yourself some time and still write an effective letter, the more power to you. As your letters become more elaborate, you may find that working with a written outline helps to remind you of all the facts and the best order in which to present them.

When you analyze the subject matter to be covered in your letter, you should also keep in mind the research you did on your customer. Your research can serve as a brief analysis of your customer's personality, interests, and values. What is important to you may not necessarily be as important to your reader. Your letter must be aimed toward your reader. As a result, it is important to keep all of your research in mind as you outline and write your letter.

With outline in hand or in your head, you can now begin to write your letter. Keep in mind that, in order to be as clear as possible, you should write simple sentences, avoiding any unnecessary information. Don't try to combine ideas in sentences. In order to get your point across most clearly, write about one thing at a time.

Avoid any excess in the sentences of your letter. If you start rambling, you are bound to get off the track and lose your reader. Remember, to be effective in letter writing you must be able to grab your reader's attention and make that reader react positively to whatever it is you are writing about.

Another important thing to remember is that ideas placed at the beginning or end of a paragraph will often stand out most clearly to the reader. This placement of ideas is a good practice to use for emphasis in your letter writing.

Knowing Your Objectives and How to Accomplish Them

Set an objective for every letter you write. As you choose the order of each paragraph and the wording of each sentence, you should keep your goal clearly in mind.

The research you did before beginning to write your customer can help you decide how best to write the letter that will be most effective in getting your reader to react the way you would like. Your research can help to make you familiar with your reader and what might have moved that reader to act in the past.

The objectives of your follow-up letter to Sam Johnson are to thank him and to attract his business to your bank. You know the value he places on loyalty to existing banking relationships and a personal relationship between banker and customer, so you might express your understanding of these values. It also might be a good idea, knowing Mr. Johnson's ability to make good suggestions, to react to a suggestion he might have made at your original meeting. Since your goal is to attract his business to your bank, closing your letter by telling him you will call him to set up another meeting is a good approach. Such a closing lets Mr. Johnson know you are appreciative of his ideas and anxious to meet with him again to discuss the possibility of your bank handling his business. Consider the following example of the complete text of a letter to Johnson:

> Thank you for an interesting meeting yesterday. I appreciate the time and information you shared with me. I can understand your sense of loyalty to existing banking relationships and the priority you place on knowing and being known by your banker.
>
> During our discussion you suggested that a lock box arrangement might speed up the collection of cash available for investment. I would like to investigate this possibility and estimate the dollar benefit to your company, considering today's high yields on monies invested for even one additional day.
>
> I will give you a call early next week to arrange lunch together as you suggested. Thanks again for your time. I look forward to doing business together.

Although Johnson is a fictitious customer, the example of the letter sent to him is one that was actually used by a banker as a follow-up letter to a customer. Judging from the final letter, the research, analysis, and knowledge of objectives were well handled by the letter writer. The result of careful planning in the construction of a letter, such as in the example above, is the increased chance of a positive response from the letter's reader.

Attitude: Components of an Effective Letter 2

Planning by itself is not enough to assure you of a positive response from your reader. There are, however, essential components of any letter that *can* multiply the chances of its effectiveness.

Before you begin to worry about the basic mechanics of a letter (structure, appearance, and grammar), think seriously about the attitude you wish to convey. Your attitude is conveyed through your choice of language, tone, and focus of attention. Each of these individual components is as important as anything else that goes into making up a successful letter.

The attitude conveyed in your letter can make the difference between a letter that is tossed aside and one that is read, understood, and reacted to favorably. It is basically very simple to convey a reader-oriented attitude. Remember as you write your letters that there is a specific reader you are addressing. Your language, tone, and focus of attention must capture the reader's interest for your letter to be successful.

Language—Clearness vs. Ambiguity

Language is a means of communication. This may seem like a foolishly simple statement to make, but remember that for communication to be completed successfully a sender must send his or her message so that the receiver not only receives, but also *understands* the message as well. If language is not used clearly and accurately, the communication process cannot be successfully completed.

A simple rule to remember is that the English you use in your everyday banking business should be the same good English used by people in all walks of life. Granted, there are terms intrinsic to the banking industry, but there is not a special type of "banking English" to be learned and used when writing bank letters. Good English is good English.

Be clear and straightforward in your letters. Write what you mean. Don't write in circles making your reader guess what you mean.

Take the following example of a writer who wants to tell a customer about an important organization:

> My correspondence was initiated to inform you of the high caliber programs and activities of an organization in which I have enjoyed being involved over the past few years. The County Business Association has served to keep me informed of, and actively involved in, the current political and economic issues affecting small businesses through its monthly breakfast meetings with interesting and impressive speakers, its newsletter on legislative activities in Washington, and several other programs outlined in the attached letter.

There are many problems with the above example. Let's start by examining the clarity and directness of the statement. Since the writer of the letter wants to inform the reader about an important organization, why didn't the writer come right out and do so by writing:

> The County Business Association, an organization in which I have been involved for the past few years, offers high caliber programs and activities.

In the writer's version of the letter, it is not until the second sentence of the paragraph that we even learn the name of the important organization. If you are writing about a particular subject, and that subject happens to be an organization, why not get its name right up front so the reader might enjoy learning about it throughout the rest of the letter, instead of being left in suspense? If you come right out and say what you mean not only are you going to grab your reader's attention right away, but you also stand a stronger chance of convincing your reader that he or she should go on reading and find out more about what it is you have to say.

It is best to be as direct as possible in your letter writing. If you can say what you have to say in five words instead of ten, then by all means do so. The idea is to get your message across clearly and directly.

Avoid the use of pompous or inflated language in your letters. It may sound lofty to write "My correspondence was initiated to inform you of..." but you are not writing for the purpose of seeing how you can turn a catchy phrase on the page. You are writing to communicate with your reader. You should write what you mean.

Sometimes when we think we are communicating clearly in a letter, the reader receives a different message from the one we intended. If such ambiguity is present in our letters, we can never be sure that the reader will understand our message. Ambiguous language is another problem with the example paragraph from the letter on the previous page. The writer wrote:

> The County Business Association has served to keep me informed of, and actively involved in, the current political and economic issues affecting small businesses through its monthly breakfast meetings with interesting and impressive speakers, its newsletter on legislative activities in Washington, and several other programs outlined in the attached letter.

The writer did not mean to suggest that the current political and economic issues were affecting small businesses as a result of the County Business Association's monthly breakfast meetings. Because of careless wording, however, the sentence could be read to mean exactly that. The writer may be defensive and quip, "Well, you knew what I meant," and in this case would be correct. But if we have to read something twice to make sure of its meaning, then the chances are that it was not written clearly in the first place. The writer could have written:

> As a result of monthly breakfast meetings with interesting speakers, a newsletter on legislative activities in Washington, and several other programs, the County Business Association has kept me informed of and involved in the current political and economic issues affecting smaller businesses.

This version would leave little doubt in the reader's mind about the writer's intended meaning.

The meaning of an ambiguous passage often cannot be as easily detected as it was in the above example. A classic example is the following:

> The loan officer approved the loan for David McDonnell because he was obviously of superior moral fiber.

From what is written above we cannot tell who is of superior moral fiber, the loan officer or Mr. McDonnell. The pronoun "he" can refer to either the loan officer or Mr. McDonnell in the above example. To avoid ambiguity, the sentence could be written:

> Because David McDonnell was obviously of superior moral fiber, the loan officer approved the loan.

or:

> Because the loan officer was of superior moral fiber, he approved the loan for David McDonnell.

Be clear, direct, and unambiguous in your letter writing.

Tone

The tone or personality of a letter can help you get a positive reaction from a reader. The tone should be set at the very start of a letter and maintained throughout. The tone of any bank letter should be courteous and friendly, and written as if you were talking with the reader. You don't want to get too technical in a letter, but rather write in language that the reader can understand.

The tone should help to show that someone with a personality—a human being—is writing the letter. If the reader believes that the writer is genuinely concerned about how the topic of the letter affects him or her, a positive response is likely.

Consider the loan letter in sample letter 2.1. The letter writer sets a tone emphasizing efficiency and personal response to the reader from the very start of the letter by addressing both his past involvement with the customer and the customer's needs. Loan officer Nilges comes directly to the point by announcing that his letter contains a credit proposal for his customer's company.

SAMPLE LETTER 2.1. Loan letter with an efficient and personal tone.

May 10, 19X2

Mr. David McDonnell
Vice President
DMI, Inc.
3542 Bethany Road
Crawford, New Jersey 01234

Dear Dave:

PROPOSED CREDIT LINE

As a follow-up to our recent conversation, I've drawn up a credit proposal that would address a portion of DMI's financing needs. If this proposal is acceptable, we'll begin the formal approval process necessary to convert it to a commitment.

Dave, we would like to propose a $1 million unsecured line of credit that gives DMI tremendous flexibility. The line may be used for:

1. Direct borrowings priced at prime
2. Acceptance financing with a 1% commission rate
3. Fixed rate borrowings priced at LIBOR plus 1%

Five percent balances would be required on the line.

The proposal outlined above illustrates how we feel about DMI. Using New National Bank will give you flexibility as well as assure DMI of getting current market rates. If you feel it is appropriate I would like to meet with Tim Smith and you to discuss the DMI, New National relationship.

Sample Letter 2.1 continued

```
I hope to hear from you soon.

                                Best regards,


                                Max Nilges
                                Loan Officer

MN/js

Enclosure
```

In the second paragraph, Nilges addresses his customer by the first name, maintaining a personal courteous tone. Paragraph four reinforces the tone of the letter:

```
The proposal outlined above illustrates how we feel about
DMI.
```

Not only does Nilges express positive feelings about his customer in this sentence, but he also suggests that the tone of the entire letter has been one of positive feelings toward DMI.

The "You Attitude"

An important concept that is discussed in many articles, books, and courses on letter writing is something called the "you attitude." The "you attitude" insists that the focus of attention in your letters be directed toward the reader, the "you" to whom you are writing.

Directing a letter toward a reader may seem very simple, but a letter writer too often incorrectly assumes his or her interests and knowledge are the same as the reader's. Some legwork needs to be done when you are deciding how to make a letter reader-oriented. This legwork may come at the planning stage of your letter discussed in chapter 1.

What you need to know are answers to basic questions such as: "What will motivate this reader to react favorably to my letter?" "What interests this reader?" "What is this reader's viewpoint on issues I am addressing in my letter?"

Sometimes you will not know the answers to these questions. If you sit down, however, and think clearly about what it is that will convince your reader that what you are writing is beneficial to him or her, you have attempted to direct the focus of attention of your letter to the reader, the "you" who is receiving your message.

The reader of your letter must be convinced that what you are trying to get him or her to do or react to is of some personal value. If you are responding to someone about the lack of job openings at your bank, you don't want to scare off a potential employee by sending a cold form letter. Nothing overly elaborate is necessary, of course, but a cordial negative response to a potential employee now may pay off in the future when your bank does need someone with his or her expertise.

Sample letter 2.2 acknowledging an employment application is courteous to and considerate of the reader, even though no jobs are available. Even though no jobs are available, Ms. Smith has written a letter which reflects a sincere interest in Mr. Leigh. By writing, "We are complimented that you would consider the County Savings Bank as a place of employment," she has flattered Mr. Leigh. This might cause him to react positively to Ms. Smith's letter. If he does react positively now, and jobs should open up at a later date for which he is qualified, then Ms. Smith's letter has served a good purpose by keeping a positive relationship with a prospective employee.

SAMPLE LETTER 2.2 Form response letter reflecting use of the "you attitude."

```
August 6, 19X8
Mr. Jacob Leigh
186 Loraine Terrace
Boston, Massachusetts 02134

                    APPLICATION FOR EMPLOYMENT

Mr. Leigh, thank you for your recent employment applica-
tion. We are complimented that you would consider the
County Savings Bank as a place of employment.

Your application will be retained in our open files.
Should any appropriate opening occur you may be contacted
for an interview.

I would appreciate it if you would notify me if you wish
to cancel your application for any reason.


JESSICA SMITH—VICE PRESIDENT
HUMAN RESOURCES

mn
```

Ms. Smith also does not get caught up in the need to use only the personal pronoun "you" in her letter. The use of the pronoun "you" is certainly important in focusing the attention of a letter on a reader, but part of the whole idea of creating a personality or tone in a letter is to let the reader know a living person—an "I"—has indeed written the letter.

The use of the personal pronoun "you" makes the reader feel involved, but a letter writer should also feel free to use the pronouns "I" and "we" when appropriate as Ms. Smith did when she wrote:

```
I would appreciate it if you would notify me if you wish
to cancel your application for any reason.
```

If Ms. Smith had used a passive voice here and had written, "It would be appreciated," instead of "I would appreciate," she would have risked the possibility of taking the personality out of her letter, almost as if she were reluctant to admit her involvement in any of the process.

A writer must focus the attention of a letter on the reader. If you choose the language and tone for your letter to convey an attitude of commitment to and interest in your reader, you will find that your letters will be more successful in grasping your readers' attention and encouraging them to respond favorably.

Structure: The Parts of a Letter

3

As you are reading Chapter 3, you will find it helpful to refer to Chapter 4 where various letter formats are discussed. Different formats require different placement of various parts of a letter. Although placement may vary, the content and function of these parts of a letter remain constant. You will easily be able to apply the principles learned in Chapter 3 to the formats discussed in Chapter 4.

Dateline

Every letter should have a dateline. The date appears on a single line two to eight lines below the letterhead or the top margin of the page. With the exception of the simplified letter format, three lines down from the letterhead is the usual space allotted in most letter formats. Because a letter should be well-framed on a page, the placement of the dateline is flexible.

The date typed on a letter should be the date on which the letter was dictated, no matter when it is to be typed or mailed, unless, of course, the letter is a standard form letter sent out time and time again. The months of the year should always be spelled out, and the day should always be indicated by a cardinal number (e.g., 1, 2, 3), never using "nd," "th," or "st" after the number as you would with ordinal numbers.

The order of the dateline is month, day followed by a comma, and year.

```
August 31, 19X8
```

Sometimes government and foreign correspondence will feature a reverse in the order of day and month, omitting the comma.

```
31 August 19X8
```

The most standard order, however, for the elements in the dateline is month, day followed by a comma, and year.

The placement of the dateline varies depending upon the letter format used. In the full-block format (see sample letter 4.1), the dateline is typed flush with the left margin, or sometimes centered, if centering the date blends well with the letterhead. In the simplified letter format (see sample letter 4.4), the dateline is typed flush with the left margin, six lines below the letterhead.

The dateline in the block (see sample letter 4.2), semiblock (see sample letter 4.3), official style (see sample letter 4.5), and hanging-indented (see sample letter 4.6) formats is flush with the right margin. The last figure of the year should never overrun the right margin.

In the block or semiblock letter formats the date can also be either centered under the letterhead or between five and ten spaces to the right of the center of the page. Unless centering the date adds to the balanced look of the letter, the date in the block and semiblock letters should be flush right.

Reference Line

The reference line is an optional addition to a bank letter. It is a number or a series of numbers and letters referring to previous correspondence. It is usually included for the benefit of a person who must file all correspondence dealing with the same specific issues or topics.

The number is aligned with and typed directly below the dateline. It is usually typed one to four lines beneath the date unless bank policy stipulates that it should be placed elsewhere. (See sample letter 4.1 for an example of a reference line.)

If your letter is to be more than one page long, the reference number must be carried over to all continuation sheets. On these sheets, the location of the reference line should correspond to its location on the first sheet, or as indicated by bank policy.

Personal or Confidential Note

The inclusion of a personal or confidential note is optional. When such a notation is used however, it should always be because the writer wants the letter to remain confidential between him or her and the reader. If such notations are used as come-on gimmicks to attract a reader to a letter, they will lose their effectiveness.

Except with the official style format, the personal or confidential note should be located four lines above the inside address. (See sample letter 16.9) It does not need to be underlined or typed all in capital letters. If a writer feels it necessary to underline or capitalize, he or she should choose one or the other (i.e., either all capital letters or underlining), but not both.

The personal note would rarely be used in the official style format because this format is usually reserved for personal letters. Should you decide it is necessary to include a personal note in the official style format, it should be typed four lines above the salutation.

Inside Address

The inside address must be included in all letters. With the exception of the official style format, the inside address is typed two to twelve lines beneath the dateline (or reference line or confidential note should there be such notations). The placement of the inside address is flexible depending upon the length of the letter.

In the simplified letter format, the inside address is typed three lines below the dateline or the last previous notation. In the official style letter, the inside address is typed two to five lines below the last line of the signature block.

The inside address is always typed flush with the left margin of the letter. It should be no longer than five lines. No line should cross over the center margin of the page. If a line is too long, it should be broken in half, indented two spaces, and continued on the next line.

The inside address of a letter addressed to an individual should include that individual's courtesy title and full name, professional title, company name, and full address. If a woman's courtesy title is unknown, "Ms." should be used.

```
Ms. Nancy Coleman
Production Editor
Bankers Publishing Company
210 South Street
Boston, Massachusetts 02111
```

Even if the courtesy title, "Mrs." is used in a business letter, a woman's and not her husband's first name should be used.

If a person's name and professional title are short enough, they can be separated by a comma and placed together on the first line of the inside address.

```
Ms. Nancy Coleman, Editor
```

If the professional title and company name are short enough, the title separated by a comma from the company name can be placed together on the second line of the inside address.

```
Mr. John H. Sayers
Designer, Modern Optics, Inc.
```

When a company is being addressed, the inside address should include the name of the company, the individual department desired, and the full address of the company.

```
County Savings & Loan
Commercial Loan Department
119 Roosevelt Street
Lichfield, West Virginia 02134
```

You should always use the company's official name in the inside address including any ampersands, abbreviations, or other items the company uses in its name when it is printed.

When the address is too long, the person's title is sometimes omitted. If you are addressing two or more people, you can either list the names alphabetically on separate lines or use the designation "Messrs." (Messieurs) for all men or "Mesdames," "Mmes.," or "Mses." for all women. When using Messrs. or Mesdames (and its abbreviations), you omit the addressees' first names.

```
Mesdames Ahern, Coleman, and Long
```

or

```
Ms. Marie Ahern
Ms. Nancy Coleman
Ms. Annmarie Long
```

Sometimes a company uses both a street address and a post office box in its letterhead. If such is the case, use the post office box number in the inside address of your letter and on the envelope. This will insure that the post office sends your letter to the proper place.

The names of numbered streets should be spelled out for streets number one through twelve. Arabic numerals should be used for streets numbered 13 and above.

```
186 First Street
186 - 13th Avenue
```

Arabic numerals should be used for all house, building, or office numbers, with the exception of the number "one," which always should be spelled out.

```
One South Street
210 South Street
```

When compass directions appear before numbered streets, cardinal numbers (e.g., 16, 17, 18) should be used. If compass directions don't appear before a numbered street, ordinal numbers (e.g., 16th, 17th, 18th) should be used.

```
186 East 30 Street
186 - 30th Street
```

When a compass direction appears before a street name, it should be spelled out. If the compass direction follows the street name, it should be abbreviated.

```
186 East 30 Street
3233 - 38th Street N.W.
```

If a building or house number appears immediately before a numbered street, separate the two with a spaced hyphen.

```
186 - 30th Street
```

A suite or apartment number following a street address should be placed on the same line as the street address separated by a comma or two spaces.

```
25 Huntington Avenue, Suite 408
25 Huntington Avenue  Suite 408
```

Although the inside address should match the address on the envelope, it generally looks more attractive to spell out the state name in the inside address. On the envelope, the two-letter state abbreviation should be used. (See appendix III for a list of two-letter state abbreviations.) The zip code should be included two spaces after the state in the inside address.

Attention Note

If you are addressing a letter to a firm but wish to direct it to the attention of a specific person, you may include an attention note. The attention note is typed two lines below the last line of the inside address and two lines above the salutation.

In the full-block, block, or simplified letter formats, the attention note is typed either flush with the left margin or centered. The attention note is usually not included in the official style format since this format is generally used for a personal letter and it would already be clear to whom the letter is addressed. The attention note can be included in a hanging-indented letter, but because this format is generally reserved for sales letters, the inclusion of an attention note would not be common.

The attention note can be written with or without a colon following the word "attention." The main elements of the attention note should have the first letter capitalized.

```
Attention: David McDonnell
Attention David McDonnell
```

Salutation

The salutation appears in all letters but those using the simplified letter format. It is usually typed two to four lines below the inside address or the attention note (if there is one). Two spaces is most typical.

In the official style format, the salutation is typed four to six lines below the dateline since the inside address appears at the bottom of the letter in this format.

The word "dear" before the person's courtesy title and name is standard. The phrase "my dear" is no longer in style. The word "dear" should be capitalized and typed flush with the left margin. If the letter is informal you address the person by his or her first name in the salutation.

Courtesy titles such as Ms., Miss, Mrs., and Mr. should be used where appropriate. If you are unsure about a woman's marital status or her courtesy title preference, it is best to use "Ms." before her name in the salutation.

Professional or academic titles (e.g., "Dr.") take precedence over courtesy titles for both men and women. A comma before the abbreviations "Jr." and "Sr." depends upon the preference of the individual being addressed.

The most conventional ways of addressing a group consisting of males and females are:

```
Ladies and Gentlemen:
```

or

```
Dear Sir or Madam:
```

The simplified letter format contains no salutation. As a result, this format can be used if the letter writer wishes to avoid the problems of sexist language that sometime exist in the salutation to a letter.

Subject Line

The subject line identifies the content of a letter and is an optional addition to all but the simplified letter formats. The simplified letter always includes a subject line typed three lines below the last line of the inside address.

In the full-block, block, semiblock, or hanging-indented formats, the subject line is typed either two lines above or below the salutation. It is typed either flush with the left margin or centered under the salutation, and consists of the word "subject" followed by a colon and the subject to be covered in a letter.

The subject line can be typed in all capital letters or with each important word capitalized in the first letter. Sometimes when just the important words are capitalized, the whole subject line is underlined. When the subject line is typed in all capital letters it is never underlined.

```
Subject: Proposed Credit Line
Subject: Proposed Credit Line
SUBJECT: PROPOSED CREDIT LINE
```

The subject line is generally used when only one subject is covered in a letter.

Body of Letter

The body of a letter should begin two lines below the salutation or subject line in the full-block, block, semiblock, official style, and hanging-indented formats. It should begin three lines below the subject line in the simplified letter format.

The letter should be single-spaced within paragraphs and double-spaced between paragraphs. If the letter is very short, double-spacing can be used within the paragraphs, using the semiblock style of indentation to indicate new paragraphs.

Paragraphs should be indented five or ten spaces in the official or semiblock styles. Five space indentations are usually standard. In the full-block, block, and simplified letter formats, no indentation is used.

In the hanging-indented format, the first line of the paragraph is flush left and the rest of the paragraph is indented five spaces. Single-spacing within paragraphs and double-spacing between paragraphs is used in the hanging-indented format.

Numbered material within letters should be indented five spaces or centered. The numbers should be placed in parenthesis or followed by a period. Double-spacing should be used between each item. Punctuation is used after each item listed in the numbered material or it is used after none of the items.

Long quotations should be blocked in the letter, setting the quotation off by indenting all of it five spaces and keeping it single-spaced.

Long paragraphs should be avoided in letters. Of course, the use of brief paragraphs should not be carried to a ridiculous extent by writing a letter full of one-sentence paragraphs causing it to sound like a machine gun because of the staccato rhythm. Be sensible about paragraph length. Say what you have to say and move on avoiding any padding or inconsequential information.

The first paragraph should introduce a letter's subject or refer to a previous correspondence or conversation to which you are responding. The following paragraphs of your letter should elaborate on the subject set up in paragraph one. The closing paragraph should briefly summarize the topic and close on a positive note, encouraging a positive working relationship with the letter's reader.

Continuation Sheets

The printed letterhead is used only for the first page of a letter. The second and following pages are typed on plain sheets of paper matching the letterhead.

The heading on a continuation sheet is typed six lines below the top of the page and includes the addressee's name, the page number, and the date. At least two lines of text, preferably more, should be carried over for a continuation sheet to be used.

In the full-block format, the information in the continuation sheet heading should be typed flush with the left margin. It should include the page number on the first line, the addressee's courtesy title and full name on the second, and the date on the third.

```
Page 2
Mr. David McDonnell
August 23, 19X2
```

The block, semiblock, official style, or hanging-indented formats can use either the flush left continuation sheet heading shown above, or be typed on one line with the addressee's name typed flush left, the page number centered and set off by spaced hyphens, and the date flush with the right margin.

```
Mr. David McDonnell        -2-        August 23, 19X2
```

Complimentary Close

The complimentary close must be included in all but the simplified letter format. It is typed two lines below the last line of the body of the letter.

In the full-block format the complimentary close should be flush with the left margin. In the block, semiblock, official style, and hanging-indented formats, the complimentary close should be flush with the right margin, directly under the dateline, or about five spaces to the right of the center of the page. It should never cross over the right margin. The simplified letter has no complimentary close.

The first letter of the first word of the complimentary close should be capitalized. The entire complimentary close should be followed by a comma.

The choice of the proper complimentary close depends upon the degree of formality of your letter. If the letter is formal the choices for a proper complimentary close include:

```
Very truly yours
Yours truly
Yours very truly
```

If the letter is less formal, but still not friendly or informal, among the complimentary closes to choose from are:

```
Yours sincerely
Very sincerely yours
Sincerely yours
Sincerely
Cordially
Most sincerely
Most cordially
Cordially yours
```

A friendly or informal letter to a person with whom you are on a first name basis can end with a complimentary close such as:

```
As ever
Best regards
Kindest regards
Best wishes
Regards
```

Signature Block

Directly under the complimentary close, the letter writer signs his or her name. Four lines below and aligned with the complimentary close in the full-block, block, semiblock, official style, and the hanging-indented formats, the writer's name is typed, usually the same way it has been signed. In the simplified letter format, the letter writer's name is typed in all capital letters five lines below the last line of the letter, flush with the left margin.

Single-spaced beneath the typed name, the letter writer's title is typed, unless it is short enough to fit on the same line as the name separated by a comma.

If the letterhead includes the letter writer's business title and the bank's name, these are not typed again in the signature block. If a letterhead is not used and your letter is a formal one requiring the bank's name, type the bank's name in all capital letters two lines below and aligned with the complimentary close, or, in the case of the simplified letter format, two lines below the last line of the letter.

Directly below the typed bank name should be the signature. Four lines below the typed bank name, the letter writer's name should be typed. If the bank's name is long it can be centered beneath the complimentary close in the block and semiblock letters.

```
Yours truly,
NEW NATIONAL BANK

Max Nilges, Loan Officer
```

If a woman wishes to use a courtesy title before her name, then Ms., Mrs., or Miss should be enclosed in parenthesis before the typed name. These are the only titles that may precede the name in the signature block. Academic degrees (e.g., Ph.D., M.B.A.) or professional ratings (e.g., C.P.A.) follow the typed name and are separated by a comma.

A person signing the letter for someone else should initial just below and to the right of the signature.

```
Yours truly,

Max Nilges, Loan Officer
```

If a secretary signs a letter in his or her name for someone else, the secretary's surname and title are typed below the signature.

```
Yours truly,

Simon Algon
Assistant to Mr. Nilges
```

Identification Line

The identification line is an optional addition to any letter. It consists of either the initials of the typist or of the writer and the typist, and is typed flush with the left margin two lines below the signature block. Many professionals believe the identification line should be omitted since it does little but identify a secretary to blame for typos.

If bank policy dictates that you use an identification line, it can be typed in a variety of ways. The typist's lowercase initials may be typed alone.

```
js
```

The writer's initials may be typed uppercase followed by a colon or virgule followed by the typist's lowercase initials.

```
MN:js
MN/js
```

The writer's initials and the typist's initials can both be uppercase, or both lowercase.

```
MN:JS
MN/JS
mn:js
mn/js
```

Any version of the identification lines above can be used as long as it serves the purpose of identifying the typist of the letter.

In the odd case that a letter should be dictated by one person, typed by another, and signed by a third, the identification line should include the signer's uppercase initials followed by a colon followed by the dictator's uppercase initials, followed by another colon, followed by the typist's lowercase initials.

```
MN:JS:ms
```

Enclosure Notations

If an enclosure is included with the letter, one of the following should be typed two lines below the identification line of the signature block if there is no identification line:

```
Enclosure
Enc.
Encl.
enc.
encl.
```

If there is more than one enclosure the plural of one of the above notations is used, with the number of enclosures indicated after the notation in parenthesis or before the notation.

```
Enclosures (2)
2 Enclosures
encs. (2)
2 encs.
Encs. (2)
2 Encs.
```

The enclosures should be placed behind the letter in order of importance. If a check is one of the enclosures it should be placed in front of the letter.

The enclosures can be numbered and listed next to the enclosure notation, one per line. If they are to be returned, indicate such in parenthesis next to the item.

```
encs.  (2) 1. Credit analysis worksheet (please return)
           2. International financing brochure
```

Distribution Notation

If you would like the recipient of your letter to know to whom you are sending copies of the letter, a distribution notation is used. Sometimes distribution notations only appear on copies of the letter.

The distribution notation consists of the words "Copy to" (or "Copies to") or the abbreviation and colon, "cc:" followed by the recipient's or recipients' names.

```
Copy to Max Nilges
cc: Max Nilges
```

Multiple recipients are listed alphabetically by full name or by initials, depending upon the letter writer's preference or bank policy.

```
Copies to: Dave McDonnell
Max Nilges
cc: DM
MN
```

If other information about the recipient is useful (e.g., a company's name) it should be placed next to the person's name in parenthesis.

```
Copies to:  Dave McDonnell (DMI, Inc.)
            Max Nilges (New National Bank)

cc: DM (DMI, Inc.)
    MN (New National Bank)
```

If space is tight and a distribution notation is essential, it can be typed a single-space above either the enclosure notation or the identification line.

Postscript

A postscript is rarely used in a bank letter unless it is used in a sales letter to emphasize a point or to make a special offer. It is typed flush with the left margin two to four lines below the last notation in a letter. The writer should initial the postscript. The abbreviation "P.S." should not be used before a postscript.

Appearance of the Letter

4

Appearance is very important in letter writing. The message you are sending is obviously the most important aspect of your letter. If the reader opens an envelope and finds a note scrawled across a piece of notebook paper torn from a notebook, however, the most important of messages is not going to get through to the reader.

There are certain conventions used in letter writing that are fairly well established, yet they are flexible enough to allow you to communicate exactly what you want to your reader. If you take into consideration the appearance of your letter—the stationery, format, length, and envelope—your reader will be drawn to your letter by its appearance. Once your reader gives your letter his or her attention, your message is sure to get through.

Stationery

Letterhead design varies from bank to bank, but it usually consists of at least the following items:

- bank logo
- bank's full, legal name
- full street address and/or post office box number
- city, state, and zip code
- telephone number

A bank's letterhead sometimes includes the bank's cable or telex number.

There are important considerations to make when choosing a letterhead design. The information included should be uncluttered and readable. The design should be simple enough for the reader to get the information he or she needs without being distracted from reading the rest of the letter.

A bank's stationery is usually white or some other conservative color. The standard size of the stationery is 8-1/2" x 11".

Margins on the typed letter should be consistent. The margins on the top and the bottom of the letter should be equal to one another. The side margins should also be equal to one another. The size of the margins depends upon the length of the letter to be written. Long letters typically have smaller margins than short letters. Using margins of one inch for long letters and two inches for short letters is a good rule of thumb to follow.

If a letter is very short, containing a few short sentences or a couple of short paragraphs, then a half-sheet of stationery can be used. The half-sheet measures 8-1/2" x 5-1/2". It is usually printed as a miniature version of the letterhead with the same letterhead design at the top as the normal size stationery.

The full-block, block, or semiblock letter formats discussed in this chapter can be used on the half-sheet. The techniques and rules governing bank letter writing all apply to letters written on a half-sheet.

Some bank executives will use an executive letterhead. In addition to the basic elements contained in a letterhead, the executive letterhead features the executive's printed name and title beneath the letterhead.

With all types of letters, the letterhead is always only used as the first sheet of a letter. If the typed letter is more than one page, a plain sheet of paper matching the letterhead should be used for subsequent pages. (See the section on continuation sheets in chapter 3 for more information.)

Various Formats for Letters

The format used for a letter is typically determined by the person writing the letter. Sometimes a bank will have a house style for a format in which letters must be written, but typically the writer must choose the format.

The full-block, block, semiblock, and simplified letter formats presented here can all be used effectively for writing any bank letter. Some letter writers find that the simplified letter is not traditional enough for their taste; others find it a perfect solution to the problem of sexist language in letter salutations. Be that as it may, these four formats are the standard ones used for most bank letters written today.

The hanging-indented and official style formats discussed here are not used for everyday bank letters. Their use indicates that a particular type of letter is being written. A discussion of the appropriate use of these formats is included in this chapter.

Chapter 3 discusses the placement and function of the parts of each of the letter formats discussed in this chapter. You might find it useful to look back at Chapter 3 for reference when you are studying the various letter formats in Chapter 4.

Full block

The full-block format, sometimes called "complete block" or simply "block," is shown in sample letter 4.1.

SAMPLE LETTER 4.1. Example of full-block format letter.

November 3, 19X2
A-456-78

Mr. Ralph Embry
Thomson Enterprises
1111 Prospect Street
Hamilton, California 00012

Dear Mr. Embry:

Your checking account has had five returns and has not been handled in a mutually satisfactory manner. Therefore, I am requesting that you close it within seven days from the date of this letter.

After that date, New National Bank will no longer pay checks presented on the account, and they will be returned marked ''Account Closed.'' Any collected funds remaining in the account will be returned to you at that time after deducting any fees owed to us.

Sincerely,

Jeffrey Kraus
Branch Manager

nlc

In this format, all the lines of the letter, from the dateline to the last notation, are flush with the left margin.

Paragraphs are not indented but rather begin flush with the left margin. Single-spacing is used within the paragraphs, and double-spacing between.

The dateline is most often typed three lines below the letterhead. Depending upon the length of the letter, however, it may be typed anywhere from two to six lines below the letterhead. If there is a reference line, it should be typed directly below the dateline.

The inside address is most often typed four lines below the dateline (or reference line if there is one) but may be typed anywhere from two to twelve lines below the dateline depending upon the length of the letter. If there is an attention line it should be typed two lines below the address and two lines above the salutation.

The salutation should be typed four lines below the inside address or attention line if there is one. If there is a subject line, it is typed two lines above or below the salutation. The body of the letter begins two lines below the salutation or subject line if there is one.

Two lines below the last line of the letter, the complimentary close is typed. The signature block is typed four lines below the complimentary close.

An identification line is typed two lines below the signature block. All other notations (e.g., enclosure, distribution) are typed two lines below the identification line.

Block

The block format, sometimes called "modified block," is shown in sample letter 4.2. This format differs from the full-block format because the dateline (and reference line if there is one), complimentary close, and signature block are aligned with the right margin. Paragraphs are not indented. The spacing of various parts of the letter in the block format is the same as it is in the full-block format.

SAMPLE LETTER 4.2. Example of block format letter.

May 10, 19X2

Mr. David McDonnell
Vice President
DMI, Inc.
3542 Bethany Road
Crawford, New Jersey 01234

Dear Dave:

PROPOSED CREDIT LINE

As a follow-up to our recent conversation, I've drawn up a credit proposal that would address a portion of DMI's financing needs. If this proposal is acceptable, we'll begin the formal approval process necessary to convert it to a commitment.

Dave, we would like to propose a $1 million unsecured line of credit that gives DMI tremendous flexibility. The line may be used for:

1. direct borrowings priced at prime
2. acceptance financing with a 1% commission rate

Sample Letter 4.2 continued

3. fixed rate borrowings priced at LIBOR plus 1%

Five percent balances would be required on the line.

The proposal outlined here illustrates how we feel about DMI. Using New National Bank will give you flexibility as well as assure DMI of getting current market rates. If you feel it is appropriate, I would like to meet with Tim Smith and you to discuss the DMI, New National relationship.

I hope to hear from you soon.

Best regards,

Max Nilges
Loan Officer

MN/js

Enclosure

The block format is widely used because of the balanced look it gives to a letter. Since everything is flush with the left margin in the full-block format, it almost appears as if the letter might tip over to the left. In the block format, since the date, complimentary close, and signature block are flush with the right margin, the letter is balanced in place and not tipped to either side.

Semiblock

The semiblock format is shown in sample letter 4.3. The only difference between this and the block format is the fact that the paragraphs in the semiblock format are indented five or ten spaces. A five-space paragraph indentation is usually preferred.

SAMPLE LETTER 4.3. Example of a semiblock format letter.

December 26, 19X2

Mr. Simon Kemper
15 Douglas Road
Norristown, Idaho 00005

Dear Mr. Kemper:

Thank you for your letter and resume indicating your interest in our management training program.

Although the economy looks brighter, things are still very tight in the banking industry and it has just been decided that we will not have a management training program this year at New National.

We are also under constant pressure to reduce staff through attrition wherever possible. At this point the most we can offer you is to keep your resume at the top of our file and to promise consideration for any openings that might become available during the coming months.

Thanks again for your interest in New National. Best of luck to you in your search for suitable employment.

Cordially,

Edward J. Coleman
Personnel Director

EJC/hlm

Simplified

The simplified letter format departs from the style of the formats mentioned thus far which have been variations upon the full-block format. An example of the simplified letter format appears in sample letter 4.4.

SAMPLE LETTER 4.4. Example of a simplified letter format.

```
August 6, 19X2

Mr. Jacob Leigh
186 Loraine Terrace
Boston, Massachusetts 02134

APPLICATION FOR EMPLOYMENT

Mr. Leigh, thank you for your recent employment applica-
tion. We are complimented that you would consider the
County Savings Bank as a place of employment.

Your application will be retained in our open files.
Should any appropriate opening occur you may be contacted
for an interview.

I would appreciate it if you would notify me if you wish
to cancel your application for any reason.

JESSICA SMITH—VICE PRESIDENT
HUMAN RESOURCES

mn
```

The most obvious variation of the simplified letter format is its lack of salutation and complimentary close. The lack of salutation is a good way to avoid the problem of knowing how to address a woman if you do not know which, if any, courtesy title she prefers. It is also a good way to address an unknown audience which may consist of both men and women or only one of these two groups.

In a simplified letter all lines are flush with the left margin, including the dateline, reference line (if there is one), and the signature block. The dateline is typed six lines below the letterhead. The inside address is typed four lines below the dateline or reference line.

A subject line always is included in the simplified letter format. It is typed in all capital letters, three lines below the inside address and three lines above the body of the letter.

Paragraphs are not indented in the simplified letter format. Five lines below the body of the letter, the signature block is typed in all capital letters. The writer's signature is signed above the signature block. If there is an identification line, it is typed two lines below the signature block. If there is an enclosure notation it is typed a single-space below the identification line. Any other notations are typed two lines below the enclosure notation.

If a continuation page is needed, the heading should be the same as used with the full-block format. The addressee's name should appear six lines from the top of the plain sheet, flush with the left margin. The page number should be typed directly below the name, and the date directly below the page number.

Official style

The official style format is used mostly for personal correspondence, often written by executives on their personalized bank stationery. This format is the same as the semiblock format with the exception of the placement of the inside address which is typed two to five lines below the signature block. See sample letter 4.5 for an example of an official style letter.

If there is an identification line in the official style format, it is typed two lines below the inside address. Any enclosure notations are typed two lines below the identification line.

SAMPLE LETTER 4.5. Example of an official style format letter.

December 1, 19X1

Dear Ralph:

Mark E. Mathews, the president of our bank, and I invite you to cocktails and dinner at six o'clock on the evening of Thursday, December 10, 19X1, at the Palay Restaurant, 79 July Street, Hamilton, California.

While the evening will be principally social, I do expect that Mark will have some informal remarks after dinner on a topical aspect of the economy. We anticipate about 30 good friends of the bank joining us for the evening.

I hope you will be able to attend and I look forward to seeing you that evening.

Regards,

Joanne Tufts

Mr. Ralph Embry
Thomson Enterprises
111 Prospect Street
Hamilton, California 00012

JT:js

Hanging indented

The use of the hanging-indented letter format is reserved for sales or advertising letters. This unorthodox format, shown in sample letter 4.6, is believed to attract the attention of the reader.

SAMPLE LETTER 4.6. Example of a hanging-indented format letter.

May 9, 19X2

Ms. Joan Kenney
1978 Malden Place
Media, Pennsylvania 01005

Dear Ms. Kenney:

How do you choose a bank?

Are modern facilities most important to you? Size and resources? Or courtesy and efficiency of personnel?

Probably you'll want to consider all of these factors. So, if you'll pardon us for ''pointing with pride,'' we like to think of the New National as the bank that friends are building. Without merger, we've grown from a small private bank organized in 1916, with a capital of $20,000, to rank among the 100 largest banks in the United States.

People are important to the ''Big, Friendly Bank for Everybody.'' Here you'll find modern facilities combined with old-fashioned courtesy. We like to think of our customers as friends. We know that the patience of a bookkeeper, the warm smile of a teller, or the helpful suggestions of a loan officer are what keep customers coming back.

Without reservation, we can tell you that we're genuinely proud of the New National men and women who serve our customers. Many of them like myself are ''old timers'' who have grown up with our business. Others have joined our New National ''family'' more recently. But all of us have one goal in common: to make it easy, pleasant, and convenient to transact business here. Our officers would like very much to show you around the ''Bank That Friends Are Building.''

Cordially,

Leslie M. Renn
Vice President

LMR:JLS

The first line of each paragraph of the hanging-indented letter is flush with the left margin. The remaining lines of that paragraph are indented five spaces. Single-spacing is used within paragraphs and double-spacing between.

The dateline is flush with the right margin and typed three lines below the letterhead. The inside address and salutation are flush with the left margin and blocked exactly as in the block format discussed earlier in this chapter. The complimentary close, signature block, and all subsequent notations are placed similar to the way they are placed in the semiblock letter format.

The main difference between the hanging-indented format and the semiblock format is the difference in the indentation of paragraphs. If there is a postscript in a hanging-indented letter, it is also typed with the first line flush left and the remaining lines indented five spaces.

Length

The length of any letter affects its appearance. Bankers or clients who receive a great deal of correspondence everyday are not going to react favorably to lengthy three-page letters which could have been written in one page.

Come right to the point in your letters. They should be as concise and limited to one page if possible.

Begin discussing the main topic or topics of your letter in the first paragraph. If you do, your reader will know what to expect as soon as he or she begins to read.

Planning and clarity in your ideas can help to limit the length of your letter. Paragraphs should not be too long and difficult to follow. You should not, however, use a string of one-sentence paragraphs which would result in a staccato-like reading of your letter. A concise paragraph with a few sentences that come right to the point should keep the length of your letters manageable.

Envelopes

The appearance of the envelope adds to the overall professional appearance of your letter. The address should be typed in the approximate horizontal and vertical center of the business envelope. With the exception of using the two-letter abbreviation for the state, the address on the envelope should appear exactly as the inside address of the letter (see Chapter 3). The use of the two-letter state abbreviation will expedite postal service. (See Appendix III for a list of two-letter state abbreviations.)

The person's name should be typed as the first line of the address. If there is space, the addressee's title can be typed next to the name on the first line, separated by a comma. A single-space down on the second line, the person's title is typed if it did not fit on the first line. If the company's name will also fit on the second line, type it next to the title, separated by a comma. A single-space below, the company name is typed if it didn't fit on the second line. The complete street address or post office box number, whichever is used in the inside address, is typed on the next line. The city followed by a comma, the two-letter state abbreviation, followed by two spaces, and the zip code are typed as the last line of the address.

If you are addressing a company rather than an individual, type the company's name on the first line and the department name or attention line on the second line.

The sender's full name and address should appear in the upper left corner of the letter. Usually the bank's name will be imprinted on the envelope.

The stamp is placed in the upper right corner of the envelope. Any special mailing notations should be typed in all capital letters directly below where the stamp is to go. On-arrival notations should be typed in all capital letters about nine lines below the top left of the envelope, aligned with the end of the return address. Italics and script writing should not be used because it might confuse the postal service.

Memoranda

Memoranda are usually written as interoffice correspondence. The format of a memorandum will vary from bank to bank. Usually banks will have a memorandum form which is used.

Typically the form will be set up as a letterhead with the following information printed flush left on it:

```
TO:
FROM:
DATE:
SUBJECT:
```

Some word processing software packages have a memorandum set-up that is easily accessible by a terminal operator. Electronic mail services also provide a format on a computer screen that can be filled out and sent. If no form is available, a writer can use the above format on a blank piece of stationery. The writer writes the message below the subject line. The most important things to remember in writing a memo are:

1. *Write one only when necessary.* Bankers already have too much correspondence with which to deal. If your memorandum is not really necessary, don't write it.
2. *Make your memo as brief and to the point as possible.* A common complaint is that business people have lost the ability to write effectively. Memos are a place where effective writing is a must. If the message you want to get across is really as important as it should be, you'll want to make sure to write as clearly and to the point as you possibly can. The memo can be more than one page if it has to be, but make sure it doesn't ramble on and on.

The memos included throughout *The Banker's Handbook of Letters and Letter Writing* are not exhaustive of all memos that are written in banks. The occasions or circumstances for which a memo can be written are countless. The memos included here will give you a good idea of the proper format and style to use.

Grammar and Usage 5

People who have difficulty writing are often so frightened about making a mistake that they freeze. Grammar just might be the most frightening element of writing.

You can combat this fear. Relax and try to write as naturally as possible. In a careful proofreading you'll usually find any grammatical errors. If you find you have a real problem with grammar, there are many good, easy-to-understand simple grammar books that should be able to help you alleviate any mistakes you might be making. You'll find a list of these books in the bibliography of this book.

In the meantime, this chapter will give you the grammar basics you need to create a well-written letter.

Grammar

The rules of grammar define how to speak and write clearly. Most of these rules are logical. Some rules may not seem as logical as others, but on the whole following the rules of grammar helps your writing to be consistent and understandable.

Spoken language often is not as precise as written language. Keep this in mind when you are writing, but don't feel compelled to embellish your letter with forceful strokes of the pen. If you get the basics correct and write with clarity and precision foremost in your mind, you will most likely produce correctly written English.

All types of grammatical errors are possible. A list of several of the most common types of errors follows. Look over these common errors. Try to detect them if they occur in your own writing. Remember, most errors you make—including those listed here—can be detected in a careful proofreading after you've finished the first draft of your letter.

Wrong pronouns

When people are in a hurry they often write letters quickly without checking for simple mistakes. Use of an improper pronoun is a common error which can be detected easily in a careful proofreading.

Some writers have a tendency to want to write "I" instead of "me," even when the latter is correct. For instance, the sentence:

```
He gave the book to Eddie and I.
```

is incorrect. The sentence should properly be written:

```
He gave the book to Eddie and me.
```

The above error is common when the writer lists two people as the recipient of the action. If you find yourself having difficulty in such a case, simply say the sentence to yourself as if the pronoun were the only receiver of the action.

```
He gave the book to me.
```

It is easy to add other receivers of the action after you have determined the proper pronoun to use. This is a simple way to try to avoid using the wrong pronoun.

Another way to avoid using the wrong pronoun is to remember that there are three "cases" of pronouns. The nominative case pronouns are the *subject* of the verb. The nominative case pronouns are:

singular	*plural*
I	we
you	you
he, she, it	they

You would never write:

```
Her and me are going to the movies.
```

but rather:

```
She and I are going to the movies.
```

In the above sentence, because "She and I" is the subject of the verb, the nominative case pronouns are used.

The objective case pronouns are used as the *object* of a verb's action or as the object of a preposition. The objective case pronouns are:

singular	*plural*
me	us
you	you
him, her, it	them

The object of a verb can usually be determined by asking "What?" or "Whom?" is the receiver of the verb's action. In the sentence,

```
I gave it to her.
```

"her" is the object of the verb because it answers the question: "To whom did you give it?"

Remember that an objective case pronoun is *always* used as the object of a preposition, so when you see a sentence that includes a prepositional phrase such as "at him," "with her," or "about me," it should immediately trigger your memory to use one of the objective case pronouns.

Possessive case pronouns indicate *possession* and are used incorrectly far less often than are the nominative and objective case pronouns. The possessive case pronouns are:

singular	*plural*
my, mine	our, ours
your, yours	your, yours
his, her, his, hers, its	their, theirs

Another common error involving the incorrect use of pronouns occurs when the words "than" or "as" precede an incomplete sentence construction. For example, take the sentence

```
Mr. Nilges is richer than I.
```

To determine the proper pronoun to use, complete the sentence.

Mr. Nilges is richer *than I am.*

Use the pronoun you would use if the construction were not incomplete.

There are many more rules governing the proper use of pronouns. Those listed here represent a few that remedy some recurring problems. If you are unsure of the pronoun to use, you can usually determine whether or not your sentence is correct by listening to how the sentence sounds once you have written it. If you remain unsure, check the rules I've noted or consult a grammar reference.

Pronouns and antecedents

The most common mistake concerning pronouns and their antecedents occurs when it is unclear to what or whom a pronoun refers. To avoid any confusion in your letters, make sure that when you begin a sentence or a clause in a sentence with he, she, it, or other pronouns, it is absolutely clear to whom or what these pronouns refer.

A couple of simple examples of unclear references involving pronouns and antecedents are:

> Loren Gary and Guy Martin prepared the loan proposal and visited the customer's new office building. It was a handsome piece of work. (*What* was a handsome piece of work? The loan proposal? The office building?)

> Donald E. McFarland spoke with Robert Long about the possibility of working together. He thought it was a good idea. (*Who* thought it was a good idea? Donald? Robert?)

Subject and verb agreement

Sentences consisting of a disagreement in number (plural vs. singular) between subject and verb often results from quick, careless writing.

Basically a word that is said to be singular in number refers to only one person or thing, whereas a word that is plural in number refers to more than one person or thing.

singular	*plural*
check	checks
this	these
loan	loans
client	clients

Remember these two basic rules:

1. Singular subjects take singular verbs.

```
The check is here
This is unsatisfactory.
The loan is adequate.
The client coughs a great deal.
```

2. Plural subjects take plural verbs.

```
The checks are here.
These are unsatisfactory.
The loans are adequate.
The clients cough a great deal.
```

In a simple sentence, making subjects and verbs agree is not too difficult. But when a phrase appears between the subject and the verb or a word whose number you are unsure of is in a sentence, it becomes more difficult.

Remember that the verb must always agree with the subject. No matter how many words separate the subject and the verb, check to make sure they agree.

```
The cancellation was final.
The cancellation of the contracts was final.
```

Even though "contracts" would take a plural verb if it were the subject of the sentence, it only modifies a singular subject in the sentence above. "Cancellation" is still the subject, so you still use a singular verb.

When you use indefinite pronouns as the subject of a sentence, it is sometimes difficult to tell whether the pronoun is singular or plural. Some take a singular verb while others take a plural.

These indefinite pronouns take a singular verb:

anybody

anyone

each

either

everybody

everyone

neither

no one

one

somebody

someone

These indefinite pronouns take a plural verb:

both

few

many

several

With the following indefinite pronouns you must judge from the context of the sentence whether to use a singular or plural verb:

all

any

most

none

some

For example:

1. `All of the secretaries are talented.`
   `All of the money is green.`
2. `Any desk is fine.`
   `Must any of the proceedings be taped?`
3. `Most of my days are busy.`
   `Most of my dinner is cold.`
4. `None of the banks were open.`
   `None of the ledger was saved.`
5. `Some of our loans are processed incorrectly.`
   `Some of the book is missing.`

Another simple rule to remember is that *compound subjects always take a plural verb.*

```
Mr. Bumby has arrived.
Mr. Bumby and Mr. Grimes have arrived.
```

When "or" or "nor" connects the two subjects, however, a singular verb is used.

```
Mr. Bumby or Mr. Grimes has arrived.
```

If you carefully check to make sure that the subjects and verbs of the sentences you write agree in number, you will most likely not make any errors. Sometimes, however, when it is difficult to determine whether a singular or plural verb should be used, a quick reference to my pointers above or a grammar book will set you straight.

Dangling modifiers

A phrase modifying the subject of a sentence should make sense. When a modifier doesn't clearly refer to the word it is modifying in a sentence, it is said to be a dangling modifier. In the sentence,

```
Preoccupied with the mortgage negotiation, her secretary
surprised her.
```

it is unclear what the phrase, "preoccupied with the mortgage negotiation," modifies. It is a dangling modifier. It appears to modify "secretary," but it's more likely that it's meant to modify the "her" of the sentence. A word that the modifier can refer to sensibly in the sentence is needed:

```
Preoccupied with the mortgage negotiation, she was sur-
prised by her secretary.
```

The sentence could also be written:

```
Because she was preoccupied with the mortgage negotia-
tion, she was surprised by her secretary.
```

When you write a sentence that contains a modifying phrase, always make sure that it clearly modifies what it is supposed to in the sentence. Most dangling modifiers result from carelessness. You can usually tell after a careful proofreading of your letter whether or not the sentences you have written make sense.

Split infinitives

Splitting infinitives is not always wrong. Some people will go to such great lengths to make sure infinitives are not split that the sentences they write are awkwardly constructed.

As a rule of thumb, you should not split an infinitive when it results in an awkwardly constructed sentence. For example, in the following sentence, the infinitive "to pass" is awkwardly split:

```
The legislation is the proper one to, whether or not you
approve of deficit spending, pass in the upcoming elec-
tion.
```

A better way to write the above sentence is:

```
Whether or not you approve of deficit spending, the legis-
lation is the proper one to pass in the upcoming election.
```

If splitting an infinitive is less awkward than leaving it intact, however, it is acceptable to split it. For example:

```
For the client to never lose is unusual.
The loan officer wanted to properly process the forms.
```

Parallel structure

Probably the most common error made involving parallel structure occurs when a writer lists items in a series and neglects to put all of these items in the same grammatical form. When you write a sentence that consists of a list or series of items, make sure these items are written in the same grammatical form. The use of parallel structure makes your writing more consistent and clearer to your reader.

In the groups of sentences below you will notice the first sentence of each group consists of a faulty parallel structure. Note how the faulty structure is rewritten in the second sentence of each group.

```
Faulty parallel structure: To sell her proposal, the mar-
keting director presented her marketing plan, asked for
```

reactions to her presentation, and many other things to involve her audience.

Better: To sell her proposal, the marketing director presented her marketing plan, asked for reactions to her presentation, and did many other things to involve her audience.

The above example was made parallel by adding a verb to the last item listed in the series. This addition made the item consistent with the other items in the series.

Faulty parallel structure: The personnel director was requested to handle terminations of employees as well as writing commendations.

Better: The personnel director was requested to handle terminations of employees as well as to write commendations.

The above sentence was made parallel by using an infinitive in the second item in the series, thus making it parallel to the first item in the series which contains an infinitive.

Faulty parallel structure can be corrected whether the items in a series are active verbs, infinitives, nouns, objectives, or any other part of speech. The important thing to remember is to be consistent with the grammatical form you use for writing items in a series.

Usage

Sometimes when we are reading a letter from someone or listening to a person speak, we are struck by the way in which the person has worded whatever he or she has said. "That doesn't sound correct," we say to ourselves. The standard which sets how we speak or write as educated people is called *usage.*

Usage guides us in the correct way of writing the English language. Usage is not static. What is accepted as correct today may be obsolete fifty years from now. Slang words which might not even have been created yet may be acceptable to use as good English ten or fifteen years from now. To write effectively you should be aware of current English usage.

One of the classic books on usage is William Strunk, Jr., and E. B. White's *The Elements of Style.* Although there are more thorough usage references available, such as Theodore M. Bernstein's *The Careful Writer,* Strunk and White's book is straightforward, simple to use, and helpful as a reference on any banker's desk. (See the bibliography for more about usage references.)

Some words are commonly misused by many letter writers. You will find a list of some of the most commonly misused words and phrases in Appendix I of *The Banker's Handbook of Letters and Letter Writing.*

Punctuation

Punctuation is used in writing to distinguish or separate one group of words from another to convey some meaning to a reader. The use of punctuation creates pauses and stresses where the writer feels they are necessary.

Appendix II goes over various aspects of punctuation that will help you use it correctly and effectively in your letter writing. Chapter 4 discusses how to use punctuation in each of the various letter formats.

Remember never to overuse punctuation. Omit punctuation when it is not necessary for clarity in your writing. Sentences needing little punctuation usually read more smoothly.

Consistency is important when using punctuation. If you decide to use punctuation in your letters, make sure you are consistent in how you use it. Ralph Waldo Emerson might have thought that "foolish consistency is the hobgoblin of little minds," but you can rest assured that consistency in the use of punctuation is not foolish. It helps to clarify your message to your reader.

Capitalization

Capitalization is another area which calls for consistency. Obviously you should capitalize the beginning of sentences as well as proper nouns and proper adjectives. There are, however, many quirks to the proper use of capitalization. When in doubt, it is usually best to lowercase or check a reference such as a dictionary. For proper capitalization within the various letter formats, see Chapter 4.

Spelling

Many books have been written to help writers with spelling problems. Most often, however, the best book to help a writer with spelling is a dictionary. To avoid careless spelling mistakes, a writer should look up those words about which he or she has the slightest doubt. The two best tools to guard against spelling errors in your letters are care in writing and a dictionary at your side.

Most word processing software packages feature a "spellcheck" function. If you have any doubts about your spelling ability, a spellcheck can be a saving grace. It will highlight any misspelled words and help you choose a correctly spelled alternative.

Jargon

Jargon is a curse to any writer who wants to get a clear, precise message across to a reader. The word "jargon" has two meanings. The first is "incoherent language." The second is "the technical language of a profession." Usually both of these types of jargon should be avoided in letter writing. Of course the first, "incoherent language," must be avoided at all costs. Technical language should be kept to a minimum in your letters to avoid confusing your reader.

A person who writes jargon is usually more impressed with the way the words sound than with getting a message across. You are writing to convey a message, not to impress your reader with how many big words you know. People who write in lofty language or jargon will often string together complex words that sound great but mean nothing.

Avoid pretention and strive for clarity in your letter writing. Forget about using jargon. Use simple language if you can. Your reader will appreciate it.

Cliches

Cliches are words or expressions that become stale from overuse. Cliches often take the form of metaphors or comparisons, such as "big as an ox" or "slept like a log." They are trite and show a lack of originality in writing.

In business, expressions such as "put on the back burner" and "caught between a rock and a hard place" have been used so often that they can be considered cliches. Nothing is grammatically wrong with these trite expressions. They are just so stale that they really have lost the power to convey much meaning to a reader.

Avoid cliches by trying to write exactly what it is you are trying to convey in your message to your reader. Make every word you write in your letters mean something. After you've written your first draft, clarify your letter's message by deleting any cliches or trite expressions you might have written.

Be original in your letter writing. If you need to make a comparison, try to make an original one. Avoid drawing from the stock of cliches that have been used for years.

Wordiness

If you don't come right out and write what you mean, your writing will be full of ambiguity. I can't emphasize this point too much. Write what you mean, not what you think sounds good.

The following pointers may be helpful in guiding you away from the curse of wordiness. Remember the following five "avoids" and you will be on your way to writing in a clear, direct style:

1. *Avoid pretentiousness.* Don't overcomplicate your writing by trying to impress the reader with your knowledge or vocabulary. Your reader most likely will not be impressed if you try to write with a great literary flair. Write simply, clearly, and directly.

2. *Avoid redundancy.* Don't use superfluous or repetitious words. Write what your reader needs to know and he or she will most likely get the message. There is no need to repeat your message over and over.

3. *Avoid padding.* Be direct in your letter writing. Strike out all unnecessary words or sentences. If you write more than you have to, your reader might become impatient. Strive for clarity and precision.

4. *Avoid weak intensifiers.* Words like "very," "quite," and "completely" usually add little or nothing to the meaning of your sentences. Don't use intensifiers unless they add to your letter's meaning.

5. *Avoid unnecessary definitions or explanations.* Explain only what absolutely needs to be explained. Don't insult your reader by explaining something he or she obviously would already know.

Revisions can help you eliminate any problem with wordiness you may be having. In the revision process you should: 1) reread the letter to make sure you've said what you wanted to say; 2) edit out all unnecessary words and phrases; and 3) clarify until your letter is precise enough to get the proper message across to your reader.

Word Processing 6

Try as some might to fight it, the day of the word processor has arrived. What many have found, much to their surprise, is that word processors actually can simplify work without taking away any of the user's individuality or creativity.

Typing Skills Are Key

The biggest difficulty for many first-time users of word processors is not learning how to turn on the machine, nor is it formatting a disk or learning how to boot the system. No, for many users, the most difficult aspect is never having learned to type. Perhaps this is why many writers, although they fought the age of the computer as much as any other group, have been admirably successful in getting up to speed on word processing skills. They already knew how to type.

In a day and age when electronic mail allows us to type a message onto a screen and send it to a correspondent on a different floor in our building or in a different city in the country, executives who learn the basic skill of typing will be able to use a word processor to increase their efficiency without sacrificing the quality of their writing.

Using the Machine

There are those who would argue that because word processors are computers, it is essential to learn how the computer works to be able to use it effectively. This would include learning to program and presumably learning how to add a chip or two to the inside of the machine should you want to upgrade its capabilities. While those who wish to tackle this endeavor have admirable ambitions, I am among those who hold to the argument, "I'm not really concerned with how it works. I just want to be able to use it."

I have a coffee maker which I can time to brew the coffee just before I wake up in the morning or just around the time I think my dinner guest may want a cup of coffee, but I don't have any idea how the timing mechanism in the machine works. All I know is that I put the coffee, filter, and water in the machine, press a few buttons, and I'll have coffee when I set the timer to make it.

It's a similar story with my computer. I know how to get it to do what I want it to do, but I've very little idea about what a chip is made from, or how all the boards inside the computer are wired.

Word Processing Software

As those of you who have been using word processors for some time already know, as you use your machine more and more you will learn new things. In the first several months of using a computer for word processing, you'll learn more and more and more. But after six months, you'll know probably 80% of what you'll ever have to know to use the machine as a word processor.

There are many different types of word processing software packages available. While some may be more frequently used than others, if you are in a larger bank, the chances are you'll probably be subjected to the software that someone else has chosen. While some software is easier to use than others either because its instructional literature is more clearly written, it doesn't involve as many multiple key hits to get the software to do something, or its bells and whistles are fancier, most word processing software will get the job done when you want to use it for letter writing.

Using Model Letters

The same letter is often written to different bank customers. Rather than retype the letter every time you want to use it, you can store those letters you use frequently on a computer disk and call it up each time the appropriate situation to send it out arises.

Take for example the letter that is sent out to a customer when a new account is opened. (See sample letter 6.1.) Rather than have the same letter retyped each time a customer opens a new account, you can simply call up the letter from a master file of letters you have stored either on a floppy or hard disk, and tailor it to reflect the particular situation. Since most word processing software packages feature what is called a "mail merge" function, you can often simply type in a coded name and address, instruct the machine which letter you want it attached to, and create a custom-tailored letter.

SAMPLE LETTER 6.1. New account thank you letter.

June 23, 19X6

Ms. Daphne Modugno
Vice President
Modugno-Yatsko Enterprises
One Pucaro Street
Norristown, Pennsylvania 43234

Dear Ms. Modugno:

Thank you for opening your account at New National Bank. Now that your account is open, we will mail periodic account statements which will provide you with current account balance information and transaction activity. And let me remind you that savings accounts are insured up to $100,000 by the FDIC, an agency of the federal government.

We value your business and will do our best to give you accurate and responsive service. Please call me at 434-3434 or use our toll-free number, 1-800-989-0909, if you need additional assistance or information.

Sincerely,

Mark Simons
Senior Vice President

ms/ar

There are dozens of letters in *The Banker's Handbook of Letters and Letter Writing* that are suitable for tailoring to your needs and storing on a master disk for frequent use. Since each bank's needs are different, you'll want to go through the letters to determine which ones are appropriate for storage in your system.

Remember, however, that one of the goals of letter writing is to give the impression that there is an actual person writing the letter specifically to the person addressed. Simply printing out the same letter to customer after customer is not always appropriate. There are other solutions.

For instance, one bank created a "private" file and a "public" file on its computer system. There are five personal computers networked together to a hard disk. Each terminal user can access anything on the public file. But if that user wants to tailor a letter or memo to reflect his or her personality, or to add specific items he or she believes to be necessary, or even just to duplicate a few paragraphs to be used in a different letter, the user can copy the document from a public file onto a private file which can only be accessed if the user types a personal code into the system. No one else can tamper with the changes that person made in his or her private file. But each user has access to whatever model letters are stored in the public file. The user is able not only to use a model letter, but also to add a personal touch.

One of the critical things to remember about word processing is that no matter how proficient you become with the machine, it is not a substitute for good writing. The letters you send out will not be magically transformed into good prose by the mere fact that you are using an expensive machine to create them or to retrieve them. The letters you retrieve will only be as good as the letters that were stored in your system in the first place.

A particularly useful aspect of a system set up to have a public vs. private file function is that long form letters which in the past required that the sender check off various appropriate paragraphs can now be tailored to include just those paragraphs which are appropriate to be included. The result will be a letter that is shorter and easier for the receiver to understand.

For example, a form letter which one bank uses as a loan approval consists of several pages of possible terms and conditions. Each appropriate term or condition is checked off. But the reader still has to plow through many pages to get to the appropriate material. (see sample letter 6.2.)

SAMPLE LETTER 6.2. Loan approval consisting of several-page list of possible terms and conditions.

November 9, 19X1

Mr. Terrence Henries
134 Leone Drive
Millersville, North Dakota 66632

Dear Mr. Henries:

We are pleased to have approved your application for a $59,600 loan subject to all of the terms and conditions which follow. For simplicity, County Savings Bank will be referred to as ''CSB,'' you as ''Borrower,'' the $59,600 loan as ''Loan,'' and the specific security as ''Security Property.''

After we receive your acceptance of our commitment, we will advise the closing attorney to prepare the loan instruments.

We are pleased to have the opportunity to serve you. If you have questions about this commitment, please call us.

Sincerely,

John Savithson
Vice President

js/nc

encs.: 1. Terms of Loan
2. Requirements and Conditions of Loan

Mr. Terrence Henries -2- November 9, 19X1

TERMS OF LOAN

Borrower: Mr. Terrence Henries

Amount of Loan: $59,600

Purpose: Residential Construction

Endorsers or Guarantors: None

Security: First deed of trust on land and improvements known as Lot 5-U, Grand Forks, Route 76, Millersville, North Dakota

Amortization: On demand
(The closing attorney is to prepare the deed of trust and deed of trust note to read ''Payable on Demand.'')

Maturity: 6 months from the date of our initial disbursement

Extensions: To be negotiated

Interest Rate: 10 1/2% per annum, payable monthly

Service Charge: 1% ($596), non-refundable

Payee and Place of Payment: County Savings Bank,
Real Estate Finance Department,
County Shopping Center,
Grand Forks, North Dakota 66630

Trustees: Henry Janeway and Curtiss Leroy, Residents of the City of Millersville

Release Provisions: Not applicable

Closing Attorney: Ms. Nanette Mathis

REQUIREMENTS

Prior to the disbursement of any portion of the loan proceeds, Borrower will have satisfied completely the following documentation requirements and other conditions as listed (only those checked):

✓ NOTE AND DEED OF TRUST (CSB Standard Form)
The loan is to be evidenced by a deed of trust note of the Borrower and secured by a first deed of trust on the Security Property, the substance of each of which is subject to approval by CSB.

The deed of trust note and deed of trust will be submitted to and reviewed by CSB prior to execution and recording. Upon approval and recording, instead of the original deed of trust which should be forwarded to CSB as soon as available, CSB is to be furnished with a standardized copy with the original recording receipt attached.

✓ TITLE INSURANCE
Borrower will furnish to CSB a policy of title insurance issued by a company acceptable to and insuring CSB in the amount of the loan, without exception for possible unfiled mechanics' and materialmen's liens and containing only such title exceptions satisfactory to CSB. Should a binder be issued, the term of this binder will not be less than the term of the loan. The title insurance policy or binder must be submitted to and reviewed by CSB prior to loan closing. If the original title policy is not available at loan closing, a marked-up binder initialed by the title company will be acceptable, providing the original policy is promptly forwarded to CSB.

✓ HAZARD INSURANCE
Borrower will furnish to CSB a standard fire insurance policy issued by a company acceptable to CSB (together with ''Paid'' premium invoice) in an amount which is the greater of the amount of the loan or 100% of the insurable value of the Security Property, with extended coverage, vandalism and malicious mischief insurance. The policy will contain standard mortgagee loss payable clause in favor of CSB, Real Estate Finance Department.

✓ FLOOD INSURANCE
[ ] Flood insurance is not required.
[ ] Flood insurance is required. Borrower is to provide CSB with a standard flood insurance policy issued under the National Flood Insurance Program naming CSB as loss payee.

✓ BUILDING LOAN AGREEMENT
Borrower will furnish to CSB a building loan agreement, the substance of which is subject to approval by CSB.

✓ CURRENT SURVEY
Borrower will furnish to CSB a current survey showing no encroachments and otherwise acceptable to CSB, prepared and certified by a certified land

Mr. Terrence Henries -4- November 9, 19X1

surveyor, which survey will designate, without limitation, (i) the dimensions of the Security Property, (ii) the dimensions and location of the buildings and other improvements constructed on the property, (iii) the dimensions of the parking areas as well as the total number of on-site parking spaces, (iv) the location of all easements of record affecting the Security Property, specifying the holder of each such easement and the pertinent recordation information, (v) any and all building restriction and/or setback lines, and (vi) means of ingress and egress. Borrower will furnish to CSB within ten (10) days after being requested to do so updated surveys of the Security Property acceptable to CSB showing all improvements then constructed on the property, prepared and certified by a certified land surveyor. If the loan is a construction loan, the above required survey is also to be furnished to CSB upon completion of construction and prior to final disbursement of the loan proceeds.

✓ SUBDIVISION PLATS
Borrower will furnish to CSB a copy of all subdivision plats recorded or to be recorded of the Security Property which plats must be acceptable to CSB. With regard to all subdivision plats to be recorded, Borrower will furnish evidence acceptable to CSB that all such plats have been approved by all necessary governmental agencies.

✓ APPRAISAL
Borrower will furnish to CSB an appraisal made by an appraiser acceptable to CSB and which appraisal must be in an amount not less than $ ___________ and otherwise acceptable to CSB.

✓ AUTHORITY TO BORROW
Borrower will furnish to CSB its Corporate Borrowing Resolution (CSB standard form or other resolution in form and substance acceptable to CSB) and acceptable evidence that Borrower is a_corporation in good standing.

OR If the Borrower is a partnership, general or limited, Borrower will furnish to CSB a copy of the partnership agreement and any existing or future amendments thereto, a certified copy of the recorded partnership certificate and such other documents as CSB may require.

✓ ASSURANCE OF UTILITY AVAILABILITY
Borrower will furnish evidence acceptable to CSB that all utilities (including drainage both on-site and off-site) necessary for the operation or occupancy of the Security Property are available to the Security Property, that the Security Property is connected thereto, and that all requisite tap-on or connection fees have been paid.

✓ PLANS AND SPECIFICATIONS
Borrower will furnish to CSB a complete and final set of working plans and specifications in respect of the Security Property. Borrower will also furnish to CSB evidence acceptable to CSB that all plans and specifications have been approved by all necessary governmental agencies.

✓ COMPLIANCE WITH GOVERNMENTAL REGULATIONS
Prior to the commencement of construction and the initial loan disbursement, Borrower will furnish evidence acceptable to CSB that the Security Property and the improvements to be constructed thereon comply with all applicable zoning ordinances, building codes and all other applicable local, state, and federal laws, rules, regulations and/or requirements.

✓ STARTS AHEAD OF SALES LIMITATION
Units started but unsold under this loan as well as all other loans to Borrower may not exceed ______________, including model units.

✓ OTHER DOCUMENTS
Borrower will furnish such other instruments, documents, opinions and/or assurances as CSB may require.

DISBURSEMENT PROCEDURE

Upon receipt and approval by CSB of all requisite loan documents, and/or provided and so long as Borrower complies with all obligations imposed upon Borrower in the loan documents and in this commitment:

✓ a. We agree to disburse funds as construction progresses and based upon inspections acceptable to CSB. In this regard Borrower must notify CSB a minimum of three business days in advance so that CSB may schedule an inspection of the improvements. Borrower will also simultaneously

Mr. Terrence Henries -6- November 9, 19X1

notify the closing attorney to up-date title to the Security Property through the date the requested loan disbursement is to be made and to give telephone advice to CSB of the results of such up-date. An endorsement to the title policy extending the effective date through the date of CSB's disbursement must promptly be furnished to CSB. CSB reserves the right to require receipt of the title up-date endorsement prior to the requested disbursement of loan proceeds.

✓ b. CSB agrees to disburse the loan proceeds in accordance with the General Contractor's Requisition for Payment, which must be approved and certified by the supervising architect or engineer of the work performed. The requisition and certification (it is suggested that American Institute of Architects' standard forms be used) must be in a form acceptable to CSB and all items included under the requisition will be subject to CSB's final approval.

✓ c. Property inspections and/or loan disbursements will be limited to one per month.

✓ d. Other:

APPROVAL OF LOAN DOCUMENTATION & FEES & EXPENSES
The loan will be made without cost to CSB. Borrower will pay all costs and expenses incurred in connection with this loan whether or not the loan is closed, including, but not limited to, title insurance premiums, surveyor's fees, appraiser's fees and legal fees. All requisite loan documents and related instruments will, at the option of CSB, be submitted to CSB's attorney for review and approval. Borrower will be deemed to have expressly agreed to pay all legal fees incurred by CSB in connection with this review.

REPRESENTATIONS OF BORROWER
The validity of this commitment is subject to the accuracy of all information, representations and materials submitted with, and in support of, Borrower's application for the loan. In the event CSB determines that any information or representations contained in the loan application are not accurate or correct, CSB will have the right to terminate this commitment, whereupon CSB will have no further obligations.

Mr. Terrence Henries -7- November 9, 19X1

ASSIGNMENT OR MODIFICATION
Neither this commitment nor the loan can be modified or assigned without prior written consent of CSB.

ACCEPTANCE OF THIS COMMITMENT
In order for this commitment to remain effective, the acceptance copy of this commitment must be executed by Borrower and returned to CSB at Grand Forks, North Dakota on or before the expiration of ten (10) days from the date of this letter. Any extension for acceptance must be in writing and signed by CSB.

EXPIRATION OF COMMITMENT
To cause this commitment to remain in effect, the loan must be closed and CSB must disburse loan proceeds prior to ____________________ and any extension of such date must be in writing and signed by CSB.

The terms and conditions of this commitment will survive settlement and any violation of these terms and conditions will constitute default under the note and deed of trust.

Very truly yours,
COUNTY SAVINGS BANK

BY: ______________________

The undersigned accepts the commitment and the terms, and requirements set forth in this agreement.

____

BY: _______________________ DATE: _______________

OTHER POSSIBLE TERMS AND REQUIREMENTS

ASSIGNMENT OF STOCK
CSB will be provided with a pledge of 100% of the capital stock of Borrower as additional collateral for the loan. The pledge must be in form and substance acceptable to CSB and must grant to CSB a perfected first security interest in all of the capital stock of Borrower.

AGREEMENT NOT TO DISPOSE OF PARTNERSHIP INTEREST

CROSS-COLLATERALIZATION
The documents evidencing and/or securing the indebtedness of the Borrower will be drawn in such a manner that the Security Property for this loan will also act as security for all other debt of the Borrower and, further, all col-

Mr. Terrence Henries -8- November 9, 19X1

lateral taken as security for any other debt of the Borrower will be deemed to secure this loan as well.

CROSS-DEFAULT
The note and deed of trust will contain a provision to the effect that any default will constitute a default under all other existing loans of the Borrower, and that any default under any one or all of the existing loans will constitute default under this note and deed of trust.

COMMISSIONS
All commissions, brokerage claims or other compensation, if any, due or payable to any person, firm or corporation by reason of the making of the loan will be paid by Borrower and the Borrower indemnifies CSB against any claims or liability for the payment of any such commission, brokerage claims or other compensation. This obligation will survive the payment in full of the principal and interest of the loan.

EQUITY REQUIREMENTS
Borrower will provide evidence of its ability to satisfy certain equity requirements as determined by CSB in connection with the loan and deposit these in escrow.

ESCROWS
Sufficient escrows for real estate taxes and hazard insurance must be prepaid prior to the commencement of the first monthly mortgage payment so that when added to subsequent monthly escrow collections, the escrow account will be adequate to pay the tax assessment and insurance premiums on month prior to their respective due dates.

GUARANTY
CSB standard form or other agreement in form and substance acceptable to CSB.

FINANCIAL STATEMENTS
Borrower will furnish to CSB a copy of all financial statements including an itemized account of gross annual income and expenditures reflecting in detail the operations of the property. This statement will be prepared in accordance with then current and generally accepted accounting principles by an accountant satisfactory to CSB.

OR For as long as the loan remains outstanding, Borrower, at his expense, agrees to deliver to CSB an income statement, balance sheet and other financial information reasonably required by CSB as soon as available but in no event more than 90 days after the end of each of its fiscal years. Borrower is also responsible for providing CSB with annual personal financial statements of all endorsers and/or guarantors of the loan.

NO ADVERSE CHANGE
No part of the Security Property will be damaged and not repaired to the satisfaction of CSB, nor taken in condemnation or other like proceeding, nor shall any such proceeding be pending. Neither Borrower nor any tenant under any assigned lease, nor any guarantor on the loan, or of any such lease, will be involved in any bankruptcy, reorganization, dissolution, or insolvency proceeding.

NON-ASSUMPTION
The loan is subject to call in full or its terms may be modified in the event of sale or conveyance of the Security Property.

SALES REPORT
Borrower hereby agrees to provide CSB, in writing, a monthly status report indicating the number of units, lots, etc., sold, settled and remaining to be sold. This report should be effective on the last week of each month and should be submitted to CSB within ten (10) days of the report date.

SOIL REPORT
Borrower will submit a soil engineer's report acceptable to CSB. CSB reserves the right to require certification that grading and foundation construction work were performed in accordance with recommendations contained in the report.

BUILDING PERMITS

CERTIFICATION OF OFF-SITE DRAINAGE AVAILABILITY AND CAPACITY

ENGINEER'S FEASIBILITY REPORT

ENVIRONMENTAL IMPACT REPORTS AND/OR HEALTH CERTIFICATES

EXISTING DEEDS OF TRUST OR PURCHASE MONEY DEEDS OF TRUST
Borrower will provide to CSB certified true copies of any deeds of trust encumbering the Security Property subject to the lien of CSB.

LINE OF CREDIT
This loan is considered a part of your ________________ line of credit and advances on this and all other loans made under this line may not exceed ________________ at any one time.

Mr. Terrence Henries -10- November 9, 19X1

MARKETING FEASIBILITY STUDIES

PERCOLATION REPORTS
Where septic tanks are to be used.

PRO-FORMA CASH FLOW PROJECTIONS

RECISION AGREEMENT

REGULATION Z
Truth in Lending Statement.

RESTRICTION ON ADDITIONAL BORROWINGS

RIGHT OF FIRST REFUSAL FOR ADDITIONAL CONSTRUCTION FINANCING SIGNS
CSB reserves the right to erect signs on the Security Property identifying all participating lenders.

SUBORDINATION AGREEMENTS

CONDOMINIUM DOCUMENTATION (Condominium loans only)
All necessary documents for the establishment of a condominium regime in accordance with the Horizontal Property Law will be submitted to CSB's counsel for approval. Upon approval, the Borrower must properly record these documents evidenced by recorder's receipts, and title policy endorsements. Additionally, the foregoing documents should be submitted to the Title Insurance Company for review and approval and the policy of title insurance should include an affirmative statement that the Horizontal Property regime has been created in accordance with and complies with state law. The policy of title insurance should also insure CSB against any loss or damage due to inadequacies of the condominium documentation.

DISBURSEMENTS
Physical inspections by representatives of CSB and construction advances will be limited to one per month and the first advance will not be made until completion of all foundation work and the concrete slab or platform is in place. Aggregate construction advances will be limited to ninety percent (90%) of the loan amount and no further advances will be made until final completion as determined by CSB.

NOTE: This provision has been designed for use on single family residential loans. It is used primarily for the one shot loan to an individual constructing his personal residence. However, it should be considered for use with small builders and builders that CSB has limited previous experience.

FOR OUT OF STATE TRANSACTIONS

Attorney's Opinion Letter
Borrower will furnish CSB with an attorney's opinion letter setting forth that the Borrowing corporation (partnership) is duly recognized and existing under (State) _______________ law and all fees, charges, and taxes required to be paid by it to permit it to operate and own any mortgage real property has been paid, that the instruments used to implement this transaction were signed by duly elected and still qualified officers of the Borrowing corporation (partnership) and are in proper legal form and order and executed so as to be valid, binding and enforceable and are according to their tenor under (State) ______________ law that the subject transaction does not constitute ''doing business'' in (State) ______________ (even were we to engage in more than one or several transactions of the same general type), that we would have access to the Courts of (State) ______________ to qualify to ''do business'' there or to pay any fees or taxes other than normal court costs, that the interest rate and all fees collected are permissible in (State) ____________ and do not constitute usury and that the mortgage or Deed of Trust is being recorded as required and will be effective without re-recording for the term of the note as a first lien on all mortgaged premises.

By using the same letter on the word processor and tailoring it to include only those conditions appropriate to this particular loan approval, the letter is much shorter and to the point. (See sample letter 6.3.)

SAMPLE LETTER 6.3. Loan approval tailored from a model letter stored in the computer.

November 9, 19X1

Mr. Terrence Henries
134 Leone Drive
Millersville, North Dakota 66632

Dear Mr. Henries:

We are pleased to have approved your application for a $59,600 loan subject to all of the terms and conditions which follow. For simplicity, County Savings Bank will be referred to as ''CSB,'' you as ''Borrower,'' the $59,600 as ''Loan,'' and the specific security as ''Security Property.''

After we receive your acceptance of our commitment, we will advise the closing attorney to prepare the loan instruments.

We are pleased to have the opportunity to serve you. If you have any questions about this commitment, please call us.

Sincerely,

John Savithson
Vice President

js/nc

encs.: 1. Terms of Loan
2. Requirements and Conditions of Loan

Terms of Loan

Borrower: Mr. Terrence Henries

Amount of Loan: $59,600

Purpose: Residential Construction

Endorsers or Guarantors: None

Security: First deed of trust on land and improvements known as Lot 5-U, Grand Forks, Route 76, Millersville, North Dakota

Mr. Terrence Henries -2- November 9, 19X1

Amortization: On demand
(The closing attorney is to prepare the deed of trust and deed of trust note to read ''Payable on Demand.'')

Maturity: 6 months from the date of our initial disbursement

Extensions: To be negotiated

Interest Rate: 10.5% per annum, payable monthly

Service Charge: 1% ($596), non-refundable

Payee and Place of Payment: County Savings Bank, Real Estate Finance Department, County Shopping Center, Grand Forks, North Dakota 66630

Trustees: Henry Janeway and Curtiss Leroy, Residents of the City of Millersville

Release Provisions: Not applicable

Closing Attorney: Ms. Nanette Mathis

REQUIREMENTS

Prior to the disbursement of any portion of the loan proceeds, Borrower will have satisfied completely the following documentation requirements and other conditions as listed:

NOTE AND DEED OF TRUST (CSB Standard Form)
The loan is to be evidenced by a deed of trust note of the Borrower and secured by a first deed of trust on the Security Property, the substance of each of which is subject to approval by CSB. The deed of trust note and deed of trust will be submitted to and reviewed by CSB prior to execution and recording. Upon approval and recording, instead of the original deed of trust which should be forwarded to CSB as soon as available, CSB is to be furnished with a standardized copy with the original recording receipt attached.

Mr. Terrence Henries -3- November 9, 19X1

TITLE INSURANCE
Borrower will furnish to CSB a policy of title insurance issued by a company acceptable to and insuring CSB in the amount of the loan, without exception for possible unfiled mechanics' and materialmen's liens and containing only such title exceptions satisfactory to CSB. Should a binder be issued, the term of this binder will not be less than the term of the loan. The title insurance policy or binder must be submitted to and reviewed by CSB prior to closing. If the original title policy is not available at loan closing, a marked-up binder initialed by the title company will be acceptable, providing the original policy is promptly forwarded to CSB.

APPRAISAL
Borrower will furnish to CSB an appraisal made by an appraiser acceptable to CSB and which appraisal must be in an amount not less than $___________ and otherwise acceptable to CSB.

AUTHORITY TO BORROW
Borrower will furnish to CSB its Corporate Borrowing Resolution (CSB standard form or other resolution in form and substance acceptable to CSB) and acceptable evidence that Borrower is a corporation in good standing.

PLANS AND SPECIFICATIONS
Borrower will furnish to CSB a complete and final set of working plans and specifications in respect of the Security Property. Borrower will also furnish to CSB evidence acceptable to CSB that all plans and specifications have been approved by all necessary governmental agencies.

COMPLIANCE WITH GOVERNMENTAL REGULATIONS
Prior to the commencement of construction and the initial loan disbursement, Borrower will furnish evidence acceptable to CSB that the Security Property and the improvements to be constructed thereon comply with all applicable zoning ordinances, building codes and all other applicable local, state, and federal laws, rules, regulations and/or requirements.

DISBURSEMENT PROCEDURE
Upon receipt and approval by CSB of all requisite loan documents, and/or provided and so long as Borrower complies with all obligations imposed upon Borrower in the loan documents and in this commitment:

Mr. Terrence Henries -4- November 9, 19X1

a. We agree to disburse funds as construction progresses and based upon inspections acceptable to CSB. In this regard Borrower must notify CSB a minimum of three business days in advance so that CSB may schedule an inspection of the improvements. Borrower will also simultaneously notify the closing attorney to up-date title to the Security Property through the date the requested loan disbursement is to be made and to give telephone advice to CSB of the results of such up-date. An endorsement to thetitle policy extending the effective date through the date of CSB's disbursement must promptly be furnished to CSB. CSB reserves the right to require receipt of the title up-date endorsement prior to the requested disbursement of loan proceeds.

b. CSB agrees to disburse the loan proceeds in accordance with the General Contractor's Requisition for Payment, which must be approved and certified by the supervising architect or engineer of the work performed. The requisition and certification (it is suggested that American Institute of Architects' standard forms be used) must be in a form acceptable to CSB and all items included under the requisition will be subject to CSB's final approval.

c. Property inspections and/or loan disbursements will be limited to one per month.

Very truly yours,

COUNTY SAVINGS BANK
BY: ______________

The undersigned hereby accepts the foregoing commitment and the terms, and requirements herein set forth, and agrees to be bound thereby.

____

BY: DATE: ______________

Word processing may not be the answer for every banker who reads this book. For those who wish to use it as a book of model letters on which to base their own, *The Banker's Handbook of Letters and Letter Writing* will still prove very useful.

But for those who are committed to automating their offices and increasing their efficiency without losing their personal touch, *The Banker's Handbook of Letters and Letter Writing* should prove a helpful tool when it comes to setting up a database of frequently used model letters that can be called up by all users and tailored to particular needs.

PART II
THE LETTERS

Sales & Marketing— General Letters 7

When you write a sales or marketing letter, your fundamental objective is to get your reader to react positively and use your bank's services. To successfully achieve this objective, these letters must grab your readers' attention and convince them that your bank is able to provide the best services for their needs.

Sales and marketing letters should be written in a friendly, personal tone. Too formal a letter might convince your readers that you are not going to provide the personal attention they need.

The letters in Chapters 7 and 8 are all geared primarily toward selling and marketing bank products and services. Chapter 7 includes general sales and marketing letters including those used for follow-ups, cross-selling, referral calls, and setting up additional calls. Chapter 8 includes letters that were written to sell specific retail products or services of a bank. These are categorized according to the type of product or service that is being marketed.

Sales Letters

Sample letter 7.1, written in the hanging-indented format, was written to sell the general services of a community bank. The hanging-indented format is used to attract the reader's attention. The contents of the letter are organized to effectively attract the reader's attention. The writer asks a question that is designed to draw the reader into the letter and to become involved in the decision-making process used to choose a bank. The remainder of the letter highlights why this particular bank is the best one to provide the services the customer needs, and urges the reader to take action by coming in to let the banker discuss more about what the bank can offer.

SAMPLE LETTER 7.1. Sales of services letter (hanging-indented format).

May 9, 19X2

Ms. Joan Kenney
1978 Malden Place
Media, Pennsylvania 01005

Dear Ms. Kenney:

How do you choose a bank?

Are modern facilities most important to you? Size and resources? Or courtesy and efficiency of personnel?

Probably you'll want to consider all of these factors. So, if you'll pardon us for ''pointing with pride,'' we like to think of the New National as the bank that friends are building. Without merger, we've grown from a small private bank organized in 1916, with a capital of $20,000, to rank among the 100 largest banks in the United States.

People are important to us. Here you'll find modern facilities combined with old-fashioned courtesy. We like to think of our customers as friends. We know that the patience of a bookkeeper, the warm smile of a teller, or the helpful suggestions of a loan officer are what keep customers coming back.

Without reservation, we can tell you that we're genuinely proud of the New National women and men who serve our customers. Many of them like myself are ''old timers'' who have grown up with our business. Others have joined our New National ''family'' more recently. But all of us have one goal in common: to make it easy, pleasant, and convenient to transact business here. Our officers would like very much to

Sample Letter 7.1 continued

show you around the ''bank that friends are building.''

Cordially,

Pearl Mahaffey
Vice President

PM:JS

Another method of attracting business is to approach newcomers to the community. For the small savings bank in a community a letter such as the one in sample letter 7.2 is a perfect way to show a personal interest in a customer and attract his or her business.

SAMPLE LETTER 7.2. Sales letter welcoming newcomer to community (block format).

January 29, 19X1

Ms. Patricia Palay
134 Howard Place
Flushing, Connecticut 02098

Dear Ms. Palay:

It is a pleasure to learn that you have moved to Flushing. I welcome you to the city and hope that you will
enjoy living among us.

As a representative of County Savings Bank, I'd like very
much to receive your personal banking business. I am confident that County Savings Bank's complete banking services, which can serve you in all of your banking needs,
would prove beneficial to you. Whether you are ready to
make a local banking connection or merely need information, I'd be interested in assisting you.

I hope you will come in sometime soon and give me the opportunity of meeting you personally. If I am not in when
you call, this letter will serve as an introduction to
any one of our officers.

Cordially,

Bethany J. Coleman
Assistant Vice President

bjc:nlc

Once a customer decides to use your services, you have an ideal candidate to whom you can sell other services. Be careful not to bombard the new customer with a hard sell. You want the customer to know that you are thankful he or she decided to use your bank, and that you are anxious to describe the many services your bank can provide. Sample letter 7.3 is a good example of an effective sales letter written to a customer who recently decided to use some of the bank's services.

All good salespeople do their homework. If you want to make a good impression with prospective customers, learn something about them. An ideal occasion on which to write a sales letter is when you learn of a prospective customer's promotion or new job. (See sample letter 7.4.)

SAMPLE LETTER 7.3. Sales letter to customer already using services (full-block format).

March 30, 19X2

Mr. Louis Volpe
Treasurer
General Hospital
100 Harlan Drive
Cambridge, Wisconsin 54321

Dear Mr. Volpe:

Thank you for placing a certificate of deposit with New National Bank yesterday.

As vice president of our Institutional and Professional Department, I handle most of our relationships with the healthcare industry including lending, cash management, and other related banking services. My associates at New National and I would be pleased to provide any services we can, or act as a sounding board on financial matters. We do business with many hospitals in the Cambridge area and are familiar with the trials and tribulations of operating within this adverse regulatory environment.

To familiarize you with New National, I enclose a copy of our 19X1 annual report for your perusal and files. Please feel free to call me or any of my associates on the enclosed list at any time. I'll call you within the next few days to introduce myself by phone.

I look forward to meeting you.

Very truly yours,

Wallace W. Whipher
Vice President

Sample Letter 7.3 continued

grl

Enclosure

SAMPLE LETTER 7.4. Sales letter congratulating customer on promotion (semiblock format).

October 8, 19X2

Ms. Elizabeth Gruber, CPA
Long & Berrigan
200 Andover Street
Bar Harbor, Michigan 67892

Dear Ms. Gruber:

Congratulations on being named a partner of Long & Berrigan. While I realize that you are restricted in the amount of banking you can do with clients, I would be delighted to assist you in any way I can.

New National Bank tailor-makes lines of credit to professionals like you. We also have a reasonably fast response time to any business referrals.

Good luck to you with your new responsibilities. I hope I can be helpful to you with any service or question no matter how big or small.

Kindest regards,

Brett Kannapaux
Vice President

Sample letter 7.5 describes services available to a customer. The writer uses a metaphor for estate planning that draws the reader in to learn about estate services available at the bank.

SAMPLE LETTER 7.5. Sales letter for estate planning services of a bank's trust department (simplified format).

September 20, 19X3

Ms. Nancy Kenworthy
54 Garland Drive
Hamilton, California 00012

ESTATE PLANNING FOR FINANCIAL SECURITY

Ms. Kenworthy, it takes a plan to build a house. If you build a home you know the necessity of an architect's plan. Specialized knowledge is required to get the best results.

The same is true of the estate you leave for your family's protection. A well-thought-out program, prepared now with the aid of your lawyer and New National Bank's Trust Department, is important to your family's financial security.

Furthermore, an estate plan—like a house—does not automatically keep itself up to date. Investment conditions, increased taxes, changing individual needs, require new provisions to meet these new and different situations. New National's Trust Department is ready and willing to help you set up a modern program for your family's future financial welfare.

You are welcome to come in and talk over New National's trust services at any time.

PAMELA A. HOGAN
TRUST OFFICER

pah/trw

Another way to sell your bank's services to a customer is to set yourself up against the competition as being a bank that can offer superior and more diverse services. Sample letter 7.6's writer explains how the bank has met the challenge of the competitive industry. The letter writer is willing to match his bank against any other. Sample letter 7.6 not only sets up the writer's bank as one that can offer quality service, but also as one that the writer is willing to stake his reputation on.

SAMPLE LETTER 7.6. Sales letter comparing your bank to competition (full-block format).

March 9, 19X2

Mr. Emil Modugno
John Wagner & Associates
One Park Place
Sibling, Ohio 02222

Dear Mr. Modugno:

Competition is the foundation of our country's economic system. As such, it has been the catalyst to tremendous economic growth and development.

In recent years, the competitive spirit in the banking industry has grown progressively keener. This competition has created an excitement which has attracted more talented personnel into the profession and led to the development of a wide range of new products and services for the corporate and consumer markets.

As a New National Corporation Bank, New National Bank has benefited from competition in national, international, regional, and local markets. In each market we have met the challenge. As a result, the New National Bank has developed a reputation as a commercial banking group with highly skilled personnel and a broad range of sophisticated corporate services.

New National Bank is your present bank's competition. We would like to have an opportunity to visit with you to discuss the ways in which our skills and services could benefit your fine company.

I will call you next week for an appointment. If all New National does is keep your present bank competitive, it will be a good investment of your time.

Sincerely,
Quentin Compson
Vice President

qc/rm

Sample letters 7.7 and 7.8 try to attract customers who either have not used their banking privileges in some time or have recently closed their accounts at the bank. Sample letter 7.7 encourages the customer to continue using his privileges more frequently because of the positive results which will occur. Sample letter 7.8 tries to draw the former account holder back into the fold by describing other services that might be more useful.

SAMPLE LETTER 7.7. Sales letter to customer who hasn't used services in some time (full-block format).

November 9, 19X2

Mr. John Hill
327 Richmond Avenue
San Diego, California 90006

Dear Mr. Hill:

It has been a long time since we've seen you at our savings windows. Our interest in you as one of our depositors makes us want to mention it.

Most people start a savings account with some definite aim in view, intending to make regular deposits from their earnings or income. We know, of course, that circumstances often cause changes in plans, yet in our nearly 100 years of experience watching savings grow, we have seen the value of thrift—a habit formed through determination and sometimes a little self-denial.

Our savings department could weave romantic tales about the ''end of the rainbow'' by telling of the education of children, the purchase of homes, hospital bills paid-in-full, long awaited travel, and financial independence—all of which were accomplished through systematic savings.

Your savings account can be a bright spot in your future. Begin anew by making regular deposits. And when you bring in your passbook the accumulated interest will be added.

Very sincerely yours,

Lindsey Harlan
Vice President

SAMPLE LETTER 7.8. Sales letter to holder of closed account (semiblock format).

May 9, 19X5

Mr. John Waggoner
456 Allegheny Road
Southside, New Jersey 09090

Dear Mr. Waggoner:

When you closed your checking account with us a few months ago, we placed your name in our inactive file, hoping you would find occasion to reopen it.

We would very much like to have your name on our ledgers again. Some of our other services include: money market accounts; loans (personal, automobile, business, home repair); NOW accounts; bank-by-mail service; automated teller service; Christmas savings club; bank money orders; travelers checks; safe deposit services; and trust department services. Perhaps this list suggests some other ways in which we can be of assistance to you.

We hope you decide to continue your association with us. If you would like more information, give me a call.

Sincerely,

Beverly G. Krauss
Vice President

bgk/jls

Follow-up Letters

Follow-up letters to meetings or phone calls let your prospective customer know you are truly interested in doing business. If the follow-up letter provides information requested by a customer, you should describe what you've enclosed in the letter and remind the reader how it will help his or her financial business. Anything you might have promised to look into at a meeting or a discussion should be addressed in your follow-up letter.

Sample letters 7.9-7.14 are all good examples of effective follow-up letters to meetings or discussions. The title in the figure legend to each of these examples will give you an idea of the type of letter that follows.

SAMPLE LETTER 7.9. Follow-up letter to meeting enclosing promised information (full-block format).

June 10, 19X1

Robert Kane
Treasurer
General Hospital
75 Lathrop Avenue
Wilmington, Kansas 99911

Dear Bob:

Loren Gary and I enjoyed meeting you and Lisa Tieszen. Thank you for taking so much of your valuable time to become acquainted.

As promised, I have placed your and Lisa's names on the mailing list for our weekly money market rate summary and newsletter. The past six weeks' mailings are also enclosed for your review. I hope you find them helpful in your budgeting process and that future mailings will be informative and useful.

I would be happy to arrange a meeting for you with our economist, Katharine Cox, any time that is convenient for you. Please call me and I will arrange a meeting.

I will be sending you a summary of some of the features of our fully automated Cash Management and Reporting System, in which you expressed an interest. I have given your name to Richard Kenney who will be glad to discuss the details of the system at your convenience.

Please feel free to call on me at any time.

As ever,

Mitchell Nevin
Vice President

MN:KL

Enclosures (6)

SAMPLE LETTER 7.10. Follow-up letter to luncheon (block format).

May 20, 19X1

Mr. Erik Heen
Brians, Daniels & Company
Certified Public Accountants
1045 Starcross Plaza
Norristown, Pennsylvania 11582

Dear Erik:

Thank you for the luncheon at the College Club on Thursday, April 23. It was a pleasure for Max Nilges and me to meet with you and the other partners of your firm. I hope this is just a beginning of the relationship between our bank and your firm.

As I told you, my department at New National specializes in serving the financial needs of your profession. Please feel free to call on me at any time to discuss your banking needs. I would be glad to meet with you or your partners to review any situation you would like to discuss.

Thank you again for inviting us to lunch. I hope to be able to work with you in the not too distant future.

Best regards,

Thomas Smith
Vice President

TS:kl

SAMPLE LETTER 7.11. Follow-up letter to meeting with plans for future meeting (full-block format).

August 25, 19X2

Ms. Joanne Thomson
Thomson Tools, Inc.
72 Congregation Avenue
Boonton, Massachusetts 12543

Dear Joanne:

It was a pleasure meeting you last week. I appreciate the time and information you shared and am impressed with you and your company.

Sample Letter 7.11 continued

I'd like to continue the process of getting to know one another and will call you early next week to arrange another visit. Perhaps at that time we could discuss the Automatic Investment and Account Reconcilement Services that I mentioned to you.

Thanks again for your time and conversation. I hope our relationship continues to be a productive one.

As ever,

Yvonne Surrette
Vice President

ys/jw

SAMPLE LETTER 7.12. Follow-up letter to meeting reacting to customer's suggestions (block format).

August 22, 19X3

Mr. Samuel Johnson
19 Court Road
Lichfield, Georgia 09090

Dear Mr. Johnson:

Thank you for an interesting meeting yesterday. I appreciate the time and information you shared with me. I can understand your sense of loyalty to existing banking relationships and the priority you place on knowing and being known by your banker.

During our discussion you suggested that a lock box arrangement might speed up the collection of cash available for investment. I would like to investigate this possibility and estimate the dollar benefit to your company, considering today's high yields on monies invested for even one additional day.

I will give you a call early next week to arrange lunch together as you suggested. Thanks again for your time. I look forward to doing business together.

Cordially yours,

Jim Boswell
Vice President

JB/VT

SAMPLE LETTER 7.13. Follow-up letter to meeting responding to customer's request for services (semiblock format).

June 17, 19X2

Mr. Justin J. Marshall, CPA
85 Stone Street
Truth or Consequences, New Mexico 00007

Dear Justin:

It was a pleasure meeting with you at the University Club that soggy evening. I was delighted to learn that New National and your firm appear to have a healthy, mutual respect. We will try to strengthen that relationship.

You mentioned needing a local account. I am taking the liberty of enclosing some signature cards for a regular checking account and a NOW account. I know that we at the main New National office would welcome your account, but you may wish to deal with a more convenient branch office.

If you need further assistance, please don't hesitate to call or write me.

Best wishes,

Martha Jewett
Vice President

MJ/kl

Enclosures (2)

SAMPLE LETTER 7.14. Follow-up letter to welcoming note (semiblock format).

July 16, 19X2

Mrs. Lorraine Gatto
Long & Berrigan
200 Andover Street
Bar Harbor, Michigan 67892

Dear Mrs. Gatto:

Thank you for your thoughtful note welcoming me to the New National Bank. I would like very much to get acquainted as you suggested and welcome that opportunity either here or in Bar Harbor.

Sample Letter 7.14 continued

Should you have any questions before we meet, please call me. I look forward to hearing from you.

Very truly yours,

Robert Long
Vice President

rm

Sometimes when you make a move from one bank to another it is wise to follow-up old business relationships you might have had. Sample letter 7.15 is an example of a follow-up letter used to rekindle old business acquaintances. The letter writer reacquaints himself with the customer, then tells her how he can help her in his new position at the bank.

SAMPLE LETTER 7.15. Follow-up letter to former business acquaintance (block format).

January 29, 19X2

Mrs. Bess Cooperburg
John Wagner & Associates
One Park Place
Sibling, Ohio 02222

Dear Bess:

It was a pleasure to learn that you have become an associate of the firm. Please accept my warmest best wishes from those of us at New National as you undertake your new responsibilities.

You may remember that we talked on the phone several times when you were counsel to the State University. Since then my duties have changed from leasing equipment to handling New National's relationship to professional firms such as John Wagner & Associates.

Please let me know if I can be of assistance to you or help you to better serve your clients in any way.

We at New National are committed to providing the quality banking and personal attention that professional people like you require to support a continuously successful practice. Feel free to give me a call.

Again, I wish you continued success.

Kindest regards,

Sample Letter 7.15 continued

William Berrigan
Vice President

wb/kl

One of the simplest follow-up letters to write is one that responds to a customer's request for information. Sample letter 7.16 is a response to a customer's inquiry about deposit rates. The banker also takes the opportunity to enclose a brochure describing the other services of his bank.

SAMPLE LETTER 7.16. Follow-up letter to inquiry about deposit rates (full-block format).

June 30, 19X6

Mrs. Alison Krawiec
186 Trampian Way
Dorchester, North Carolina 23232

Dear Mrs. Krawiec:

In response to your inquiry, I am enclosing a copy of New National Bank's current deposit rate sheet along with a new account application and a bank-by-mail envelope. As you can see, the bank continues to offer competitive interest rates on savings accounts, with the added security of FDIC insurance.

I've also enclosed a brochure which explains our banking philosophy. I believe you'll appreciate our emphasis on personalized, responsive service and higher rates paid on savings accounts.

I am ready to assist you and your friends who might be interested in banking with New National Bank. We will value your business and do our best to give you accurate and responsive service.

Please call me at 1-800-555-1324 if you have any questions.

Sincerely,

Justin Long
Senior Vice President

jl/mn

Enclosures

You can also write a follow-up letter to a prospective customer you have tried to reach by phone several times with no success. Sample letter 7.17 gives an example of such a letter. The letter writer shows her knowledge of the customer's needs and prepares the customer for a follow-up call. Although the letter writer still hasn't spoken to the customer, he has been able to make his sales pitch through a short letter to be followed by a phone call.

SAMPLE LETTER 7.17. Follow-up letter to prospective customer you have tried to reach unsuccessfully (semiblock format).

December 20, 19X2

Mr. George Dendrinos
Lewis James Inc.
1966 Myron Boulevard
Goddard, New Jersey 57000

Dear Mr. Dendrinos:

I have attempted to call you several times during this past month with no success. I can appreciate how busy you must be handling all of the financial and operational matters of your company.

County Savings Bank is keenly aware of the heightened competition in banking and is committed to responding with more creative and attentive service to corporate customers such as you. We combine the personal touch and convenience of a local bank with all of the sophisticated resources of our major regional banking corporation.

I will call you in the near future to try to schedule a visit at your convenience. I look forward to meeting with you.

Cordially,

Cheryl G. Mead
Vice President

CGM:PAH

Cross-Selling

Cross-selling is a perfect way for different departments of a bank to work together to increase the overall business done with a particular customer. Sample letter 7.3 shows the result of cross-selling. Someone in the money market division of the bank knew that the customer could probably use the services of the institutional and professional department, so he told that department. Sample letter 7.3 is the result of the reference.

Sample letters 7.18 and 7.19 are more direct examples of cross-selling. The writer of sample letter 7.19 describes some services from various departments of his bank which might be useful to the customer. The result of this cross-selling might be an increase in his bank's overall business. The cross-selling letter in sample letter 7.18 was written as a follow-up to a lunch meeting. Sample letters 7.20 and 7.21 are both letters used to cross-sell financial planning services offered by a bank. Sample letter 7.20 is a follow-up to a referral by a member of a different department of the bank. Sample letter 7.21 is a brief letter of agreement written as a follow-up to a meeting with a customer. Both are prime examples of letters that can be used to sell nontraditional bank services.

SAMPLE LETTER 7.18. Cross-selling letter as follow-up to meeting (block format).

May 18, 19X3

Hiram Lester, Esq.
Georgia, Simons & Peterson
100 Newton Street
Binghamton, Maine 80098

Dear Hiram:

Thanks for lunching with Brian Palay and me today. It was a pleasure to meet you. Enclosed are copies of our brochure on cash management services at County Savings Bank.

When you are reviewing the financial aspects of your firm's administration, please feel free to call upon me if you think I might be of help. It appears that a cash management system combining controlled disbursements with speedier receivables could free up significant working capital that may answer some of the concerns you voiced at lunch about efficient control of the liquidity of your firm.

In the interim, do you feel it would be of mutual benefit for you and me to act as matchmakers to introduce members of your firm to one of County Savings' commercial loan officers? Perhaps a small luncheon here would be appropriate. Let me know what you think.

Thanks again for a good luncheon. It was a pleasure to meet you.

Kindest regards,

Bethany J. Coleman
Vice President

Sample Letter 7.18 continued

bjc:bdp

2 encs.

cc: Brian Palay

SAMPLE LETTER 7.19. Cross-selling letter as follow-up to phone call or letter (semiblock format).

October 29, 19X2

Mr. Nathaniel J. Waggoner
Keith, Simons, and Underhaul
555 Twilite Drive
Encino, Oregon 09832

Dear Nathaniel:

New National Bank has a wide range of products to meet the needs of the middle market company. Not only are our commercial banking services innovative, but our cash management, international, and trust services also address the needs of the $10 million to $50 million company.

New National's cash management services include lock box provisions with a liquidity management system that maximizes working capital dollars. Cash management is a fee-based service that may be paid for with free balances.

Our international services aid your import financing with letters of credit, banker's acceptances, and New National's extensive correspondent banking relationships.

New National's trust services are highly regarded in the industry. We have recently widened our involvement with pension funds in the $10 million range. I will talk to one of our trust professionals and arrange a meeting for the three of us next month.

I looked forward to meeting with you soon. If you have any questions before then, do not hesitate to call.

Best regards,

Max Nilges
Loan Officer

mn/ls

SAMPLE LETTER 7.20. Cross-selling financial planning services as a result of a referral (full-block format).

July 30, 19X6

Mr. James Lewis
President
Boonton Film Studios, Inc.
312 Lathrop Avenue
Boonton, New Jersey 07005

Dear Jim:

I'm delighted that Bob Rosner suggested we meet to see if working together makes sense.

I have enclosed some materials which describe me and the financial planning service which I run for The County Savings Bank. My compensation is on a fee-only basis, which insures that my advice to you is objective.

A financial planning data set is also enclosed. You should review this material and fill out the forms that request information about you and your personal finances. This is the first step in the financial planning process.

I will call next week to set up a convenient time to meet. If you have any questions before then, feel free to give me a call.

Sincerely,

Louis Volpe, CFP

lv/js

Enclosures

SAMPLE LETTER 7.21. Cross-selling financial planning services—a brief letter of agreement as a follow-up to a meeting (full-block format).

August 19, 19X6

Mr. James Lewis
President
Boonton Film Studios, Inc.
312 Lathrop Avenue
Boonton, New Jersey 07005

Dear Jim:

I enjoyed meeting with you at my office at County Savings Bank and discussing our working relationship. This short note will formalize that working agreement.

As your financial planner, I will coordinate all of your personal financial affairs. These will include budgets, insurance, savings and investments, tax planning, and retirement and estate planning. After my comprehensive review, we will develop an action plan with specific objectives tailored to meet your goals. The action plan will be prepared by December 19X6.

While I will be available to you on an ongoing basis in 19X7 and beyond, we will meet at least semiannually on a scheduled basis and more often if necessary.

My compensation is on a fee-only basis. It will be paid on a retainer basis reflecting an estimation of the professional time I will spend providing financial planning services to you. Fees for the comprehensive review and action plan will be $3,600, payable in three equal installments on September 1, November 1, and January 1. Thereafter, my retainer will be $1,600 annually, payable quarterly.

I'll see you in your office in Boonton on September 10 at 2 p.m. and at the Morristown Business Club's breakfast meeting at the Governor Morris Inn at 7:30 a.m. on Wednesday, September 3.

If you have any questions before then, please feel free to call me.

Sincerely,

Louis Volpe, CFP

lv/js

Referrals

Thanking a customer for a referral is good business practice. Sample letter 7.22 is included with the sales letters because such a letter, although it doesn't sell any specific services, helps to convince the customer you're thanking that you appreciate the business lead. When the customer who gave you the referral is ready for more banking services, you are likely to be remembered. Such a letter might also be considered a good customer service letter (see Chapter 10).

SAMPLE LETTER 7.22. Thank you for referral letter (full-block format).

March 15, 19X1

Mr. Scott Brewster
435 Marshall Street
Cosgrove, Idaho 88899

Dear Mr. Brewster:

It always pleases me when one of our customers recommends County Savings Bank to a friend. This is evidence of confidence which is greatly appreciated.

We were pleased yesterday when Patricia Palay informed us that your recommendation led her to select our bank. I want to assure you that all of us at the County Savings Bank will do our best to live up to your recommendation.

Sincerely yours,

Alana Berg
Branch Manager

ab:pp

Setting Up Additional Calls

Often you'll have to set up additional calls when selling your bank's services. Nothing elaborate is necessary in a letter setting up an additional call. Sample letter 7.23 is an example of a straightforward letter confirming another meeting with a customer. The official style format used in the letter shows that a personal relationship exists between the letter writer and the reader, suggesting that this business relationship has been going on for some time.

SAMPLE LETTER 7.23. Letter for setting up additional calls (official style format).

April 10, 19X2

Dear Ralph:

I am confirming our appointment of May 8 at 9:30 p.m. Enclosed are the rate comparisons that I spoke about last week. These rates are all inclusive and do not require compensating balances or fees.

I look forward to our next meeting and to developing a relationship beneficial to both Thomson Enterprises and New National Bank.

Regards,

Gene O'Connor

Mr. Ralph Hamilton
Thomson Enterprises
111 Prospect Street
Hamilton, California 00012

JT:JS

Interest In Customer's Projects

Sometimes you might learn of a project your customer is undertaking that could require some banking services. Rather than wait for a customer to get around to getting in touch with you about the project, it is a good idea to show your interest in becoming involved with the project. Sample letter 7.24 was written to display such an interest.

SAMPLE LETTER 7.24. Letter showing an interest in a customer's project (block format).

April 10, 19X1

Mr. Howard Palay
Z.T.X., Inc.
Grand Forks Drive
Levittown, Texas 08754

Dear Mr. Palay:

It was interesting to learn of your plan to develop an extended care nursing facility to be affiliated with General Hospital in Levittown.

As your bankers, we would, of course, like to become more thoroughly informed of your plans as they continue to develop and become firm. We would also like to receive a copy of your financing proposal when it is ready for review and consideration. Any commitment on our part for financial support of the project would naturally be contingent upon analysis of your final plan and the circumstances existing at that time.

We wish you well in your ongoing endeavors.

Very truly yours,

Catherine C. Long
Vice President

CL:JS

Sales Memos

Memoranda 7.25-7.28 deal with the business referral program within a bank. Memorandum 7.25 discusses the program for the year; memorandum 7.26 a final program for the year; and memorandum 7.27 an update on information on new referrals.

MEMORANDUM 7.25. Memorandum discussing business referral program for the year.

TO: Division Officers
FROM: James Marks
DATE: February 11, 19X2
SUBJECT: Attorney/Accountant Contact and Referral Program 19X2 Calendar

Our program to build contacts with legal and accounting professionals continues to expand our pool of professional resources and referral sources. Enclosed you'll find the first half of the 19X2 Calendar of Proposed Events. Please review the series of dates and make note of the specific events that involve you.

JM:ED

Enclosure

MEMORANDUM 7.26. Memorandum discussing a final business referral program for the year.

TO: Division Officers
FROM: Gene O'Connor
DATE: December 9, 19X1
SUBJECT: Presentation Meeting on December 14 with Wagner & Associates

The final attorney/accountant event for 19X1 will be an afternoon presentation. It will be held in the directors' room at 4 p.m., Monday, December 14, with cocktails and hors d'oeuvres to be served at 5:30 p.m.

John Wagner & Associates will give an overview of the specialties of their sibling office and the special industries they serve. There will also be a discussion conducted by their Human Resources and Employee Benefit Consulting Group about trends they observe in methods of executive compensation and pension programs in middle market companies.

Our Personal Trust Division will give a capsule discussion of new products and services to middle market companies and their owners from trust to pension services. They will also discuss New National's investment philosophy and new tools available, including immunization funds and their various applications.

Memorandum 7.26 continued

As we are all aware, the underlying reason for this meeting is to provide a vehicle for building referrals between the two institutions. In spite of the pressures that various holiday galas may cause, please put aside time for this event and attend. Thanks!

It will be appreciated if district heads would provide a list of their personnel who will attend so we may process a master list for distribution to Wagner's people. Name tags should also be worn.

GO:JS

MEMORANDUM 7.27. Memorandum updating information on new business referrals.

TO: Division Officers
FROM: Gene O'Connor
DATE: December 3, 19X1
SUBJECT: Referral Data on Recently Booked Business

Please indicate in the space provided on the attached sheet if the new businesses listed were referrals, and, if so, their sources. Please also indicate the law firm which rendered our documentation and the fee involved. Thanks.

Enclosure

GO/JS

Memorandum 7.28 is from one department to another explaining how the business referral program can help the other department's customers.

MEMORANDUM 7.28. Memorandum from one department to another discussing how business referral program can help customer.

TO: William Runyon, Vice President
New National Leasing Company
FROM: James Marks, Vice President
Institutional and Professional Development
DATE: September 23, 19X2
SUBJECT: IPD's Services Available to Wagner & Associates

You've asked what we at New National could do for John Wagner & Associates. In response, I've attached to this memo a partial list of services we regularly provide to attorneys.

Perhaps the best thing we can offer them is ourselves. The members of the firm should feel comfortable dealing with people who have been relating to professionals for many years.

Please look over the attached list. If you think a meeting between you, me, and representatives from Wagner & Associates is appropriate, please let me know.

JM:ED

Enclosure

Sales & Marketing— Retail Services

8

The letters in chapter 8 were written to sell or market specific bank services and products. They are categorized here according to the type of service or product being marketed.

Savings, Checking, NOW, Money Market, Certificates of Deposit

Sample letters 8.1-8.19 were all written to market various types of savings, checking, and money market accounts. Sample letters 8.1-8.3 describe basic savings accounts which are available at the writer's bank. Each is clearly written, describing the benefits of the particular savings vehicle.

SAMPLE LETTER 8.1. Basic savings account sales letter (simplified format).

January 29, 19X3

Mr. Brian Palay
65 Lincoln Drive
Grand Forks, North Dakota 45161

THE COUNTY BANK'S BASIC SAVINGS ACCOUNT

Mr. Palay, when you want a basic savings account that offers interest, no monthly service charges, a low minimum balance, and security, you're looking for one of The County Bank's Basic Savings Account.

You may prefer to keep your Basic Savings Account separate from your other bank accounts and receive a quarterly statement. Then again, you may enjoy the convenience of having your savings account attached to your checking account. You'll have one account number and receive one convenient monthly statement. You can even transfer funds between the two accounts—either with a transfer slip or your County Bank ATM card.

Whether your Basic Savings Account stands alone or is combined with a transaction account, you'll earn 5.5% annual interest, paid and compounded monthly. There's no monthly service charge to worry about and just $10 opens any of our regular savings accounts, so there's no high minimum balance to maintain. With a County Bank ATM card, you can access your savings account any time of the day, any day of the week, at hundreds of ATM machines throughout the state.

To open your Basic Savings Account, visit a County Bank office. A customer service representative will be happy to assist you with all of your banking needs.

KERM IDDE
ASSISTANT VICE PRESIDENT

KI:JS

SAMPLE LETTER 8.2. Savings and investment options (hanging-indented format).

August 19, 19X6

Mr. Loren Gary
43 Lorraine Terrace
Eufaula, Alabama 54345

Dear Mr. Gary:

At The County Savings Bank we let you choose the savings or investment plan that's best for your personal needs.

Our regular passbook savings account lets you make deposits and withdrawals as often as you wish. Interest is compounded continuously and credited to your account monthly at the rate of 5.5%.

County Savings Bank's statement savings account gives you a detailed monthly statement instead of a passbook. You can make unlimited transactions, and have access to your money 24 hours a day through our County Bank ATM Network. Interest is compounded continuously and paid monthly at the rate of 5.5%.

The County Money Market Account combines money market rates with easy access to your money. The rate earned varies weekly to insure that it remains competitive with other high yield investments. Your money is accessible through any County Bank ATM, and you receive a monthly statement itemizing all transactions and interest earned. With $2,500 or more, you may open a County Money Market Account and make additional deposits of any amount at any time. There is no limit to the number of withdrawals within the branches. You are limited to three third party checks per statement period. Your account earns the full high rate of interest as long as your balance is at least $2,500. If your balance falls below that amount, your account will earn the regular 5.25% NOW Account rate. If it falls below $1,000, you will also be charged $3 per month.

County Bank Certificates of Deposit are designed to accommodate your particular investment goals. You can choose terms ranging anywhere from three to thirty-six months, so you'll be certain that the money you need for retirement, college tuition, or some other goal will be there when you need it. Interest rates for all certificates are set periodically according to current rates on U.S. Treasury Bills with similar maturities. The rate in effect on the date of

Mr. Loren Gary 2 August 19, 19X6

purchase is fixed and guaranteed for the full term of the certificate.

Jumbo Certificates of Deposit are available for $100,000 or more. Both rate and term are set daily and interest may be withdrawn either monthly or quarterly.

The County Bank has a savings or investment plan for everyone. All County Bank Accounts are FDIC insured up to $100,000 per account. For current rates, call our Rate Hotline at 323-5654. For more detailed information, give me a call or stop by and see a customer service representative in any of our conveniently located branch offices.

Cordially,

Lisa Tieszen
Vice President

lt:ns

SAMPLE LETTER 8.3. Passbook-plus savings (full-block format).

May 9, 19X4

Mr. Relneth Liplar
Liplar/Malhem Associates
34 Eatex Road
Revodna, Massachusetts 01810

Dear Mr. Liplar:

A passbook savings account gives you tangible evidence of the progress you're making in your savings. Until now, however, passbook savings accounts offered less than attractive interest rates. New National Bank offers the Passbook-Plus Savings Account, the high-rate account for the intelligent saver.

The Passbook-Plus Savings Account gives premium rates, even in comparison to money market accounts. To start earning New National's high passbook account rates right away, simply fill out the enclosed coupon and mail it with your initial deposit of $1,000 or more. We'll send you an account information packet and your new Passbook-Plus Savings Account Passbook.

If you have any questions, please call me at 432-9821. You can also stop by any of our conveniently located

Sample Letter 8.3 continued

branch offices where a customer service representative will answers any of your savings questions.

Sincerely,

Muffy Ramsdell
Vice President

mr:js

Enclosure

Sample letter 8.4 and 8.5 were written to market special types of savings accounts. Like the earlier savings account letters, the benefits of this type of account are described.

SAMPLE LETTER 8.4. Seasons greetings savings accounts (block format).

January 5, 19X4

Ms. Bethany Coleman
4545 Razzmatazz Way
Ft. Wayne, Illinois 45321

Dear Ms. Coleman:

New National Seasons Greetings Savings Accounts help you save for the holidays. You can open your account at any time of the year with as little as $10. Make additional contributions in person or have a set amount automatically transferred to your Seasons Greetings Savings Account from your New National checking account. You save year-round, earn interest on your deposits, and we mail you a check for your balance in October.

Your Seasons Greetings Savings Account will earn 5.5% annual interest, paid and compounded monthly. You'll receive a quarterly statement for the account showing all deposits and your earned interest.

With a New National Seasons Greetings Savings Account, you won't have to worry about high minimum balance requirements or monthly service charges because there are none. You can be sure your deposits are safe. FDIC insurance guarantees the security of all your New National deposits up to $100,000.

Don't let another holiday season catch you unprepared. A customer service representative will be happy to open your Seasons Greetings Savings Account for you and to an-

Sample Letter 8.4 continued

swer any questions you may have about New National Bank's other banking products and services.

Best regards,

William Berrigan
Vice President

wb/mn

SAMPLE LETTER 8.5. Special savings account (full-block format).

September 9, 19X1

Ms. Lauren J. Palay
1918 Seerd Drive
Grand Forks, Minnesota 10285

Dear Ms. Palay:

Our Household Passbook Savings Account is a special account we've created at County Savings to help customers with modest incomes save money while they pay their bills. We designed Household Passbook for our customers who strive to save for their future, but, because of steep minimum balance requirements on most accounts, find saving extremely difficult.

With Household Passbook, there are no fees or minimum balance requirements, so you needn't worry that the money you work hard to save will be eaten up by steep bank fees. What's more, you can open a Household Passbook account with as little as $20. And to make paying bills even easier, we offer our Household Passbook customers 60 free money orders a year that can be drawn on their accounts to pay specific bills each month. To be eligible to open a Household Passbook Savings Account, your household income must be $30,000 or less.

If you want more information or to open a Household Passbook Savings Account today, visit any County Savings customer service representative or give me a call at our downtown branch to set up an appointment.

Sincerely,

Ignatz Krauss
Vice President

mk

Sample letters 8.6 through 8.10 were written to market checking services offered by a bank. Sample letters 8.6 and 8.7 details the various checking options his bank offers. Sample letter 8.8 describes a basic checking account service. Sample letter 8.9 was written to market a new type of checking account with a variable rate schedule. Sample letter 8.10 was written to market a checking account with overdraft protection.

SAMPLE LETTER 8.6. Checking account plans (simplified letter format).

August 6, 19X3

Mr. Robert Bradley
Vice President
Bookmakers of America
1435 Anders Way
Chicago, Illinois 30322

PERSONAL BANKING PLANS AT NEW NATIONAL

At New National, our checking account plans take checking account services a step further. Whether you select a checking, NOW, or Super NOW account, each plan is individually designed to provide the flexibility and service you need to make managing your money easier.

New National Checking Account Plans include several special features, including:

1. A $1,500 line of credit that lets you avoid the embarrassment of an accidental overdraft. Your account is automatically covered up to $2,000, providing you with extra money when you need it. Of course, you must qualify for the credit line based on your good credit standing.

2. A free New National Automated Teller Machine (ATM) access card which serves a dual purpose. First, it gives you access to your New National account at hundreds of ATM locations throughout Illinois. Second, if you have a credit line, you may also use this card at merchants and banks worldwide. Through a special arrangement with MasterCard, you can use your New National card for payment at more than four million MasterCard merchants or for cash withdrawals at 100,000 banks worldwide. The charges will be automatically deducted from your checking account, just as if you had made the transaction at an ATM.

3. A single monthly statement makes your recordkeeping simple by reporting all your account activity,

including an itemized listing and description of every transaction.

4. Service charges that are based on average monthly balances mean less worry on a daily basis. We have eliminated the daily minimum balance required by many banks and replaced it with an <u>average</u> monthly balance.

5. Check processing speed that lets you use your money faster. When you deposit a check into your account from any other Illinois bank, New National credits you with available funds in just one day.

A <u>Checking Account</u> at New National is a traditional, non-interest bearing checking account with several optional features. These include a $1,500 credit line, a free New National Access Card, and a free savings account.

An average collected balance of at least $1,000 in your Checking Account is required during your statement month to avoid incurring service charges. If you do not maintain this balance, your account will be charged a service fee of $4.00 a month plus transaction fees of 40 cents per item or 30 cents for each ATM transaction.

A <u>NOW Account</u> offers the same $1,500 credit line and free ATM access card available with all of our Checking Account Plans. As long as you maintain at least a $500 average collected balance each month, your account will earn interest.

If you maintain an average collected monthly balance of at least $2,000, your account will not incur service charges. Otherwise, charges will include a service fee of $5 per month plus 40 cents per item or 30 cents for each ATM transaction.

With an average collected balance each month of at least $2,000, a <u>Super NOW Account</u> earns interest at a preferred rate. As with all of our Checking Account Plans, your Super NOW Account offers a $1,500 credit line and a free New National Access Card.

To avoid service charges you must maintain an average collected monthly balance of $10,000. If your average

Mr. Robert Bradley -3- August 6, 19X3

balance should drop below $10,000, you will incur a monthly service fee of $8 as well as fees of 40 cents for each item or 30 cents for ATM transactions.

To enroll in one of New National's Checking Account Plans, see a New National banker or call me at 555-9876. We'll help you select the plan that's right for you.

DAVID LAWRENCE PALAY
VICE PRESIDENT

psp

SAMPLE LETTER 8.7. Basic checking accounts (full-block format).

September 9, 19X1

Mr. Leonard Dewey
54 Washington Heights
York, Pennsylvania 60650

Dear Mr. Dewey:

With so many types of checking accounts available today, how can you choose the one that best meets your needs? Well, at County Savings, we've tried to make it easier by designing three easy-to-understand checking accounts to help our customers better manage their money. Regardless or whether you need a simple account for bill paying or want to earn interest on your checking account balances, we have an account for you. And with all of our checking accounts you'll have 24-hour access to your money through our automated teller machine network. Plus, you'll have the protection of FDIC insurance.

Simple Checking is our basic account. This is our no-interest checking account that's perfect for basic bill paying needs. By maintaining a $650 balance, or by having your payroll or Social Security check deposited directly, the account is free of fees. The service charge is $3.50 per month if you don't meet these criteria, plus $.15 per check cleared during the month. You can open a Simple Checking account with as little as $350.

If you write a number of checks each month, our Interest-bearing Checking account is designed to meet your needs. By keeping $1,500 in your account or by having your payroll or Social Security check directly deposited in this

Mr. Leonard Dewey -2- September 9, 19X1

account you not only earn interest, but pay no fees for checking privileges. The service charge is $3.50 per month if you don't meet these criteria, plus $.15 per check cleared during the month. You can open an Interest-bearing Checking account with as little as $350. Interest on the account is compounded and credited monthly.

Our Top Balance Checking account allows you to combine the benefits of a checking account with the earnings potential of a savings account. If you maintain a monthly balance of $3,000 or more in your Top Balance Checking account, you'll earn a higher interest rate on your balance than offered in our Interest-bearing Checking account. If you fall below a $3,000 balance, your account earns a lower, but still competitive rate of interest. And, like our Interest-bearing Checking account, your account is free if you maintain a monthly balance of $1,500 or more, or have your payroll or Social Security check directly deposited in the account. As with our other accounts, the service charge is $3.50 per month if you don't meet these criteria, plus $.15 per check cleared during the month. You can open an Interest-bearing Checking account with as little as $350. Interest on the account is compounded and credited monthly.

You can open the checking account that best meets your needs by stopping by and seeing me or another customer service representative at County Savings. We look forward to serving your needs.

Sincerely,

Lisa Tieszen
Vice President

lt/lg

SAMPLE LETTER 8.8. Basic checking accounts (semiblock format).

April 5, 19X7

Mr. Leonard Yancey Dean
23 Manila Drive
Folder, Idaho 43212

Dear Mr. Dean:

If you don't write many checks, chances are you don't want to keep a lot of money in a checking account just to meet minimum balance requirements. To meet the needs of customers like you, The County Bank offers Simple Service Checking.

A convenient, low-cost alternative to accounts with higher monthly fees, Simple Service Checking costs as little as $2.50 per month. You can make up to 10 withdrawals each month, including checks written against your account and cash withdrawals.

Additional Simple Service Checking services include electronic funds transfers, automatic loan payments, and preauthorized transfers, such as direct deposit of payroll or social security checks.

After a 30-day new account waiting period, your funds will be available for withdrawal on the next business day after deposit.

With a County Bank Card you can make routine Simple Service Checking Account transactions any time of the day, any day of the week, at hundreds of County Bank machines.

Start taking advantage of low-cost banking services w ith a County Bank Simple Service Checking Account. Give us a call and we'll be happy to help you open your account or to answer any of your savings or checking questions.

Cordially,

Lisa Tieszen
Vice President

lt/lg

SAMPLE LETTER 8.9. Sales letter for checking account (simplified format).

November 9, 19X2

Ms. Gina Zachman
908 Pomegranite Place
Bernardsville, Idaho 80808

NEW SMART SAVER ACCOUNT

Ms. Zachman, New National Bank is pleased to announce a totally new concept in checking account service—a plan that lets you control the service charges you pay by offering credits against those charges for funds you keep in both checking and savings accounts with us.

The new plan is called the Smart Saver Checking Account. All checking customers will be changing to this new plan. One month from now, your statement will reflect this new method of computing service charges.

How will it affect you? Good news! The balance you normally keep in your checking account suggests that you will not incur any service charges whatsoever.

But to assure you that you don't, we urge you to keep your balance from going below $300 at any time. As long as you do not fall below that minimum balance, no charges will be incurred.

Here's how Smart Saver works. It's simple:

	Monthly Service Charge for Checking
Keep at least $300 in your checking account at all times	None
Keep $200–$299 in your checking account at all times	$1.50 fee, plus 10¢ per check written
Keep $100–$199 in your checking account at all times	$2.00 fee, plus 10¢ per check written
Have less than $100 in your checking account at all times	$2.50 fee, plus 10¢ per check written

And, here's why we call this new checking account the Smart Saver Checking Account. For each $1,000 you maintain in a 5% Statement Savings Account, you will receive

Ms. Gina Zachman -2- November 9, 19X2

$1 credit against your monthly checking acount service charges. Keep $4,000 in a Statement Account and all activity charges will be eliminated. If your savings are now in another type of savings account or in another financial institution, ask about changing them to a Statement Account, so you can qualify for this extra discount.

Again, it appears that you are accustomed to keeping sufficient funds in your checking account to eliminate all service charges under the new plan. But we thought you'd like to know how this new service is designed. Please be assured that this change will not affect your existing accounts in any other way. You will keep your same account numbers, use the same printed checks you have been using, and receive your statements just like always.

If you have further questions about the new Smart Saver Account, stop by any New National office or call us and ask for the Smart Saver Center. We appreciate the opportunity to serve you and we hope you will always rely on us for all of your banking needs.

RENE BRONDES
VICE PRESIDENT

RB:JS

SAMPLE LETTER 8.10. Checking account options letter sent to existing account holder (full-block format).

December 26, 19X1

Mr. Peter Jessic
43 Lorraine Terrace
Mountain Lakes, New Jersey 07005

Dear Mr. Jessic:

We value your business as a checking account customer at New National Bank. That's why we want to make sure that you've got the checking account that best meets your needs. New National's wide variety of checking account options makes it easy for you to get the account that's perfect for you.

With our Simple-Fee Checking account, you pay one small fee a month and receive unlimited check writing and automated teller machine transaction privileges. If you write

Sample Letter 8.10 continued

very few checks each month, you might consider our Convenient Checking account, for which you'll be charged for each check written, but be charged an even lower monthly fee and face no minimum balance requirement.

Of course, you can have a charge free checking account if you take advantage of our Interest-Bearing Checking account and keep a minimum balance in either the checking account or a savings or money market account.

We also offer a central assets account—our New National Flag Account—which allows you to savings, checking, credit, and investments into one account. You can keep the bulk of your money in any of our accounts—including high-yielding certificates of deposit—and use the total balance to erase any monthly checking fees.

We want you to choose the account at New National that best meets your needs. For more information, stop by your nearest New National branch, or complete and return the enclosed postage-paid information request card.

Sincerely,

Archibald Roberts
Assistant Vice President

dd

Enclosure

Sample letters 8.11 and 8.12 present two versions of letters marketing NOW accounts to customers. Both clearly point out all the benefits of the account.

SAMPLE LETTER 8.11 NOW accounts (semiblock format).

December 26, 19X6

Mr. John Waggoner
98 Joe Bing Place
Noreaster, Maine 87654

Dear Mr. Waggoner:

A County Bank NOW Account pays 5.25% interest, compounded continuously to an annual yield of 5.47%, so you can enjoy the convenience of checking without sacrificing a return on your checking dollars.

Your County Bank NOW Account will be free of all regular monthly service charges when you maintain a minimum balance of $1,000, throughout the statement month.

If your balance goes below $1,000, but not below $500, a $4 account maintenance fee is applied. If your balance goes below $500 at any time during the statement month a 30 cent per check charge will also be applied.

With your NOW Account at The County Bank, you may also apply for overdraft protection, which will save you the embarrassment and inconvenience of having a check returned for insufficient funds. Overdraft protection doesn't cost you anything until you use it. When you draw a check for more than your account balance, within your approved credit line, we will automatically deposit increments of $100 to your account to cover the overdraft. You pay interest only on the amount you borrow, while the amount is outstanding. Each month, you may repay as little as 5% of your balance ($25 minimum). All transactions are conveniently reported on your regular monthly NOW Account statement.

If you'd like more information on The County Bank's NOW Account, feel free to give me a call at 543-6543, or stop by any of our conveniently located branch offices and speak with a customer service representative.

Cordially,

Archibald Roberts
Assistant Vice President

ar:dd

SAMPLE LETTER 8.12 NOW accounts (block format).

October 7, 19X4

Mr. Bud Genry
54 Flipfile Road
Soft Pines, Tennessee 54343

Dear Mr. Genry:

When you want your checking account to earn competitive interest, have the convenience and liquidity of unlimited check writing, and give you 24-hour access to your funds, New National's NOW Account fits the bill.

Your personal NOW Account earns 5.25% interest, paid and compounded monthly. If you maintain a minimum daily balance of just $500 in your NOW Account, we will wave the $8 monthly fee. If you are assessed a monthly fee, it can be reduced to just $6 if you set up a direct payroll deposit, social security deposit, or other government deposit to your NOW Account.

Combine your NOW Account with one of our savings accounts and you'll have one account number and receive one easy-to-follow monthly statement. You can transfer funds between accounts—either with a transfer slip or a New National Bank Card.

Your money starts earning interest in your NOW Account on the next business day following deposit. No more waiting days, or sometimes weeks for deposited checks to clear, even if they are out-of-state checks.

To open your NOW Account, or to inquire about any of our checking, savings, or investment products, call me or visit a customer service representative at one of our branch locations today. We'll be happy to help you decide which New National Bank accounts are right for you.

Sincerely,

Andrew Taro Aoyama
Assistant Vice President

ATA:JHG

Sample letters 8.13 and 8.14 was written to market a money market deposit account. Sample letters 8.15 and 8.16 both market money market checking accounts. Each carefully spells out the benefits and parameters of the account being marketed, leaving little room for confusion in the prospective customer's mind.

SAMPLE LETTER 8.13. Money market account (semiblock format).

February 29, 19X0

Ms. Lisa Tieszen Gary
32 Hinsdale Road
Chicago, Illinois 89765

Dear Ms. Gary:

If you're looking for an account that pays high money market rates, offers you the security of FDIC insurance and ready access to your funds, New National Banks' Money Market Account could be your answer.

Our Money Market Account pays money market rates. There's no high balance requirement to meet. Interest is compounded and credited to your account each month. The rate is reviewed and may change weekly to remain competitive.

You can open your Money Market Account with as l ittle as $500. You may make unlimited withdrawals at any branch or automated teller machine. You are also allowed up to six special transactions during each monthly statement period. Three may be special Money Market Account Checks. The others may be preauthorized withdrawals, such as telephone transfers or automatic bill payments.

You can avoid the $5 monthly fee by keeping a $1,000 minimum daily balance in your account. Your money starts earning interest and your funds will be available for withdrawal in your Money Market Account on the first business day following your deposit.
You can rest assured that the money you deposit in your New National Money Market Account is protected. FDIC insurance guarantees the security of all of your New National deposits up to $100,000.

To find out more about our Money Market Account, or to open an account, visit a New National office today. A customer service representative will be happy to assist you in determining what accounts are right for you and to answer any questions you may have about New National's banking services and products.

Sincerely,

Nancy Long
Senior Vice President

nl:jm

SAMPLE LETTER 8.14. Money market savings account (full-block format).

September 10, 19X1

Mr. Ralph Embry
1111 Prospect Street
Hamilton, California 00012

Dear Mr. Embry:

Tired of steep monthly service fees on your money market accounts? Have we got an offer for you. Open a New National Money Market Account between now and December 31 and we'll waive all monthly service fees for the first sixth months, no matter what your monthly balances are, if you also sign up for New National's Fixed Savings Strategy. By marrying a money market account to a checking account, you'll continue to have 24-hour access to your money, plus you'll enjoy the higher rates our money market accounts earn.

Over the next six months, you'll be able to save up to $50 in service charges, no matter what balances you keep. And by linking your Money Market Account with a Fixed Savings Strategy, you'll be able to meet the monthly minimum balance that will waive service fees in the future.

Our Fixed Savings Strategy is simple. You choose a set amount you want to have transferred each month from your New National checking account into your Money Market Account. Simple, right? Regular savings that adds up fast to whatever goal you might have, from education to retirement.

You can open a New National Money Market Account today by completing and returning the enclosed postage-paid application, or by dropping in at any New National office. We look forward to doing business with you.

Sincerely,

Jeffrey Karus
Vice President
nlc

Enclosure

SAMPLE LETTER 8.15. Money market checking account (block format).

July 14, 19X0

Mr. Peter Jensen
98 Bethany Road
Sunvale, Maryland 90909

Dear Peter:

WRITE-NOTE CHECK CREDIT

Write-Note Check Credit, available with your County Bank Money Market Account, gives you the ability to request a line of credit from $500 to $5,000.

You borrow by just writing your own personal checks. You never need to reapply for a loan or complete another application. There is no charge until you use the line of credit. When you make monthly payments you rebuild your available line of credit. A monthly statement will show your checking account transactions and your check credit transactions.

Write-Note Check Credit is most useful for those unexpected bills or emergencies when you don't have the time to call your bank for a conventional loan.

County Bank offers the easiest and fastest way to borrow in the comfort and convenience of your own home. Simply complete the enclosed application for Write-Note Check Credit and return it to County Bank today.

Best regards,

Max Nilges
Loan Officer

mn/js

Enclosure

SAMPLE LETTER 8.16. Money market checking account (full-block format).

September 5, 19X4

Mr. Efraín Calderon
67 Desire Street
Marlon, Massachusetts 02112

Dear Mr. Calderon:

New National Bank's Money Market Checking Account offers you high money market interest, plus the convenience and liquidity of unlimited check writing and 24-hour access to your funds.

Our Money Market Checking Account earns market rates, and there's no high minimum balance required. You can open your Money Market Checking Account with as little as $10. You can also combine your Money Market Checking Account with one of our savings accounts. You'll have one account number and receive one easy-to-follow statement. You can transfer funds between accounts either with a transfer slip or with your New National Bank Card.

Your money starts earning interest and will be available for withdrawal on your Money Market Checking Account on the next business day following deposit. You won't have to wait days for deposited checks to clear, even if they are out-of-state checks.

We will waive the $10 monthly fee if you maintain a minimum daily balance of $1,500 in your Money Market Checking Account. You can also avoid monthly fees by attaching your Money Market Checking Account to a New National Savings Account with a minimum daily balance of $5,000.

You can access you Money Market Checking Account any time of the day with a New National Bank Card at the hundreds of New National Automated Teller Machines around the state.

To open your Money Market Checking Account, or to find out more about our banking services, visit a New National Branch Office today. A customer service representative will be happy to help you determine what accounts are right for you.

Sincerely,

Kali Mahoney
Vice President

mn

Sample letters 8.17 and 8.18 were written to market special accounts. Sample letter 8.17 markets a Super NOW account while sample letter 8.18 markets a central assets account.

SAMPLE LETTER 8.17. Super NOW checking (block format).

May 9, 19X4

Ms. Amy Little
65 Pedestrian Way
Boston, New Jersey 07005

Dear Ms. Little:

The County Bank's Super NOW Account is an all-purpose checking account that combines convenience, unlimited check writing, and high interest rates. Your funds will always be readily accessible through approximately 1,000 automated teller machines statewide. Each month you will receive your canceled checks along with a detailed statement showing all deposits and withdrawals and interest earned. All funds are fully insured by FDIC up to $100,000 per account.

Super NOW Accounts can be opened for as little as $10 and require an average daily balance of $2,000 to earn current market rates. If the average daily balance falls below $2,000, the account will earn 5.25% interest.

There are several ways you can have a Super NOW Account free of monthly service charges. Just maintain a $500 minimum balance or have your paycheck, Social Security, or other recurring payments electronically deposited directly into your account.

When you open this account, you may apply for a free County Bank Card, which gives you access to almost 6,500 automated teller machines nationwide. You can even use your card at American Express machines located at most major airports nationwide.

Aside from getting up to $300 per day in cash at all automated teller machine locations, you can also make deposits, loan payments, mortgage payments, life insurance payments, and transfer funds between accounts at designated locations.

For further information, give me a call or stop by any of our conveniently located offices.

Best regards,

Sample Letter 8.17 continued

Max Nilges
Vice President

mn/js

SAMPLE LETTER 8.18. Central assets accounts (hanging-indented format).

January 30, 19X5

Mr. Jack Waggoner
45 Surrette Way
Quincy, Maryland 43434

Dear Mr. Waggoner:

New National's Central Assets Account is a vehicle for today's investor that provides both excellent value and great convenience. When you open a New National Central Assets Account with a minimum deposit of $5,000 you can take advantage of these outstanding benefits:

– Money market interest rates.
– FDIC insurance protection up to $100,000.
– Access to your funds by check, mail, or phone.
– A gold VISA Card with no annual fee.
– Automatic monthly payment of your monthly VISA purchases.
– Access to your cash through hundreds of ATMs in our ATM network.

Our Central Assets Account was designed expressly for people who need more than just a money market account. Take advantage of this unique opportunity today. Send in the enclosed application with your deposit, or call me at 890-5656. I'll be glad to answer any questions.

Cordially,

Lynn Stein
Assistant Vice President

ls/js

Enclosure

Sample letter 8.19 was written to describe the certificates of deposit offered by a bank.

SAMPLE LETTER 8.19. Certificates of deposit (full-block format).

September 10, 19X1

Mrs. Catherine C. Long
485 Dow Lane
Roxbury, Massachusetts 93939

Dear Mrs. Long:

If you're trying to reach specific financial goals, consider County Savings Bank's wide variety of certificates of deposit (CDs). Our CDs let you lock in a guaranteed interest rate for a set period of time. So no matter what market rates do, you'll earn the rate of interest you're locked into.

You can choose whatever CD term length you want, from 30 days to 5 years. And, you can open most of our CDs with as little as $1,000. If you need to have the funds available on a certain day, you can set up your CD to come due on that day. So County Savings CDs can be a great way to save for tuition, weddings, vacations, or that nestegg you've always wanted to accumulate. For your safety, all of our CDs are backed by the FDIC.

If you want to use the interest earned on your CD to meet your monthly expenses, you'll have the option of having the interest transferred to any County Savings checking or savings account, or to have an interest check sent directly to you.

Minimum deposit for County Savings CDs is $1,000, except for our Jumbo CD, which has a $100,000 initial deposit requirement. Rates vary depending on length of maturity and prevailing market rates. For your convenience we've set up a 24-hour County CD Hotline. Call 800-CDSRATES to find out today's rates.

For more information about County Savings CDs, or to open an account, stop by any County Savings Bank branch. We'll help you to open the appropriate CD and to start earning well.

Sincerely,

William Berrigan
Vice President

jcb

Loans—Consumer, Mortgage, Home Equity, Auto, & Student

Sample letters 8.20-8.37 were all written to market loan services.

Sample letters 8.20 and 8.21 discuss general consumer loans available at each writer's bank. While the writer of sample letter 8.20 chose to list the various types of loans his bank offers within the letter, the writer of sample letter 8.21 opted to incorporate the offerings in the text of the letter. Both methods are effective if they give the reader enough information to make an intelligent decision about loan needs. Sample letter 8.22 markets three types of consumer loans.

SAMPLE LETTER 8.20. Consumer loans (hanging-indented format).

August 16, 19X3

Mr. Ron Carrington
5678 Palay Place
East Grand Forks, Minnesota 57980

Dear Mr. Carrington:

The County Bank offers loans for all worthwhile purposes. Whether it's for a new car, a home improvement, that vacation you've worked hard for, or an unexpected expense, we have a loan that's right for you.

Simply complete the enclosed application if you're interested in securing any of the following loans:

Personal loans can be used for new appliances, furniture, a dream vacation, your family's medical or dental work, a personal computer, and many other purposes.

Auto loans can be used for that car you've been looking for.

Home improvement loans can be used for repairs and improvements you want to make around the house.

Home equity loans let you put the equity in your home to good use towards a college tuition, major home remodeling, or perhaps a second home.

Once you've completed the enclosed application, bring it to any County Bank office, or mail it to: County Bank, Loan Approval Department, 56 Benjamin Street, Nottingham, Minnesota 01120. Feel free to call me if you have any questions.

Sample Letter 8.20 continued

Cordially,

David K. Goods
Loan Officer

dkg/hlm

Enclosures

SAMPLE LETTER 8.21. Consumer loans (semiblock format).

February 14, 19X8

Mr. Colman Long
5454 Fenstermeister Road
West Hartford, Oregon 08765

Dear Mr. Long:

The reasons why you might want a bank loan are as varied as the events of your life. For your borrowing needs, the answer is New National Bank.

You may want to set up your own personal line of credit to be available whenever you need it. Our Cash Reserve is used in conjunction with your New National personal checking account. You create your own loan by simply writing a check for an amount larger than your existing checking account balance. You may borrow as often as you like, up to your preestablished loan level.

Our Soon-As-You-Need-It Credit plan establishes a similar loan level, and we provide you with a Soon-As-You-Need-It checkbook to activate your credit line. New National is ready to meet your everyday money requirements. Ask one of our helpful loan experts to assist you in designing a low-cost loan to suit your needs.

Give us a call at 555-6798, or stop in at any one of our conveniently located bank branches.

Sincerely,

Francis Cooke
Assistant Vice President

fc/ec

SAMPLE LETTER 8.22. Three types of loans available (full-block format).

September 10, 19X1

Mr. Peter Kasnar
43 Douglas Road
Far Hills, New Jersey 09008

Dear Mr. Kasnar:

If you're looking for a loan to finance your education, buy a boat or car, or remodel your kitchen, we've just made the application process easier. County Savings' Triple-Duty Loan Application lets you to apply for every kind of credit we offer—from loans to cash reserves.

You can choose from three types of credit County Savings Bank offers. You can use an installment loan for any personal money needs, from paying for a child's education costs or buying a car, to completing home improvements or taking a vacation.

For major home improvements, you can borrow with the home improvement loan we offer. Designed for those who own their own home and have solid credit records, the home improvement loan lets you borrow from $3,000 to $25,000.

If it's a line of credit you want to draw on when a particular needs crops up, you might want to consider our cash reserves loan, which allows you to do just that.

To apply for the loan that's right for your needs, complete the enclosed application, indicating which types of credit you would like. Bring or mail the completed application to any of County Savings branches. We look forward to having your business.

Sincerely,

Alan Radnor
Vice President

ltc
Enclosure

Sample letters 8.23 through 8.31 all market mortgage-type loans. Sample letter 8.23 markets a basic first mortgage on a home. The bank's new mortgage company subsidiary is featured in the letter which sells the reader on the personal, professional service she will receive from the bank. Sample letter 8.24, on the other hand, tries to market both first mortgages and home equity credit lines. This approach might help the bank to attract customers who already own their own home but are looking for ways to tap into the equity they've built up. Sample letter 8.25 sells the customer on the idea of taking advantage of low interest rates and also offers a discount on mortgage closing fees. Sample letter 8.26 spells out the variety of mortgage options available. Sample letter 8.27 was written to promote biweekly mortgages. Sample letter 8.28 was written to a current mortgage loan customer encouraging him or her to consider refinancing. And sample letter 8.29 was written as a cover letter to accompany a computer analysis of the customer's mortgage financing needs.

SAMPLE LETTER 8.23. Mortgage loans (block format).

May 10, 19X4

Ms. Hayley Rowe Henderson
567 Holliston Road
Brookline, Massachusetts 07654

Dear Ms. Henderson:

Quite often finding the right mortgage can be even harder than finding just the right home. But not at The County Bank.

Through our new subsidiary, MacIntyre Mortgage Company, we offer you one of the widest selections of fixed rate and adjustable rate mortgage plans available anywhere for any type of house or condominium—single family or multi-family; owner occupied or investment property; first homes or vacation homes.

Because mortgages are MacIntyre's only business, you can be sure the person you talk with is someone who knows your needs and can help you get the mortgage financing you want, at the terms you can afford.

If you're in the market for your first home, you know that the down payment can represent a substantial investment. When you come to MacIntyre Mortgage Company, you'll find we have included a choice of very low-down-payment mortgages. That means you have flexibility to help you buy more house, and arrange terms that best fit your budget.

We realize it is not always convenient to come to our office to fill out an application. That's why we will arrange to have a mortgage specialist meet with you where you work or in your home. Just name the time and day.

If you prefer you can schedule an appointment at one of our offices. We have three MacIntyre Mortgage Company offices, as well as Mortgage Service Centers at each of

Sample Letter 8.23 continued

our County Bank offices. Just pick one that's most convenient for you.

If you're interested in knowing just how much house you should be looking for, we can help. Call us at 678-8976 and we'll answer your questions over the phone. When it's time to apply for your mortgage, we'll help you prepare the necessary paperwork so we can process your application quickly.

Sincerely,

Jeremy Westerman
Senior Vice President

JW:JH

SAMPLE LETTER 8.24. Mortgage loans (semiblock format).

August 16, 19X0

Mr. Roger Tarras
Hungadunga, Hungadunga & McCormick
23 Spaulding Territory
Teaneck, New Jersey 90088

Dear Mr. Tarras:

The County Bank has made real estate lending its specialty for more than 40 years. More than 75% of our deposits are invested in real estate loans in communities throughout New Jersey.

With fixed and adjustable rate first mortgage loans, fixed term second mortgages, construction loans, and bridge loans, The County Bank offers a full range of residential mortgage plans to quickly satisfy even the most unusual financing need.

Once you've selected a new home you want to move in just as soon as you can. That's why at The County Bank, we've combined our competitive mortgage rates with a loan processing system the competition can't beat.

When you apply for a residential mortgage loan at The County Bank you'll have our answer within seven days and a finished loan just thirty days later.

Sample Letter 8.24 continued

Conforming Home Mortgages are available with terms up to 30 years. They are routinely made for amounts up to 95% of market value.

If you already own a home, you can use the equity you've built in it to secure a County Capital Credit Line ranging from $5,000 to $125,000. You may do so without disturbing any existing first mortgage you may have.

County Capital Credit is a preapproved, revolving credit line available to you anytime and anywhere. To borrow, you simple write one of your County Capital Credit checks. There are no additional forms and no waiting for separate loans to be approved. With County Capital Credit, you can finally turn you greatest capital asset, the equity in your home, into immediate cash.

For more information, stop in or give me a call at 675-0909.

Cordially,

Leslie Rawls
Mortgage Officer

mhf

SAMPLE LETTER 8.25. Mortgage loans (full-block format).

May 9, 19X1

Ms. Annmarie Long
95 Dix Street
Boonton, New Jersey 07005

Dear Ms. Long:

If you're planning to buy or refinance a home, now is the perfect time to turn to New National Bank's mortgage professionals. Because we're not only offering low interest rates, but if you apply before July 4, we're discounting the attorney closing fees by 25%, which could save you up to $250. And if you have your monthly mortgage payments deducted from your New National account, we won't charge you the normal $200 application fee. So by applying now, you could saving up to $450.

Sample Letter 8.25 continued

Choose to apply to any of the mortgage types we offer—fixed, adjustable, biweekly, or jumbo. We also continue to offer a 24-hour turnaround time on decisions to speed up your closing. And we'll let you lock in your rate for 90 days on the day you apply.

Our mortgage professionals will help you decide what type of mortgage is best for you. Plus they'll walk you through the prequalification test to see how much you'll be able to borrow and answer any questions you have.

For New National's current rates or a prequalification, call us today or stop by any branch. You can also set up an appointment with a New National mortgage professional. Or, to get more information by mail, fill out and return the enclosed postage-paid card.

Sincerely,

Edward Coleman
Vice President

nlc

Enclosure

SAMPLE LETTER 8.26. Mortgage loans (full-block format).

July 14, 19X1

Mr. Scott Idyll
45 Waltham Boulevard
Sastown, Idaho 59595

Dear Mr. Idyll:

If you're in the market to buy a house, County Savings Bank has a variety of mortgage options to fit your needs. Consider some of the alternatives.

Many homebuyers find adjustable rate mortgages (ARMs) appealing since the initial interest rate is lower than the rate on fixed rate loans of the same term. ARM interest rates and monthly payments will change periodically depending on where market interest rates are. Our one-year ARM, for example, changes rates on a present date every year. Changes are tied to market indexes, like the prime lending rate, so your mortgage rate may go up or down every year. We put a cap on how high our ARM rates can go

Sample Letter 8.26 continued

during the life of your mortgage loan, so you'll know how much the most is you'll ever have to pay.

Our fixed-rate mortgages lock in a rate for the whole term of the mortgage loan. County Savings offers fixed-rate mortgages from 10-year to 30-year terms. With a 30-year mortgage, you'll have a lower monthly payment and you can usually qualify for a larger amount. With a 10-year mortgage, you can repay your loan in a third of the time, and your interest savings can be considerable.

Call on one of our mortgage specialists today to help you determine the mortgage loan that best meets your needs. They'll also be able to tell you how much you prequalify for. Stop in at any branch or give a call to set up an appointment.

Sincerely,

Nancy Wilson
Vice President

bi

SAMPLE LETTER 8.27. Biweekly mortgages (full-block format).

March 20, 19X8

Ms. Jeanne Berrigan
24 Waterside Street
Marblehead, Hawaii 40440

Dear Ms. Berrigan:

Many of our customers who'd like to speed up the time it takes to own their homes have chosen County Savings Bank's biweekly mortgage option which can shave around 10 years off of a 30-year fixed mortgage. Here's how it works.

When you take out a biweekly mortgage, you make a payment—equal to about half of your typical monthly payment—every two weeks. Since a traditional 30-year fixed-rate mortgage requires 12 payments a year and with the biweekly mortgage you end up making 26 monthly payments a year, you wind up make 1 extra monthly payment a year.

Because you're making extra payments and you're making them more frequently, you'll end up paying off a traditional 30-year mortgage loan much faster than normal. The

Sample Letter 8.27 continued

biweekly option will enable you to pay off a mortgage in 19 to 21 years what would have taken 30 years had you opted for traditional monthly payments.

The cost to you? About one extra monthly payment per year.

To apply for a County Savings Bank biweekly mortgage or to find out more, simply stop by any one of our branches. We look forward to doing business with you.

Sincerely,

Lorraine Gatto
Vice President

jg

SAMPLE LETTER 8.28. Mortgage refinancing (full-block format).

April 23, 19X3

Mr. Nathaniel Waggoner
43 Blossom Court
Hampden, New Jersey 03030

Dear Mr. Waggoner:

If you have a mortgage and are wondering whether or not now is the right time to refinance, County Savings Bank has designed a short quiz for you to determine the answer.

1. Do you have an adjustable rate mortgage on which the rates are now 2% or more higher than our current fixed-rate mortgage rates?

2. Do you have an home equity line of credit that's tied to a market index that causes monthly payments to be alarmingly high?

3. Do you panic when you think about where you're going to get the money to send your kids to college?

4. Do you fret each month over all of your outstanding loans, thinking it would be simpler to consolidate all of them into one?

5. Do you regret that your mortgage rate is now more than 12%?

If you answered yes to any of these questions, now may be the time to consider refinancing your mortgage. And County Savings Bank's mortgage professionals can help you

Sample Letter 8.28 continued

explore the options and make an informed decision. To set up an appoint, give me a call, or stop by any of our branch offices.

Sincerely,

Maurice Lowe
Vice President

SAMPLE LETTER 8.29. Mortgage loan analysis (full-block format).

August 9, 19X0

Mr. Gary Loren
90 Adams Street
Eufaula, Arkansas 09087

Dear Mr. Loren:

Thank you in your interest in New National as a mortgage source. Based on our recent meeting and the figures you provided us, we have created a computer analysis of what you can expect your downpayment, mortgage balance, and monthly payments to be should New National provide you with a mortgage.

A couple of pieces of information might help you understand the analysis better. The ''payment ratio'' is the percent of your gross income that will be devoted to housing payments, and in most cases must be less than 28%. The ''all debts ratio'' is the percentage of your gross income that will be devoted to all monthly obligations. Generally this ratio must be less than 36%.

We hope this information will be helpful to you as you are preparing to apply for a mortgage. Please do not hesitate to call me for any other assistance.

Sincerely,

Lisa Tieszen
Vice President

jtg

Enclosure

Sample letters 8.30 and 8.31 are two versions of letters offering home equity loans. Sample letter 8.30 is a bit longer and plays up the low interest rate. Sample letter 8.31 is more to the point, but still covers the essential information that the reader should know.

SAMPLE LETTER 8.30. Home equity loan (simplified format).

August 11, 19X9

Mr. Justin Long
408 Huntington Avenue
Boston, Massachusetts 02114

HOME EQUITY LOAN

Mr. Long, a County Bank Home Equity Credit Line can help you turn the equity you've built up in your home into instant cash. It gives you a line of credit from $10,000 to $125,000 secured by your home equity.

You can use the money to pay for the things you want—like an addition to your home or college education—when you want them.

All you have to do to get your cash is write a special check ($500 minimum). Unlike many other banks which restrict borrowing to 70% or 75% of the appraised value of your home, The County Bank lets you borrow up to 80%.

Not only do you have instant access to your money, you pay less to borrow it. Our rate is just 1.5% above The County Bank prime rate, adjusted monthly. For example, if our prime rate on the first business day of the month is 9.5%, your rate for that month will be 11%. And with a County Bank Home Equity Credit Line there is no limit to how low your rate can go because we have no minimum rate. Naturally, you pay interest only on the money you actually borrow—not on the unused portion of your line of credit.

There are no annual fees or origination fees (''points'') for your County Bank Home Equity Credit Line. There is a one-time application fee which covers the bank's appraisal costs and expenses related to closing, such as attorney's fees, title search, and recording fees.

To apply for a County Bank Home Equity Credit Line, simply complete and return the enclosed application and include the most recent copy of your real estate tax bill. Once we receive your application, we'll let you know exactly how much your total application fee will be and pro-

Sample Letter 8.30 continued

cess your County Bank Home Equity Credit Line request. If you have any questions, please call me at 876-9809.

JOSEPH BING
LOAN OFFICER

mn

enc.

SAMPLE LETTER 8.31. Home equity loan (hanging-indented format).

May 9, 19X6

Ms. Sue Millard
56 Forest Lane
Lake Forest, Wisconsin 90876

Dear Ms. Millard:

New National Bank's Easy-Equity Credit Line could be the perfect way to finance your borrowing needs. It is a personal line of credit that lets you use the equity in your home whenever you need money. You apply only once. When the credit line is approved, you gain access to your money, any time, simply by writing a check. It's an excellent way to pay for home improvements, a college education, a second home, starting a business, or for any other purpose you may have in mind.

Easy-Equity Credit Line is easy to use. Once your application is approved, you will be granted a line of credit for up to $100,000. You will receive an Easy-Equity Credit Line checkbook. Whenever you need money, you just write a check.

Our rate is just 1% over the national prime rate. The interest rate will be adjusted monthly as the prime rate changes. After a one-time start-up fee, you pay only interest on the amount you actually use. There are no annual fees.

To get an Easy-Equity Credit Line application, complete and mail the enclosed postpaid reply card. Feel free to call me if you have any questions.

Cordially,

Sample Letter 8.31 continued

Hayley Rowe Henderson
Loan Officer

hrh/jls

enc.

Sample letter 8.32 was written to market car loans.

SAMPLE LETTER 8.32. Car loans (full-block format).

September 11, 19X2

Mr. Anthony Delastro
54 Terrace Drive
Poskaty, Virginia 49449

Dear Mr. Delastro:

New National wants to make borrowing to purchase the car you want simple and quick. Our goal is to give you a response to your request for a car loan on the same day you apply. You needn't spend days in suspense about the outcome of your application.

All you need to do to apply for a New National loan is to call our New National Loan Line at 800-CARLOAN. Or, complete the enclosed application and bring it in to one of our branches or mail it to us in the enclosed postage paid envelope.

We offer competitive rates on all of our car loans, but we'll make the loan even more attractive if you have the monthly payments deducted from your New National savings or checking account. When you choose this option, your payment gets made automatically, and we charge you less interest on your loan.

If you'd like to find out more about the loans we offer, just drop in to one of our branches or give us a call.

Sincerely,

Jacqueline Alanson
Vice President

jls

Enclosure

Sample letters 8.33 through 8.36 market student loans. Sample letter 8.33 discusses Higher Education Loan Plans that are made directly to students. Sample letter 8.34 discusses the Parents Loans for Undergraduate Students program. Sample letter 8.35 discusses both plans in the same letter. And sample letter 8.36 discusses even a wider variety of student loan options.

SAMPLE LETTER 8.33. Student loans (full-block format).

November 3, 19X2

Mr. Alan Lavine
435 Threton Place
Ashburton, Ohio 45345

Dear Mr. Lavine:

The County Bank believes that if you're smart enough to get into college, money shouldn't keep you out. With the Higher Education Loan Plan (H.E.L.P.) those high grades you worked so hard for can earn you the loan you need.

You are eligible for H.E.L.P. if you are now enrolled or have been accepted in at least a half-time program at an educational institution approved under the Guaranteed Student Loan program.

Undergraduates can borrow up to $2,500 a year and graduate students can borrow up to $5,000 a year. Interest is deferred while you are an accredited student and for six months after graduation. You begin to pay back the loan six months after graduation or withdrawal from school.

H.E.L.P. makes it easier for you with a low annual percentage rate—8% for the first-time borrower. If you have previously borrowed from this program, your loan will continue at your original interest rate.

For more information, stop by any of The County Bank's branch location and talk to one of our customer service representatives. Or feel free to call my office at 877-4545.

Sincerely,

Max Nilges
Vice President

mn/js

SAMPLE LETTER 8.34. Student loans (block format).

April 1, 19X4

Ms. Eleanor Rigbee
65 Tyingson Road
Federal Village, Wyoming 90909

Dear Ms. Rigbee:

PARENT LOANS FOR STUDENTS PROGRAM

The County Bank helps parents meet their children's education costs with the Parent Loans for Undergraduate Students program (P.L.U.S.)

To be eligible, the student in your family must be enrolled or have been accepted for enrollment at an educational institution approved by the Guaranteed Student Loan program. Parents must also meet The County Bank's credit standards.

We will loan you up to $3,000 a year for each dependent student. The minimum loan is $1,000 each academic year. Interest rates are 12% annually on P.L.U.S. loans. The first payment is due 45 days from the date that the loan money is paid to you. The minimum monthly payment is $50.

The County Bank is the number one bank in Wyoming for college loans. We make getting a loan easy because we want you to get the loan. That's what makes us the best bank for education loans in the state.

If you'd like more information on the P.L.U.S. loans, stop by any of our conveniently located branch offices, or give me a call at 456-5656.

Best regards,

Max Nilges
Senior Vice President

mn/pj

SAMPLE LETTER 8.35. Student loans (semiblock format).

August 6, 19X4

Mr. Ted Bunnell
186 Savin Road
Belmont, Maine 90876

Dear Mr. Bunnell:

Students' loans used to be just for those attending college. But New National Bank can help you finance the cost of vocational school, technical school, an advanced degree—and, of course, college. We'll tailor a financing solution to your particular needs.

The Higher Education Loan Plan (H.E.L.P.) is a federally sponsored program administered by the Maine Higher Education Assistance Corporation. College and technical school students may borrow up to $2,500 per year for undergraduate study; graduate students may borrow up to $5,000 per year. Repayment of H.E.L.P. loans does not begin until the student has graduated. All loans are made directly to the student, with no requirements for parent cosignatures.

The Parent Loans for Undergraduate Students (P.L.U.S.) program is also federally sponsored and administered locally. P.L.U.S. loans are available to parents of dependent undergraduate students as well as independent undergraduate and graduate students.

Another important source of financing for many parents is the equity in their homes. With a New National Home Equity Loan you can use the money tied up in your home to finance the cost of higher education.

For help in tailoring a financing solution for your particular needs, give me a call in our Higher Education Loan Department at 335-4439, or stop in at any of our conveniently located branches.

Sincerely,

Peter E. Jensen
Senior Vice President

PEJ/dam

SAMPLE LETTER 8.36. Student loans (full-block format).

August 17, 19X0

Mr. Jonathan Strauss
445 Bayside Place
Beaverton, Oregon 59595

Dear Mr. Strauss:

New National Bank is pleased to offer the widest range of education loans available in the Beaverton region. Whether it's to finance a child's education or finance your own undergraduate or graduate degree, we can help you find the financing you need.

New National offers the Stafford Student Loan, which offers low-interest rates and deferred payments while you are in undergraduate or graduate school. If you don't qualify for a Stafford Loan, the PLUS (Parental Loan for Undergraduate Students) and SLS (Supplemental Loan for Students) may be a good alternative source for education financing. PLUS loans are available to parents, and SLS loans to graduate and undergraduate students.

With a TERI (The Educational Resources Institute) loan, you can borrow up to $20,000 a year, which is considerably more than other education loans. And with a TERI, you don't have to pass an income ''test.'' Application approval is based solely on your ability to repay the loan. Similarly PEP (Professional Education Plan) loans, available to graduate students, allow eligible students to borrow up to $20,000 a year at low interest rates. Here too, loan approval is based on your ability to repay.

We've enclosed an information sheet that contains more information about all New National's education loans. If you have any questions or need more information about any of New national's education loans programs, one of our loan representatives can select the education loan option that's right for you. Simply call one our 24-hour customer help line, stop by one of our branches, or complete and return the enclosed postage-paid card.

Sincerely,

Gannon Long
Vice President

ltg

Enclosures

Sample letter 8.37 markets a consumer credit line.

SAMPLE LETTER 8.37. Credit line (full-block format).

June 28, 19X1

Mr. Jack L. English
681 Nivas Avenue
Nostrom, Alabama 03220

Dear Mr. English:

At New National we're in the business of making banking easier for our customers. That's why we're prepared to offer you a $3,500 personal reserve credit line. All you have to do is to fill out and send back the acceptance form enclosed and we'll open your personal reserve credit line.

By marrying a New National personal reserve credit line to your checking account, you'll get the safety of overdraft protection as well as a personal line of credit. The personal reserve credit line costs you nothing until you use it.

Here's how your personal reserve credit line can work. If you inadvertently write a check for more than the balance in your checking account, your personal reserve credit line will cover the difference up to your available credit limit. You can also write a loan to yourself any time you want by writing yourself a check up to your available credit limit. What's more, you can withdraw cash from your credit line at any of our automated teller machines throughout the state.

When you complete and return the enclosed personal reserve credit line acceptance form, we'll open your account. If you have any questions, please call our customer service hotline at 800-RESERVE, or stop by any of our branches.

Sincerely,

Alexander Nebitz
Vice President

lsl

Enclosure

Credit Cards and ATM Cards

Sample letters 8.38 through 8.40 market credit card and ATM card services to bank customers. Sample letter 8.38 is a particularly easy letter to adapt for use in a word processor. Sample letters 8.39 and 8.40 are a long and short version of letters marketing ATM card services.

SAMPLE LETTER 8.38. Credit card offering (full-block format).

July 2, 19X6

Mr. Patrick McDonnell
3434 Mockingbird Lane
Russbaker, New York 21234

Dear Mr. McDonnell:

I think you will be excited about having the opportunity and the convenience to consolidate your credit card obligations with one financial institution. The County Bank now offers you the unique opportunity to enjoy the prestige of having both the Gold Premier Visa and the Gold Preferred MasterCard.

Both of these Gold Cards are honored throughout the United States and around the world. They are recognized for their versatility and indispensable for their convenience. The Gold Credit Cards combine the features of major purchases, travel, and financial services and are accepted at thousands of locations here and around the world.

Now you can have the following valuable services and features with The County Bank's Gold Credit Card program:

High credit line of $10,000
Cash availability at thousands of locations
Worldwide acceptance at thousands of locations
Emergency airline tickets
Travel reservation service
Car rental discounts
Free convenience checks
Toll-free access numbers for Gold Card services

The enclosed brochure tells you more about The County Bank's Gold Credit Card program.

To apply for both Gold Credit Cards, simply complete the enclosed application and return it in the envelope we've provided.

Sample Letter 8.38 continued

Sincerely,

Bethany Jane Coleman
President

SAMPLE LETTER 8.39. ATM cards (full-block format).

November 3, 19X7

Mr. Jack Derrida
Presidential Valve Company, Inc.
342 Parisian Highway
Tuskaloosa, Oklahoma 56784

Dear Mr. Derrida:

At The County Bank, we want to make your banking fast, easy, and convenient. Our ATM Card does just that. You receive instant cash, day or night, at approximately 500 locations in banks and supermarkets throughout Oklahoma alone. Your funds are also available at more than 1,500 ATMs nationwide.

To use the ATM, all you'll need is a N.O.W. Checking, Super N.O.W., Savings, or a Money Market Account with The County Bank. When you are ready to use an ATM, all you do is insert your ATM Card and enter your secret Personal Identification Number. Then, the ATM guides you through the transaction, and gives you a printed receipt.

You can get up to $300 per day at ATM locations in addition to making deposits, transferring funds between accounts, making loan payments, mortgage payments, and life insurance payments.

Your County Bank ATM card lets you cash personal checks up to $500 at hundreds of affiliated bank locations throughout the country. Your card is also accepted at all American Express machines located at most major airports nationwide.

To get your free County Bank ATM card, simply fill out the enclosed application and return it to the nearest County Bank office. When you receive your card, you'll begin to have banking convenience across the state and the country.

Sincerely,

Sample Letter 8.39 continued

Chaim Oared
Branch Manager

mn

Enclosure

SAMPLE LETTER 8.40. ATM cash card (full-block format).

August 20, 19X4

Mr. Joe Bolton
Three Stooge Place
Dorchester, Massachusetts 02125

Dear Mr. Bolton:

We have a New National ATM Cash Card for you.
Your Cash Card lets you withdraw cash from your Money Market Checking account. You can also make deposits with the card at more than 800 ATMs all over New England.

The machines are located in all kinds of banks, credit unions, supermarkets, and even drugstores. They are accessible day or night, weekday, or weekend. If you have not already used a card to get cash, try ours. You will probably never go back to waiting in teller lines again.

I am enclosing an application for the New National ATM Cash Card. Please complete it and return it to my attention. If you have any questions, please call me at 1-800-999-0909. I will be happy to help you.

Sincerely,

Matthew Rovner
Account Executive

enc.

Commercial Banking Services

Sample letter 8.41 is a tightly written comprehensive letter marketing commercial banking services to potential customers.

SAMPLE LETTER 8.41. Commercial banking services (official style format).

August 12, 19X3

Dear Peter:

Your inquiry the other day about The County Bank's commercial banking services is very timely. For the past several years, we've been serving the business community with business loans, real estate financing, and a variety of business banking services. Our senior officers have a highly personalized approach to service and are backed by a bank with more than $1 billion in assets.

We can provide your business with a wide range of financing options, including lines of credit, short-term working capital loans, equipment loans, and letters of credit. Our rates are competitive, and we'll design a loan plan to fit your needs.

In addition to lending you the funds you need to grow, The County Bank can make the money you already have grow. We offer corporate and payroll checking accounts, and a business checking account which allows you to sweep money into a money market account when your balance reaches $1,000. You get a detailed monthly statement that shows all your transactions plus the interest you've earned.

Whether you're looking for construction loans, permanent loans, equity investments, joint ventures, or other commercial real estate financing services, we can help. We'll do everything from finding investors for your project, handling lease-back arrangements, dealing with municipal and state agencies, arranging end loan financing or even selling bonds on Wall Street.

The County Bank's multistage financing will ease your cash flow. We offer land and land development loans, construction loans upon approval and standing loans during startup on approved development transactions.

If you'd like to set up an appointment to come in and talk in more detail about these services, please call me.

Sincerely,

Sample Letter 8.41 continued

Nancy Long

Mr. Peter Jensen, Chairman
The Son Newspapers, Inc.
98 Bethany College Place
Morlan, West Virginia 02125

NL:js

Retirement Accounts

Sample letters 8.42-8.47 are all written to market retirement accounts. Sample letters 8.42 through 8.44 deal specifically with IRA accounts. Sample letter 8.42 discusses the benefits of an IRA plan, while sample letters 8.43 and 8.44 offer IRA savings plans.

SAMPLE LETTER 8.42. IRA plans (block format).

March 5, 19X4

Ms. Andrea Rock
4545 Tremont Place
Yarmouth, Michigan 87654

Dear Ms. Rock:

Individual Retirement Accounts are tax-sheltered savings plans for wage earners or self-employed people younger than 70.5. If you are not covered by a company pension plan, IRAs are an excellent method of planning for your future retirement by having your money grow on a tax-deferred basis.

You may contribute 100% of your earned income or compensation or $2,000, whichever is less, to your IRA each year. If you have a nonworking spouse, the limit of total contribution is increased to $2,250. Couples who both work may establish separate IRAs and contribute up to $2,000 each every year.

You can begin to collect retirement benefits after you reach age 59.5. You must begin to receive funds in the year in which you reach 70.5. Withdrawals prior to age 59.5 are subject to penalties.

Sample Letter 8.42 continued

Your initial and all subsequent contributions can be made at any time before your tax return is due, usually April 15. Contribution dates are subject to change by the Internal Revenue Service; therefore we suggest you inquire at The County Bank for the most current provision.

If you have no company sponsored pension plan, the funds you contribute to your IRA may be deductible from your income taxed by the IRS. Even if you do have a company pension plan, you can set up an IRA and the interest earned on it will not be subject to Federal Tax, until distribution.

Opening an IRA plan is almost as easy as opening a savings account. Just complete a few simple forms at any of our conveniently located branch offices, or call or write and we will mail the forms to you.

If you have any questions about IRAs or our retirement options, feel free to call me at 676-9090.

Best regards,

Erik Erikson
Branch Manager

ee/hm

SAMPLE LETTER 8.43. IRA savings plan (simplified format).

August 6, 19X2

Mrs. C. C. Long
343 Interlude Way
Penobscot, Rhode Island 90765

IRA SAVINGS PLAN

Don't get caught short of IRA cash on April 15. With New National's AutoIRA Account, you don't have to because it grows an IRA for you, automatically, month by month.

AutoIRA gives you the benefit of automatic savings so you don't have to worry about big lump sum payments. It's convenient and easy. It also offers you all the benefits you'd expect from any IRA—high money market interest rates, substantial tax advantages, a growing retirement

Sample Letter 8.43 continued

income, and federally insured deposits up to $100,000 by the FDIC.

AutoIRA fits in with the way you earn your money, because it automatically puts cash away for you, month by month. You simply choose any monthly amount, from as little as $50, to contribute to your IRA. Then you choose how you'd like to save that amount. With AutoIRA, you can have your monthly amount:

- deducted from your checking account, anywhere in the country, at any bank,
- charged to any MasterCard, VISA, or American Express card, or
- deducted from your payroll.

That's all you do. AutoIRA does the rest, from transferring the funds to providing you with periodic statements of your account activity.

You can also make an additional lump sum contribution at the end of the calendar year if you wish, as long as you don't exceed the $2,000 annual maximum.

AutoIRA makes investing in your retirement easier than ever before. To apply for an AutoIRA account, use the enclosed application form. To apply by phone, or for further information, call us at 555-6789.

Sidney Beshkin
Assistant Vice President

sb/hh
Enclosure

SAMPLE LETTER 8.44. IRA plans (full-block format).

November 3, 19X3

Mr. David L. Palay
Rising Planet Inc.
543 Ries Street
Plattsburgh, New York 10023

Dear Mr. Palay:

Sample Letter 8.44 continued

Millions of Americans take advantage of the significant tax benefits Individual Retirement Accounts (IRAs) offer. But surprisingly, many millions more do not.

We suspect it's because saving has always been difficult. Saving in an IRA can be confusing as well.

People who make a single lump sum contribution to their IRA each year may find that the money may not be available when it's needed. What's more, most financial institutions offering IRA's have established substantial minimum deposit requirements to open an account.

The County Savings Bank lets you enjoy all the tax advantages of an IRA with contributions of as little as $10 a month. What's more, your contributions are made automatically.

With your tax-sheltered IRA at County Bank, you decide how much to deposit each month or payday, and that amount is transferred automatically and deposited in your County Savings IRA Money Market Account, even if you have your checking account with another bank. The only requirement is that you contribute at least $10 a month. That's it. It's as simple as payroll savings.

Each month you will receive a detailed statement listing all contributions made in your IRA, all tax-deferred interest earned, and the current balance in your plan.

Simply complete the enclosed IRA Savings Plan application and return it to us today. For more information about The County Bank's retirement plans and the many investment alternatives we offer, please give us a call at 898-3542.

Sincerely,

Florence Lewis
Assistant Vice President

fl/hm

Enclosure

Sample letter 8.45 markets IRA and Keogh accounts to prospective customers. Sample letter 8.46 markets IRA rollover provisions available. Sample letter 8.47 specifically markets Keogh accounts.

SAMPLE LETTER 8.45. Sales letter describing IRA and Keogh services available (block format).

December 26, 19X2

Mr. Leigh Jeffreys
119 Roosevelt Street
Ware, Wyoming 55569

Dear Mr. Jeffreys:

The County Savings Bank has three basic investment plans for IRA and Keogh contributions. All plans are guaranteed and offer continuous compounding of interest, the maximum allowed by law.

Plan A is the 18-Month Variable Rate Term Deposit. The interest rate on this type of term deposit will change each month on our normal dividend date (fourth Monday of the month). The maturity is 18 months and additional deposits may be made periodically without changing the maturity date. The index used to determine this rate will be the highest yield for 1 1/2 year U.S. Treasury Notes offered the Friday before our monthly dividend date.

Plan B is the Fixed Rate Term Deposit. The maturity of our fixed rate term deposit is from 1 1/2 to 2 1/2 years. The index used to determine this fixed rate will be the highest yield for 2 year U.S. Treasury Notes offered the Friday before our dividend date.

Plan C is our ''Automatic Transfer'' program. To help you build up your IRA account over time, we also offer a systematic monthly savings program whereby we will automatically transfer an amount specified by you from your NOW or regular savings account to an IRA regular savings account. Upon your instructions, we will then transfer the accumulated funds, in increments of at least $500, to our 1 1/2 year, variable rate term deposit (without changing the maturity date) or to one of our fixed rate term deposit accounts.

I hope one of our IRA/Keogh investment plans will work for you. Feel free to call me if you have any questions. I look forward to hearing from you.

Regards,

Sample Letter 8.45 continued

Loren Gary
Vice President

jls

SAMPLE LETTER 8.46. IRA rollovers and transfers (full-block format).

June 14, 19X6

Ms. Alessandra Nordstrom
38 Commercial Place
Cambridge, California 90030

Dear Ms. Nordstrom:

Over the past several years, employer-sponsored pension plans have grown dramatically. As employees go on to new jobs, they often face the prospect of reinvesting lump-sum pension payouts. These payouts are taxable in the year they are received unless they are rolled over into another retirement vehicle.

If you're facing just such a situation, you may be able to continue to defer tax payments on your retirement money by setting up a rollover IRA at County Savings Bank. The rollover IRA allows you to invest money received from an employer-sponsored pension plan or from another IRA. You'll continue deferring tax payments until you withdraw your money upon retirement. Any rollover must be completed within 60 days of the day you receive your final payment.

You can also use a rollover to consolidate IRA funds or to transfer funds from one plan to another. You can move your IRA funds to County Savings Bank by taking a distribution from your current IRA and reinvesting the funds in a County Savings IRA within 60 days of the distribution. You can rely on County Savings and your current IRA trustee to handle this transaction for you. If you'd like to consolidate your IRA funds by transferring your IRA directly to County Savings Bank, you can do it by simply transferring directly between trustees with no reportable distributions taking place.

Fill out the enclosed worksheet and we'll be able to complete your IRA transfer or rollover. Once you have completed the information, visit a customer service representative at any County Savings branch. They'll be glad to help you with any questions you might have.

Sample Letter 8.46 continued

Sincerely,

Arnold Zeith
Vice President

Enclosure

SAMPLE LETTER 8.47 Keogh plans (semiblock format).

October 10, 19X3

Mr. Ed Debev
56 Divine Avenue
Cambridge, Alabama 90876

Dear Mr. Debev:

Thank you for your interest in retirement savings options for self-employed individuals. One of your best options may be a New National Bank Keogh Plan.

A Keogh plan is a tax-qualified retirement plan approved by Congress for self-employed individuals. It allows any self-employed person to shelter a sizeable percentage of his or her income from federal tax liability until retirement.

All unincorporated proprietorships and partnerships are eligible for a Keogh plan. Attorneys, accountants, architects, writers, physicians, consultants, freelancers—anyone earning self-employed income—can establish a Keogh plan for himself and his employees. Even full-time company employees can start a Keogh plan as long as the income they invest is earned on a separate, self-employed basis.

A Keogh plan gives you all the benefits of an IRA—high, competitive interest rates, a growing tax-deferred retirement income, and FDIC-insured deposits up to $100,000. But since the investment limits of a Keogh are considerably higher than an IRA, its tax advantages are far more substantial. Depending upon the plan you choose, the maximum deductible employer contribution could be as much as 25% of total compensation up to $30,000 a year. All funds contributed up to the legal limit are deductible from federal taxes as a business expense. Your total invested income, as well as its accumulated capital growth, remain tax-free until withdrawals are made at retirement.

Sample Letter 8.47 continued

Any Keogh plan covering a business owner must also cover employees at least 21 years old who have worked for the employer for at least three consecutive years. If you have employees, you must contribute at least the same percentage of their annual salary as you invest into your own account. Depending upon the plan you choose, however, you may not be required to make contributions every year if you fail to reach your profit goals. If you withdraw funds before you are 59.5 years old, they'll be subject to a 10% early withdrawal tax penalty.

If you are serious about a New National Keogh Plan, we'll work with you to establish the plan that is best for you. Simply fill out and mail the enclosed Keogh Kit Request Form or call our Keogh Hotline at 657-9090. We'll send you everything you need to put one of our Keogh Plans to work for you.

Cordially,

Tracey Hunt
Assistant Vice President

th/mn

Enclosure

Life Insurance

Sample letter 8.48 markets Savings Bank Life Insurance to customers. Sample letters 8.49 markets mortgage life insurance to mortgage customers.

SAMPLE LETTER 8.48. Savings Bank Life Insurance (simplified format).

July 7, 19X4

Mr. Jacob Wirth
45 Boston Place
Huntsville, Massachusetts 30345

SAVINGS BANK LIFE INSURANCE

Mr. Wirth, low cost and dependable service are two good reasons to buy Savings Bank Life Insurance. Independent studies have shown, time after time, that SBLI, is one of the best insurance buys not only in Massachusetts, but in all of the United States.

Sample Letter 8.48 continued

Massachusetts state law allows you to purchase SBLI directly from The County Bank without paying an agent's commission. This, combined with our low overhead costs, means savings for you.

Any person between the ages of 15 days and 70 who lives or works regularly in Massachusetts may purchase Savings Bank Life Insurance. Once your policy is issued, you may keep it, even if you move out of the state.

The County Bank offers permanent, term, children's, group, and annuity insurance plans. These plans are designed for individuals, families, and businesses.

Premiums can be paid either annually, semiannually, or quarterly. Premium payments may be made at the bank, by mail, or automatically deducted from your savings account, whichever is most convenient for you.

SBLI representatives are located at all County Bank branch locations—every banking day. If it is inconvenient for you to visit one of our offices, you can purchase SBLI through the mail or by telephone. We're always ready to help you select the plan that's best for you.

For more information, stop by The County Bank office nearest you, call us at 675-9087, or complete the information request form I've enclosed.

DUDLEY ROSE
SENIOR VICE PRESIDENT

mn

Enclosure

SAMPLE LETTER 8.49 Mortgage life insurance (full-block format).

December 26, 19X7

Mr. Bruce Gold
47 Beaconsfield Road
Bideford, Vermont 90876

Dear Mr. Gold:

You made a wise investment when you purchased your home. Mortgage life insurance lets you safeguard that important asset and protect your family against financial hardship by paying off your mortgage loan if you should die.

Sample Letter 8.49 continued

Many of our customers rely on this plan for their family's security. It's underwritten by Nilges Mutual Life, the nation's number one provider of mortgage life insurance. Individuals are eligible for the plan. Two homeowners can apply jointly at a discount. The cost for coverage does not increase with age.

Review the enclosed brochure. Then complete the application and return it today. Send no payment now. When your application is approved, the small cost will be added to your monthly mortgage payment. If you're not fully satisfied, you may discontinue coverage by notifying us.

If you have any questions call our toll-free insurance information line any time at 800-328-9343.

Act now to protect your home and family with mortgage life insurance.

Sincerely,

Hamilton Beach
Assistant Treasurer

hb/ns

Enclosure

Stocks & Bonds

Sample letter 8.50 is a straightforward letter marketing Series EE Savings Bonds. Samples 8.51 and 8.52 market discount brokerage services and municipal securities to customers. Since both topics may be new to prospective customers it is crucial that they be explained clearly.

SAMPLE LETTER 8.50. Series EE Savings Bonds (block format).

December 26, 19X6

Ms. Yvonne Surette
75 Entrepreneurial Way
Acropolis, Washington 20009

Dear Ms. Surette:

SERIES EE SAVINGS BONDS

For as little as $25, you can get market advantages for your savings. Series EE Savings Bonds now offer savers

Sample Letter 8.50 continued

the benefits of market interest rates without any risk to principal. Interest is variable, based on 85% of market rates when a bond is held five years or longer.

There's no limit on what you can earn. For example, when market rates average 13%, bonds earn about 11%. If rates go higher, bonds earn even more. The rates are averaged every six months. You receive a cumulative average rate at redemption. Bonds held less than five years earn interest on a fixed, graduated scale.

The minimum guaranteed rate is 6%, even if market rates average lower. So there's no market risk.

Outstanding bonds retain their current guarantees, and will automatically earn prevailing higher rates if held five more years. So there's no need to cash in older bonds.

Savings Bonds continue to offer the safety, convenience, and tax advantages bond holders have always enjoyed.

There's never been a better time to buy Savings Bonds. I've enclosed a brochure on Series EE Bonds which explains their rates, safety, and tax status. If you have any questions, feel free to call me.

Sincerely,

Max Nilges, President
New National Bank

MN/rr

Enclosure

SAMPLE LETTER 8.51. Discount brokerage services (full-block format).

September 5, 19X5

Mrs. Natalie Thomson
675 Greentop Way
Alasahoochie, New Mexico 95456

Dear Mrs. Thomson:

With County Bank's discount brokerage service, you can count on saving up to 70% on brokerage commissions. There was a time when you had to pay the high commissions brokers demanded. But now the independent investor who enjoys making buy and sell decisions can save on every trade.

Sample Letter 8.51 continued

Many investors rely on their full-commission broker for sound advice when they need it. But those who are accustomed to managing their own portfolios can rely on our discount brokerage services for buying and selling stocks, bonds, and options at substantial savings.

You can trade by calling our nationwide toll-free number 1-800-555-2323. Trades are processed by our own discount brokerage firm, and are cleared by McGuffie Clearing House. Our professionals handle your transaction quickly and efficiently, without high pressure selling. If you wish, you can arrange to have proceeds from the sale of securities directly deposited into a County Bank account, where it will earn interest immediately.

Look over the commission schedule and postpaid application I've enclosed. If you need more information, call me or a service representative in our discount brokerage office at 656-7676.

Sincerely,

Evan Marshall
Vice President

em/js

Enclosure

SAMPLE LETTER 8.52. Municipal securities (simplified format).

February 5, 19X4

Mr. Peter Jensen, Chairman
The Son Newspapers, Inc.
98 Bethany College Place
Morlan, West Virginia 02125

MUNICIPAL SECURITIES AT NEW NATIONAL BANK

Mr. Jensen, are you paying taxes on your investment income? If taxes on interest income are reducing your current yields, municipal securities may be the answer. You can take advantage of many tax-free investment opportunities available directly through New National Bank.

The most important benefit of investing in municipal securities is that the interest you earn is exempt from federal income taxes. As an added benefit, in most states, interest income earned on securities issued by governmental units within the state is also exempt from state and

Sample Letter 8.52 continued

local income taxes. As a taxpayer, that means your investment yield on municipal securities remains the same—before and after April 15.

For most investors, tax-free income translates into investment yields that are considerably higher than those derived from taxable instruments. For example, an individual in a 27% income tax bracket would have to earn a before-tax rate of more than 9.5% on another investment to equal the yield of a 7% municipal security.

New National Bank has the resources you need to start making tax-free investments. Securities available through our municipal dealer desk include tax-exempt bonds, notes, commercial paper, and shares in tax-exempt unit investment trusts. You can rely on our staff of highly qualified municipal security representatives to provide sound investment advice, recommend the best tax-free securities, and execute trades promptly and accurately. All you have to do to take advantage of any of these services is make a phone call.

To make investing in tax-free securities as easy as possible, we also offer the convenience of automatic transaction settlement through any New National Bank checking or savings account. At your request, we can debit your account with the proceeds of a sale. You will not have to worry about missing settlement dates or waiting for checks to arrive in the mail.

With a New National Bank money market account your available funds will not sit idle. Between security purchases we can arrange for your funds to be automatically deposited into your money market account where they will earn money market interest rates.

Start improving your after-tax investment earnings today. For more information, call me at 980-7898.

TIM STOUT
Municipal Securities Representive

wed

Account Administration 9

The letters in this chapter cover a wide range of account-related topics. In all of these letters, the writers have kept in mind that they are dealing with customers who should receive all of the respect due them, whether the letter is dealing with a pleasant topic or an account problem.

Opening an Account

Sample letters 9.1 and 9.2 deal with opening an account. Sample letter 9.1 gives the customer information needed to open an account, while sample letter 9.2 explains to a prospective customer that an account must be opened in person at the bank.

SAMPLE LETTER 9.1. Letter enclosing documents necessary for opening account (semiblock format).

June 16, 19X2

Mr. Charles Gatto
Schwartz, Wyle, and Stevens
168 - 13th Avenue
Norristown, Idaho 00005

Dear Mr. Gatto:

Enclosed are the documents necessary for opening the account for Law Office Leasing. We will be delighted to provide you with temporary checks when you formally open the account.

If I can be of further assistance, please call me.

Cordially,

Dennis Costa
Vice President

jdg

Enclosures (2)

SAMPLE LETTER 9.2. Letter notifying customer that an account must be opened in person (full-block format).

November 3, 19X1

Ms. Jeanne Berrigan
908 Mignon Place
Hamilton, California 00012

Dear Ms. Berrigan:

We would like to accommodate your request to open an account by mail. County Savings Bank requires, however, that its customers sign the signature cards in the presence of a bank employee and present proper identification prior to the account being opened.

We also cannot approve a credit line or issue a credit card to individuals outside of our market area. Should you move into our market area, we would be glad to consider providing you with these banking services.

Sample Letter 9.2 continued

If I can be of further assistance, please call me.

Sincerely,

Beall Dozier Gary
Assistant Vice President

BDG:jls

Account Transfers

Sample letters 9.3-9.5 deal with account transfers. Sample letter 9.3 was written to a customer apologizing for the delay in transferring the customer's account. Sample letter 9.4 was written to another bank requesting that a customer's account be transferred to the writer's bank. And sample letter 9.5 is a letter to a business owner indicating the one of his vendors accounts have been changed to a new bank.

SAMPLE LETTER 9.3. Letter apologizing for delay in transferring account (block format).

July 13, 19X1

Mr. and Mrs. James C. Diamond
14 Divinity Avenue
Punxatawney, New York 90906

Dear Mr. and Mrs. Diamond:

Subject: Transfer of Account #1-342

Account #1-342 has been transferred to you effective today. Please accept my apology on behalf of County Savings Bank for any inconvenience caused you because of the mix-up in transferring this account.

If you have any questions or if I may be of further assistance, please do not hesitate to call me.

Yours truly,

Lester L. Cooper
Assistant Vice President

llc/jls

SAMPLE LETTER 9.4. Letter to another bank requesting customer's accounts be transferred (full-block format).

May 4, 19X1

Simon Legyern
Head Teller
State Savings Bank
2456 Illinois Avenue
Alabama, Illinois 09845

TRANSFER OF ANNMARIE LONG'S ACCOUNT #A02456

Enclosed are savings passbook #A02456 and customer's draft #B0298 in the name of Annmarie Long. Please close the account and forward the principal balance plus any accrued interest to County Savings Bank. A postage paid envelope is enclosed for your convenience.

Thank you for your assistance in this matter.

LESTER L. COOPER
ASSISTANT VICE PRESIDENT

jls

Encls.: 1. Passbook #A02456
2. Draft #B0298

cc: Annmarie Long

SAMPLE LETTER 9.5. Notice to business of account transferral (full-block format).

August 8, 19X5

Mr. John L. Salem
Salem Parts Company
320 Jefferson Boulevard
St. Paul, Kansas 40404
Subject: Notice of Assignment

Dear Mr. Salem:

Nimons, Inc. has transferred and assigned to New National Bank in Boonton, Kansas, all of its right, title, and interest in all of its accounts including the right to receive payment on your account which is otherwise owed to Nimons, Inc. A true copy of the instrument of assignment is enclosed.

Sample Letter 9.5 continued

Please make all payments otherwise due or to become due Nimons, Inc. to the New National Bank. Remit all payments to us at: P.O. Box 3542, Boonton, Kansas 40405, Attention: Special Services. Please sign and return to me the enclosed copy of this notice.

Sincerely,

Max Nilges
Vice President

Receipt is acknowledged of the above notice of assignment this ____ day of ___________, 19X5.

Salem Parts Company

By: ______________________

Position:________________

Special Services

Sometimes a banker will believe it is wise to offer special services to a customer of long standing. Such a decision is made on the basis of determining the long-range benefits of keeping a particularly good customer with the bank. Sample letter 9.6 is an example of an offer of special services to a local hospital. This letter is well-organized and effectively sets forth the offer the bank is willing to make. The numbered list helps to clarify the point-by-point offer.

SAMPLE LETTER 9.6. Letter offering special services (full-block format).

November 26, 19X0

Mr. Louis Vare
Treasurer
General Hospital
100 Harlan Drive
Cambridge, Wisconsin 54321

Dear Mr. Vare:

County Savings Bank proposes to provide the following services to General Hospital's central account:

1. Processing of checks.

Sample Letter 9.6 continued

2. Stopping payment on checks without charge.
3. Aligning checks in serial order if checks are magnetically encoded with the serial numbers.
4. Automatically transferring from the hospital's account an amount sufficient to cover the payment of checks, keeping a collected balance to $40,000 and providing a repurchase agreement as described in paragraph six below.
5. Mailing credit and debit tickets to the hospital each day for investment transactions, along with a list of securities purchased or offered as collateral for investments.
6. Providing the hospital with a repurchase agreement for one day (three days on normal weekends and four days on holiday weekends) in the minimum amount of $100,000 with increments of $10,000 which will be for the sale and repurchase of securities fully guaranteed by the U.S. Government or other collateral mutually acceptable maturing within less than six months and with a par value of at least equal to the sale price plus interest at a rate equal to 1% less than the Federal Funds Rate. This repurchase agreement is subject to the County Savings Bank having sufficient acceptable securities in the portfolio.
7. Providing checks for the hospital at the bank's cost.
8. Providing a daily listing of the balances in the hospital's accounts reflecting the previous day's balances.

Please advise us if there are any questions regarding this proposal.

Sincerely,

Lester L. Cooper
Assistance Vice President

LLC:jls

Problems with Accounts

Sample letters 9.6-9.16 are examples of account administration letters focusing on account problems. Some of the problems resulted from a customer error, others from a bank error. In all of the letters, no matter who was responsible for the error, the writer has focussed on the problem at hand rather than trying to establish guilt. Such an approach indicates to a customer the letter writer's commitment to a smooth and effective working relationship.

Sample letter 9.7 expresses an apology and provides an explanation for a malfunctioning automatic teller machine.

Problems with checks arise frequently. Sample letters 9.8 and 9.9 give examples of two major types of check problems—stopped checks and forged signatures. Both letters give brief explanations of the circumstances surrounding the problem and ask for clarification from the customer if it is necessary.

SAMPLE LETTER 9.7. Letter apologizing for malfunctioning automated teller machine (semiblock format).

July 9, 19X1

Ms. Nancy Hartwood
One South Street
Mount Viscount, Oklahoma 44090

Dear Ms. Hartwood:

I apologize for the inconvenience caused by the malfunctions of our downtown 24-Hour Express Machine. While mechanical breakdowns can always develop on equipment of this sort, I must acknowledge that they became excessive. Rest assured that the problems plaguing the machine have been corrected.

Once again, I apologize for this unfortunate situation and thank you for some constructive criticism.

Sincerely,

Drew McDonoghue
Vice President

DM:lk

SAMPLE LETTER 9.8. Letter to a customer about a stopped check (block format).

August 23, 19X9

William Burg
P.O. Box 565
Ford's Landing, Tennessee 00070

Dear Mr. Burg:

On August 20, County Savings Bank cashed a check for you drawn on the County Department of Highways for $280.29. Payment has been stopped on this check and returned to us.

It will be necessary for you to come in and cover this check immediately. When payment is made, the check will be turned over to you to act on accordingly.

Your prompt attention to this matter will be greatly appreciated.

Sincerely,

Lester L. Cooper
Assistant Vice President

SAMPLE LETTER 9.9. Letter to customer about a forged signature (semiblock format).

April 7, 19X2

Mrs. Louise Guff
123 Point Breeze Drive
Union, Colorado 09050

Dear Mrs. Guff:

Enclosed is check #1554 for $100.00 payable to Samuel Johnson on your account #AS4356. We have voided the check and are returning it to you for your records.

On April 6, 19X2, the payee tried to cash your check at our downtown office. While verifying your signature, the teller noted that the signature on the check did not correspond to the signature on our signature card. After talking to you by phone and verifying that this was not your signature, we refused to negotiate the check payable to Samuel Johnson.

If there are any questions, please call me.

Yours truly,

Sample Letter 9.9 continued

Larz Manneng
Vice President

lm:js

encl.

Sample letters 9.10 and 9.11 refer to the same problem which resulted in the dishonoring of a check because of a bank error. Sample letter 9.10 is a letter to a customer explaining and apologizing for the bank's error and informing him that an explanation will be sent to the creditor to whom the check was written.

SAMPLE LETTER 9.10. Letter to customer explaining bank's error in dishonoring check (full-block format).

December 21, 19X2

Mr. Jacob Leigh
186 Loraine Terrace
Boston, Massachusetts 02134

Dear Mr. Leigh:

On November 23, we returned a check made out by you to the County Electric Department in the amount of $125. This check was returned to your creditor marked ''Not Sufficient Funds.''

The action was an error on our part, and we have asked the creditor to redeposit the check, provided they have not yet received the funds for which this check was drawn. We have also requested that our error be indicated on your creditor's records so that your credit rating will not be damaged.

Please accept our apologies for this inconvenience. If you have any further questions about this matter, please call me.

Sincerely,

Oliver Marshall
Branch Manager

OM:JS

Sample letter 9.11 is the letter to the creditor explaining the bank's error and asking that the customer's check be honored and redeposited.

SAMPLE LETTER 9.11. Letter to customer's creditor explaining bank's error in dishonoring check (full-block format).

December 21, 19X2

Mr. Alan W. Wayne
County Electric Department
987 Osway Road
Beltway, New York 01121

Dear Mr. Wayne:

On November 23, 19X2, we returned a check issued to the County Electric Department in the amount of $125 by Jacob Leigh marked ''Not Sufficient Funds.'' This action was an error on our part. We are requesting that you redeposit the check, provided you have not yet received the funds for which the check was drawn.

Please mark your records so that this error will not reflect on Mr. Leigh's credit standing with you.

Please accept our apologies for this inconvenience. If you have any further questions, please call me.

Sincerely,

Oliver Marshall
Branch Manager

OM:JS

Sample letter 9.12 is a shorter version of sample letter 9.11 to a creditor explaining the bank's error in dishonoring a customer's check.

SAMPLE LETTER 9.12. Letter to customer's creditor explaining bank's error in dishonoring check. Shorter version of sample letter 9.11 (block format).

August 7, 19X1

Adolph Fleischer
County Gas Department
Collection Department
456 Van Ness Boulevard
Rodan, Delaware 050703

Dear Mr. Fleischer:

The dishonoring of a check for $135.91 drawn by Ralph Embry was an error on County Savings Bank's part and should not be considered a reflection on Mr. Embry's business habits.

Please accept my apology for any inconvenience.

Yours truly,

Lester L. Cooper
Assistant Vice President

llc:chg

cc: Ralph Embry

Sample letter 9.13 is a response to a customer's inquiry about a deposit problem, which turned out to be a bank error. Assuring the customer that the error was a slip-up which will not likely occur again is a good move to reinstate his or her confidence in the bank.

SAMPLE LETTER 9.13. Letter to customer responding to deposit problem which turned out to be bank's error (block format).

July 8, 19X1

Mr. Mack Guffie
23 Irving Street, Apt. 5
Cazenove, Illinois 00066

Dear Mr. Guffie:

Thank you for your letter of July 2, 19X1 regarding the check for $120.31 which was withdrawn from your checking account. I have personally checked into this matter and found that the withdrawal from your account occurred because of an error on the part of one of our employees. We regret any inconveniences this error has caused you.

Sample Letter 9.13 continued

I want to assure you that we do appreciate your business and will do everything we can to see that a similar incident does not occur in the future. If you feel further discussion of this matter is necessary, please call me.

Yours very truly,

Oliver Marshall
Branch Manager

om/hg

Sample letter 9.14 responds to a problem similar to the one in sample letter 9.15, except that it is a follow-up to a phone call inquiry rather than a letter.

SAMPLE LETTER 9.14. Letter to customer responding to deposit problem which turned out to be bank's error. Response to phone call (full-block format).

August 19, 19X0

Mr. Frank George
9067 Glassway Place
Sheboygin, Illinois 09555

Dear Mr. George:

A deposit receipt for interest on $3,000 at 5 1/4% for sixteen days is enclosed. This receipt should correct the error in your account we discussed on the telephone last Tuesday.

I apologize for the error concerning your deposit and any inconvenience it caused you. Proper measures have been taken to alleviate such a problem from occurring in the future.

We value your relationship to us and appreciate your loyalty to the County Savings Bank. If I can be of further assistance to you, please do not hesitate to call on me.

Very truly yours,

Larz Manneng
Vice President

lm/jjl

Sometimes a customer will make a deposit to a checking account, forgetting that the account had been closed out. The reaction a bank has to such a deposit will vary from bank to bank, but a letter explaining the circumstances is always in order. Sample letter 9.15 is a letter written on such an occasion. This bank's practice was to open a new account (thus acquiring some new business) and to explain the circumstances to the customer.

SAMPLE LETTER 9.15. Letter to customer who made deposit to closed checking account (semiblock format).

November 15, 19X0

Mr. Jeffrey Runyon
327 Francis Place
Rutherford, Ohio 77709

Dear Mr. Runyon:

We received your deposit yesterday which we assume you intended to have credited to your former checking account. Since the account you once held with our bank was closed more than two years ago, we have opened a new account for you. As a new account requires a new account number, please destroy all unused checks and deposit tickets now in your possession.

Enclosed is an initial supply of checks and deposit tickets bearing your new account number. Please use these only until your new checkbook arrives in approximately one week.

Two new signature cards are also enclosed. Each card requires both signatures. Please return the cards to us as promptly as possible in the enclosed postage paid envelope.

We take this opportunity to thank you for banking with New National.

Sincerely,

Colman Edwards
Vice President

ce:ut

Enclosures (3)

If a customer calls attention to the bank's error in his or her favor, it is good practice to thank the customer, as is done in sample letter 9.16. Thanking the customer encourages honesty and saves the bank money. It also lets the customer know how much his or her patronage is appreciated.

SAMPLE LETTER 9.16. Letter thanking customer for calling attention to bank error in his favor (block format).

April 26, 19X2

Mr. Darell Marshall
150 Turning Point Way
St. Loyisa, Michigan 77777

Dear Mr. Marshall:

Christine Ellery, our teller manager, and I would like to thank you for returning the $20 you were given in error by one of our tellers. We both appreciate that a customer would demonstrate this kind of loyalty to County Savings Bank.

It is a pleasure serving you.

Sincerely,

Alan D. Armaunde
President

lss

Service Charges

Because of many factors, service charges for checking accounts will have to change from time to time. Sample letters 9.17-9.22 are examples of letters written to explain changes in service charges to customers. Sample letters 9.17 and 9.18 are straightforward letters explaining such changes. The latter of the two letters offers an alternative checking plan to the customer which might defray any service charge.

SAMPLE LETTER 9.17. Letter to customer explaining change in service charges (simplified format).

November 15, 19X8

Mr. Arthur Cunningham
345 Wordley Road
Mayfield, Ohio 05043

CHANGE IN SERVICE CHARGES

For some time the New National Bank has been able to provide its customers with no-service-charge checking accounts. Because of increasing operating costs and the advent of automatic transfer service between savings and checking accounts, however, we have reluctantly decided to reinstitute service charges for checking accounts.

The minimal charges, which constitute our processing costs, will become effective December 1, 19X8. If you maintain a minimum balance of $300 or an average balance of $750, you will not be assessed a service charge. For those accounts that go below those amounts, a nominal charge of 10 cents per check and a monthly maintenance charge of 50 cents will be assessed.

We will continue to offer free checking accounts to our customers older than sixty-five, and to students. If you qualify under either of these categories, please make that fact known to any of our personnel.

If you have any questions concerning these changes, please call any of our officers or employees. We want to take this occasion to express our thanks for the continued opportunity of serving you.

COLMAN EDWARDS
VICE PRESIDENT

jls

SAMPLE LETTER 9.18. Letter to customer explaining change in service charges (semiblock format).

April 2, 19X9

Ms. Alison Sullivan
56 Boonton Trail, Suite 987
Santa Fe, Colorado 06532

Dear Ms. Sullivan:

We have recently completed a study of our checking accounts and have determined that, in order to maintain our quality standard of service, we must make an adjustment in our service charge policy.

Effective May 1, 19X9, a minimum balance of $500 in the savings portion of your National Account must be maintained if you wish to continue free checking services. Should your savings balance drop below $500 in a given monthly statement period, a service charge of $3 will be assessed.

In light of this increase you may be interested to know more about our National Account II Interest/Checking Plan. New National Bank is now able to offer you a zero-balance checking account linked with a 5% interest, until you need it.

In the National Account II Interest/Checking Plan, we will automatically transfer the amount needed to cover your checks when they are presented to us for payment. Only the exact amount will be transferred. Your entire balance remains in savings earning 5% interest compounded daily and paid quarterly. The National Account II Interest/Checking Plan with its zero balance checking privilege is free when you maintain a balance of at least $2000 in your 5% savings account.

If you are interested in this new service from New National Bank, stop by any of our branches or call me.

Cordially,

Colman Edwards
Vice President

jls

Sample letters 9.19 and 9.20 are from the same bank to holders of different types of checking accounts. Sample letter 9.19 explains how the customer can continue to pay a minimal service fee. Sample letter 9.20 explains the new service fee and asks the customer to consider another one of the bank's checking accounts which could lower service charges. In these two letters, it is obvious from the tone of the letter and the features offered that the bank would like its customers to shift into the Centurion Checking Account so they will maintain higher balances and receive low-cost checking.

SAMPLE LETTER 9.19. Letter to customer explaining change in service charges (simplified format).

January 9, 19X9

Mr. Jeffrey Young
45 Militant Place
Charlestown, Pennsylvania 89334

CHANGE IN CENTURION CHECKING ACCOUNT PRICING

Your satisfaction with our bank has always been important to us. In order to maintain the quality service to which you have become accustomed, we find it necessary to adopt a new method of pricing our Centurion Checking Accounts. Beginning February 19X9, the following schedule will be in effect:

Minimum Monthly Checking Balance	Monthly Fee
$ 0–$ 99	$4
$100–$199	$3
$200–$299	$1
$300 +	No Charge

This schedule may result in no additional charges to the majority of our customers because each $1,000 you maintain in your savings account will give you a $1 discount from your monthly checking account service charge.

Keep $4,000 in your savings account and you will receive no-charge checking, regardless of your checking balance. You can see that this plan will allow you the opportunity of actually reducing your monthly service charge fees, while still allowing us the opportunity of recovering our costs.

If your checking and savings accounts with us do not have the same account number, it is important that you let us know so that we can change them because the numbers must be the same in order for you to get your discount.

Sample Letter 9.19 continued

This is the first price adjustment New National Bank has put into effect on our Centurion Accounts in more than twenty years. During those years we faced many cost increases in processing personal checks. We have absorbed these and have not passed them on to you, our valued customer. Checking costs have risen to a point where we can no longer absorb all of these increased costs, however, and we are forced to adjust service charges accordingly.

If you have any questions regarding this change, or if we can be of any assistance to you, please call our Customer Service Representative, Mrs. Christine Jade. She will be happy to answer all of your questions.

COLMAN EDWARDS
VICE PRESIDENT

jls

SAMPLE LETTER 9.20. Letter to customer explaining change in service charges (block format).

January 9, 19X9

Ms. Alice Longworth
908 Smithsonian Drive
Charlestown, Pennsylvania 89334

Dear Ms. Longworth:

Your satisfaction with our bank has always been very important to us. In order to maintain the quality service to which you have become accustomed, we find it necessary to adjust the pricing schedule of our Check-O-Matic Accounts.

This is the first price adjustment New National Bank has put into effect on Check-O-Matic Accounts in more than twenty years. During those years we faced many cost increases in processing personal checks. We have absorbed them and have not passed them on to you, our valued customer. Checking costs have risen to a point where we can no longer absorb all of these increased costs, however, and we are forced to adjust service charges accordingly.

Beginning February 19X9, the following schedule will be in effect:

Sample Letter 9.20 continued

Check-O-Matic Accounts

Monthly Maintenance Service Charge	Per Check Charge
$1	$.15

As an alternative to the Check-O-Matic Account which you now have, we invite you to consider our Centurion Checking Account which entitles you to no-charge checking if you maintain a $300 minimum balance in your Centurion Checking Account or $4,000 in a regular savings account. In a Centurion Account you may write as many checks as you like without incurring any additional costs. The price schedule of our Centurion Account is:

Centurion Accounts

Minimum Monthly Checking Balance	Monthly Fee
$ 0–$ 99	$4
$100–$199	$3
$200–$299	$1
$300 +	No Charge

In addition, for each $1,000 you maintain in your savings account you will receive a $1 discount from the monthly fee.

If you have any questions regarding this change, or if we can be of any assistance to you, please call our Customer Service Representative, Mrs. Christine Jade. She will be happy to answer all of your questions.

Sincerely,

Colman Edwards
Vice President

jls

Sample letter 9.21 was written to a business to explain its credit card processings fees would be raised.

SAMPLE LETTER 9.21. Letter to customer explaining merchant card fees will be raised (full-block format).

March 1, 19X3

John Wallace
Salem Dispatch, Inc.
23 Box Road
Lincoln Park, New Jersey 32323

Dear Mr. Wallace:

New National has been informed by Visa and MasterCard that they will be increasing their interchange fees to merchant banks, effective April 1, 19X3. Based on your current Visa/MasterCard transaction volume, this will increase your discount rate by .25 percent. For example, if you rate is currently 5 percent, it will increase to 5.25 percent. This rate will be effective April 1, 19X3, and you will see the adjustment on your April month-end statement.

During the past 10 years, both Visa and MasterCard have encouraged merchants to move toward more sophisticated processing methods, including electronic authorization and faster deposit of transactions. Both Visa and MasterCard have enabled us to offer reduced discount rates to our merchants as incentives to invest in electronic processing technology. Visa and MasterCard are now planning to move away from these incentive rates and closer to actual cost-based fees.

As your Visa/MasterCard processing member, New National is committed to keeping you informed of industry changes. We will notify you of continuing developments in the future.

Sincerely,

Arlin T. Roland
Senior Vice President

ltg

When a bank believes that a customer, for one reason or another, should not be levied a service charge for a checking account, a letter stating so is, of course, in order. Sample letter 9.22 is an example of one type of these letters that can be written.

SAMPLE LETTER 9.22. Letter to customer explaining service charges will be discontinued (full-block format).

December 22, 19X1

Ms. Janet Ritter
24 Earlam Place
Mesquidez, Idaho 98943

Dear Ms. Ritter:

After reviewing your account history with New National Bank for the past year, I agree that you should not be assessed a monthly service charge. Therefore, as we discussed in our phone conversation today, I have instructed our branch manager in Mesquidez to reverse your service charges for October ($299.52) and November ($54.50).

I have also instructed the branch manager to place your account on a permanent waive status. The permanent waive status will be reviewed every six months to see if it is justified. If we should ever determine that it is not justified, we will notify you in writing prior to changing the service charge status of your account.

If you have any questions regarding this matter, please call me.

Yours truly,

John E. Gannon
Vice President

JEG/man

Insufficient Funds

Sample letters 9.23 and 9.24 are two examples of letters dealing with insufficient funds in an account. Sample letter 9.23 is a letter explaining that a check was drawn for which there were insufficient funds in the customer's account.

SAMPLE LETTER 9.23. Letter to customer explaining there are insufficient funds to cover check written (block format).

April 26, 19X2

Mr. Lester P. Prentiss
56 Discount Parkway
Cleveland, Arizona 03245

Dear Mr. Prentiss:

On April 3, 19X2, you presented check number 26543 for $125 drawn on State Savings Bank to our downtown County Savings Bank branch. On April 12, that check was returned to us by the State Savings Bank because of insufficient funds.

Under state law, you, as endorser of the item, are liable to County Savings Bank for the amount of the above item.

As a service to you, County Savings Bank has represented the above check for payment. If it is dishonored a second time, you will be notified of such dishonor.

Sincerely,

Oliver Marshall
Branch Manager

om/jj

Sample letter 9.23, above, is a good basic letter to use for any customer who has written a check with insufficient funds in an account. Some variations of the last paragraph in sample letter 9.23 that could easily be filled in depending on the circumstances and the action the bank wishes to take are:

1. A hold for the amount of the item has been placed against your account number 90909, and the above amount will be withdrawn in five days unless you have made reimbursement.
2. Please contact this office to arrange for reimbursement of the $125 received by you.
3. The amount of the dishonored item has been withdrawn from your account number 90909. The dishonored item is also included with this letter.

Sample letter 9.24 explains to a firm that the bank can no longer cover depository transfers for which there are insufficient funds in an account.

SAMPLE LETTER 9.24. Letter to firm explaining depository transfers can no longer be covered because of insufficient funds (semiblock format).

July 13, 19X2

Mr. Ralph Embry
Thomson Enterprises
111 Prospect Street
Hamilton, California 00012

Subject: Checking Account #Z22-3

Dear Mr. Embry:

Your firm's checking account #Z22-3 with us has not contained sufficient funds to cover your depository transfers in quite some time. We are no longer in a position to accommodate this situation. Therefore, beginning Wednesday, July 21, 19X2, any drafts made on this account for which there are insufficient collected funds will be returned as ''Not Sufficient Funds'' items.

We hope you understand our unwillingness to finance the float in this account. We appreciate your past patronage and look forward to a continuing, mutually beneficial relationship.
If you have any questions, please call me.

Yours very truly,

Colman Edwards
Vice President

ce:js

cc: Mr. Henry Davids

Overdrafts

Sample letters 9.25-9.27 deal with account overdrafts. Sample letter 9.25 addresses a customer who has overdrawn his account.

SAMPLE LETTER 9.25. Letter to a customer about an overdrawn account (full-block format).

July 17, 19X1

Mr. Edward Cerpo
P.O. Box 704
Allegheny, Alaska 03251

Dear Mr. Cerpo:

On July 15, 19X1, your savings account number X2702 was overdrawn for $75 through our automated teller machine at our downtown office.

Under state law, you, as withdrawer on the account, are liable to the County Savings Bank for $75.

Please reimburse us for the above amount within the next ten days. If reimbursement is not made, further action may be taken.

Sincerely,

Oliver Marshall
Branch Manager
om/js

A possible variation of sample letter 9.25, above, is to change the last paragraph to one which explains the action that has been taken, such as:

> County Savings Bank intends to withdraw this amount from your savings account on July 27 unless reimbursement is made.

Sample letter 9.26 is a follow-up to the customer written to in sample letter 9.25. Because no action was taken on his part, the bank has decided to close his account.

SAMPLE LETTER 9.26. Follow-up letter to customer with overdrawn account (block format).

July 28, 19X1

Mr. Edward Cerpo
P.O. Box 704
Allegheny, Alaska 03251

Dear Mr. Cerpo:

Your savings account number X2702 has been closed. This action results from an overdraw at the automated teller machine at our downtown office on July 15, 19X1. Notice of this condition was sent to you on July 17, 19X1. Since reimbursement was not made, the account was closed. We regret having to take this action.

If you have any questions, please call me.

Sincerely,

Oliver Marshall
Branch Manager

om/js

When overdraft charges are made, a customer will often question the reason for these charges. Sample letter 9.27 is an example of a letter written to explain overdraft charges.

SAMPLE LETTER 9.27. Letter to customer explaining overdraft charges (block format).

March 9, 19X2

Patrice A. Player
78 Dragoon Drive
Stanford, Arkansas 97534

Dear Ms. Player:

This letter is in reference to our recent telephone conversation concerning the overdraft charges we made to your Novelty Store Account.

Upon reviewing our records, I noted that your Novelty Store Account was overdrawn 12 times during the past 12-month period. In addition, your now-closed personal check-

Sample Letter 9.27 continued

ing account was overdrawn 4 times in the same time period. A total of 23 checks caused these overdrafts.

During this time, we charged you only $12. Our normal charge is $6 per check. The total charge, therefore, would normally have been $138.

Considering this, I feel that New National Bank has been more than fair with you in our issuing of past charges.

New National appreciates the balances you maintain in your two In Trust For Savings Accounts, but I recommend that you also always maintain a positive balance in your Novelty Store Account in order to avoid additional overdraft charges.

If I can be of further assistance, please do not hesitate to call.

Sincerely,

Colman Edwards
Vice President

CE:JS

cc: Mr. Frank Dawson, Branch Manager

Closing Unsatisfactory Accounts

Sample letters 9.28-9.32 deal with unsatisfactory accounts. Sample letter 9.28 was written to a customer whose account is to be closed because of an excessive number of returns.

SAMPLE LETTER 9.28. Letter to customer explaining his account is to be closed because of excessive number of returns (semiblock format).

November 15, 19X2

Mr. Edward Warner
17 Brunner Pass
Morris Gulch, New Mexico 01574

Dear Mr. Warner:

Your checking account has had 15 returns and has not been handled in a mutually satisfactory manner. Therefore, we are requesting that you close it within 7 days from the date of this letter.

After that date, we will no longer pay checks presented on the account, and they will be returned marked ''Account Closed.'' Any collected funds remaining in the account will be returned to you at that time after deducting any fees owed to us.

Sincerely,

Lester L. Cooper
Assistant Vice President

LLC:JLS

Sample letter 9.29 was written to a customer who had excessive overdrafts. A shorter version of this type of letter is shown in sample letter 9.29.

SAMPLE LETTER 9.29. Letter to a customer whose checking account has been closed because of excessive overdrafts (block format).

March 4, 19X2

Ms. Adrienne Berrigan
987 West 40 Street
Montgomery, Pennsylvania 82009

Dear Ms. Berrigan:

The County Savings Bank intends to close your checking account number 265432140-9 in seven days. This action is being taken due to an excessive number of overdrafts on the account.

On the date of closing, the available balance remaining in the account will be mailed to you at the above address. County Savings Bank regrets having to take this action.

If you would like to discuss this matter prior to the closing of the account, please call me.

Sincerely,

Lester L. Cooper
Assistant Vice President

llc/jls

SAMPLE LETTER 9.30. Letter to a customer whose checking account has been closed because of excessive overdrafts. Shorter version of letter 9.29 (semiblock format).

March 4, 19X1

Mr. and Mrs. Jonathan Drogan
P.O. Box 77
Camden, Oregon 44455

Dear Mr. and Mrs. Drogan:

Your County Savings checking account number 9676567-5 has been closed because of excessive overdrafts. Enclosed you will find a check for the available balance in the account.

Sincerely,
Lester L. Cooper

Sample Letter 9.30 continued

Assistant Vice President

llc/jls

encl.

Sample letter 9.31 was written to a customer who had accumulated excessive overdraft charges. After he made a deposit in his checking account, he was notified that the amount he owed the bank was withdrawn, a check for the balance was enclosed, and his account was being closed.

SAMPLE LETTER 9.31. Letter to customer after his deposit notifying him that overdraft charges were collected, the balance sent him, and his account closed (block format).

July 16, 19X9

Mr. Frank Gloria
P.O. Box 7089
Sleighton, Massachusetts 87675

Dear Mr. Gloria:

Subject: Checking Account #70-8

Enclosed is our cashier's check #17892 for $18.45 which represents the remaining balance in your checking account #70-8. Overdraft charges of $117.78 have been deducted from your $136.23 deposit of July 6, 19X9, and the account has been closed because of continued overdraft problems.

If you have any questions regarding this transaction please do not hesitate to call me.

Yours truly,

Lester L. Cooper
Assistant Vice President

llc/jls
encl.

Sample letter 9.32 might be a rare occurrence at most banks. The holder of the checking accounts had been keeping the bulk of his money at competing banks, while taking advantage of free checking services at the bank writing this letter. The bank felt it was not benefitting from this arrangement and decided to ask the customer to move his accounts.

SAMPLE LETTER 9.32. Letter to firm requesting it to move accounts (simplified format).

August 5, 19X2

Mr. Lawrence Z. Weimer
Beeting Cars
333 Matin Road
Ricting, New Jersey 95566

COUNTY SAVINGS BANK CHECKING ACCOUNTS
NUMBERS: 7-020-600; 7-223-698; 7-323-908

Mr. Weimer, it has come to our attention that your company is maintaining most of its accounts with New National Bank. We feel it wise to have your above-listed County Savings Bank accounts closed at this time.

We request that you stop writing checks on these accounts immediately. We will forward the proceeds of the accounts to you on August 16, 19X2. Any checks presented for payment on or after that date will be returned marked ''Account Closed.''

Thank you for your cooperation in this matter.

Lester L. Cooper
Assistant Vice President

llc:jls

Money Market Certificates & Certificates of Deposit

When a customer holds some type of savings certificates, it is necessary from time to time to write letters keeping up-to-date on the customer's plans for the certificate when it reaches maturity. Sample letter 9.33 is a personalized form letter which is used by a bank to learn the customer's wishes for reinvestment. Because of the many options offered the customer, sample letter 9.33 might also be considered an effective sales letter.

SAMPLE LETTER 9.33. Letter to customer requesting instructions for reinvestment of money market certificate (simplified format).

September 9, 19X2

Mr. Michael Kerry
87 Leonid Drive, Suite 9C
Winhelm, Texas 05556

INSTRUCTIONS FOR MONEY MARKET CERTIFICATE

Your Money Market Certificate #909778-6 for $7500 will mature on October 10, 19X2. This certificate will be renewed for 182 days at the rate prevailing on the maturity date. There is nothing you have to do to renew.

You must take action no later than 7 days after the maturity date listed above if you wish to change or redeem your certificate.

Use this letter to explain to us what you want done. Your instructions will be followed upon receipt of this form and applicable documents, but not before the maturity date. Unless you choose option A1, you must return your certificate with this signed form when requesting changes or redemption.

A. Change existing certificate:
A1. ( ) Renew my certificate for the original deposit amount, and mail me a check for the interest earned
A2. ( ) Renew my certificate for the amount shown plus the enclosed check
B. After redeeming my certificate:
B1. ( ) Purchase a tax free interest certificate ($500 minimum)
B2. ( ) Purchase an investment certificate for a term of ___weeks ($5000 minimum). (Choose one: 5,6,7,8,9,10,11, or 12 weeks.)
B3. ( ) Purchase a 30 month certificate ($1000 minimum). Send my interest: ___Monthly ___Quarterly ___Semi-annually ___Annually.
B4. ( ) Transfer my funds to my: ( ) Passbook ( ) Saver ( ) Checking ( ) Now Account number .
B5. ( ) Mail me a check for the full amount.
C. ( ) I've chosen an option not listed above. On the reverse side are my instructions and a number to call me during banking hours.

Signature ______________________________

Sample Letter 9.33 continued

If this notice is received by New National Bank more than 7 days after the maturity date, your certificate will be renewed as of the maturity date at the then prevailing rate. Call 2X1-85X0 for current rates.

COLMAN EDWARDS
VICE PRESIDENT

CE:JS

Sample letter 9.34 is a letter written to confirm a customer's intentions to use a savings certificate to pay off a loan he had at the same bank.

SAMPLE LETTER 9.34. Letter confirming customer's intentions to use savings certificates to pay off loan (full-block format).

October 23, 19X8

Mr. Paul Grimes
89 Gleason Drive, Apt. 87B
New Cameron, Arkansas 04445

Dear Mr. Grimes:

As you instructed, we have cashed in your four-year savings certificate #909. Since the certificate is being paid before its scheduled maturity, the interest rate on it reverts back to the passbook rate and all interest accrued under it is forfeited for the past three months.

The present balance of the certificate is $1,452.68. This amount, along with your check for $30, has been applied to your loan. There remains a balance of $47.32 on the loan.

Call me if you have any questions. Best regards to you and Carol.

Sincerely,

Larz Manneng
Vice President

LM:JS

Sample letter 9.35 notifies a customer that his Certificate of Deposit has matured.

SAMPLE LETTER 9.35. Certificate of Deposit maturity notification (full-block format).

June 20, 19X6

Mr. William Hard
89 Unix Square
Yuma, Arkansas 90342

Dear Mr. Hard:

Your Certificate of Deposit will be maturing on July 23, 19X6 and will be renewed at maturity, at the rate in effect at that time, unless we are instructed otherwise.

For your information, I am enclosing a copy of our latest deposit rate sheet. As you can see, the bank continues to offer competitive interest rates on savings accounts with the added security of FSLIC insurance.

We value your business and look forward to serving your banking needs. Please call me at 1-800-555-4343 for current rates or if you have any banking questions.

Sincerely,

Philip D. Eizetres
Senior Vice President

pde/mne

Enclosure

Credit Cards

Sample letter 9.36 notifies a customer that his credit card limits have been raised.

SAMPLE LETTER 9.36. Raising of credit card limits (full-block format).

December 1, 19X3

Mr. Harold L. Krauss
23 Loom Drive
Dorchester, Vermont 40455

Dear Mr. Krauss:

Because of your fine credit history, we have increased your New National MasterCard credit limit to $5,000. You can use the extra $1,000 this holiday season to make gift purchases, catalog orders, or pay for travel.

If you must pay for purchases in cash, remember New National charges no transaction fee for cash advances on your New National credit card. And, at any time, you can check your credit card balance or pay your credit card bill at any New National automated teller machine.

Now may be a good time to use your New National credit line to save money by transferring balances from other credit cards that charge higher rates to your New National credit card. It's easy to do. Simply call today for a credit card transfer certificate.

If you have any questions about your credit line increase or would like a credit card transfer certificate, please call our 24-hour credit card hotline at 800-NEWCARD.

Sincerely,

Max Nilges
Vice President

jls

IRS-related Matters

When the Internal Revenue Service requests a customer's bank records or puts a tax levy on an account, the customer must, of course, be notified. Sample letter 9.37 is an example of a letter written to a customer notifying him that the IRS has requested his records.

SAMPLE LETTER 9.37. Letter notifying customer that IRS has requested his records (full-block format).

June 14, 19X1

Joseph Ayer
89 Main Street
Virginia City, Kansas 44455

Dear Mr. Ayer:

Subject: Internal Revenue Service Summons for Bank Records

New National Bank has received a summons from the Internal Revenue Service for bank records relevant to a tax investigation of the following accounts in your name:

Savings Account #288896-7
Checking Account #5209753
Now Account #4577276

Unless there is a valid basis for challenging the summons, New National is compelled, by law, to produce the records for the accounts listed above on June 21, 19X1.

Should you have any questions regarding this summons, please get in touch with your attorney or the IRS Agent conducting your tax investigation.

Sincerely,

Colman Edwards
Vice President

ce/jjk

Sample letter 9.38 notifies a customer of a tax levy served by the IRS and the steps to be taken.

SAMPLE LETTER 9.38. Letter notifying customer of tax levy served by IRS (full-block format).

October 20, 19X8

Dr. James L. Peterson
89 Cayuga Place
Wisconsin City, Missouri 05566

Dear Dr. Peterson:

New National Bank has been served a tax levy by the Internal Revenue Service for $300. As a result, we have debited your savings account number 789006-67, and forwarded a cashier's check to the IRS for $300.

A $6.00 service charge has been imposed on your account for our handling costs.

Sincerely,

Colman Edwards
Vice President

jls

Liens

When a lien is served, the customer should be notified, as in sample letter 9.39, of the actions to be taken and any costs that will be incurred.

SAMPLE LETTER 9.39. Letter notifying customer that lien has been served (semi-block format).

June 6, 19X1

Ms. Arlene C. Newhart
3233 - 38th Street N.W.
River City, Vermont 43657

Dear Ms. Newhart:

We have been served a lien by the County Court for $250. As a result, we have attached the balance of your account up to $250.

If we do not receive from the County Court by June 13, 19X1, the law requires us to charge your account #333456-889 $250, and remit the funds to the County Court.

A $6 service charge has been imposed on your account for handling costs.

Very truly yours,

Colman Edwards
Vice President

jjk

Account Administration Memos

Memorandum 9.40 is an example of an effective account administration memo. The message is clear that the bank does not approve of its employees overdrawing their accounts. The action to be taken is spelled out.

MEMORANDUM 9.40. Memorandum to employee about overdrawn account.

TO: George C. Post
FROM: Lester L. Cooper, Assistant Vice President
DATE: November 15, 19X2
SUBJECT: Overdrawn Checking Account

Your account today reflected an overdraft of $25. Please make a deposit within three business days to bring your account back to a positive balance.

In the meantime, any additional checks presented for payment will be subject to be returned for nonsufficient funds in your account. Your account will be subject to the normal service charges that apply to nonemployee accounts.

While this is not a new policy, it will be followed more closely in the future. Your supervisor will be glad to discuss this with you if you have any questions or comments.

jls

cc: Personnel File of George C. Post

Customer Service 10

Customer service letters are some of the most important letters you will write. Every banker wants to let customers know just how important they are to the bank.

A good letter can help keep a customer's business. All of the letters in this chapter are designed to win over or strengthen the loyalty of customers.

Thanks for Business

Sample letters 10.1-10.10 are examples of "thanks for business" letters. Sample letters 10.1-10.4 thank customers for new accounts. The four examples give you a good variety of how to express your appreciation for new business. Sample letters 10.2 and 10.4 are to corporate customers, while sample letters 10.1 and 10.3 are to individual customers.

SAMPLE LETTER 10.1. New account thank you letter (full-block format).

June 23, 19X6

Ms. Claire Dunphy
One Pucaro Street
Norristown, Pennsylvania 43234

Dear Ms. Dunphy:

Thank you for opening your account at New National Bank. The bank will mail periodic account statements which will provide you with current account balance information and transaction activity. Savings accounts are insured up to $100,000 by the FDIC, an agency of the federal government.

We value your business and will do our best to give you accurate and responsive service. We are also committed to paying a competitive rate on all deposit accounts.

Please call me at 434-3434 or use our toll-free number, 1-800-989-0909, if you need additional assistance or information.

Sincerely,

Mark Stoeckle
Senior Vice President

ms/ar

SAMPLE LETTER 10.2. Thank you for new checking account letter (block format).

August 19, 19X1

Messrs. Ross Mournelly and Frank Hamel
Mournelly & Hamel CPAs
45 Woodley Place, Suite 87B
Lindsfield, Kentucky 08720

Subject: Mournelly & Hamel CPAs #5646-838-6

Dear Ross and Frank:
Thank you for the new checking account you have opened with New National Bank. Your new account number is 5646-838-6.

Enclosed you'll find a supply of temporary checks, along with a partnership authority and signature cards to be completed and returned to me at your earliest conve-

Sample Letter 10.2 continued

nience. An envelope addressed to my attention is enclosed for this purpose.

New National will be happy to service your needs on this checking account at any time. We will also be happy to provide any other assistance we can. Don't hesitate to call me if you should have any questions.

As ever,

NEW NATIONAL BANK

Otto J. Dukes

Vice President

ojd:jdg

enclosures

SAMPLE LETTER 10.3. Thank you for new account (full-block format).

November 16, 19X2

Mrs. Carol Grimes
67 Rand Place
St. Joseph, Illinois 27031

Dear Mrs. Grimes:

Thank you for selecting our bank as the home for your new account. We will provide the kind of thoughtful service that will maintain your confidence in our institution.

One's bank account is a very personal thing. I am enclosing my card in case you wish to speak to someone confidentially about your new account or any of our other banking services.

Please call me when I can be of help to you.

Sincerely,

Frederick A. Stair
Vice President

fas/jsh

Encl.

SAMPLE LETTER 10.4. Thank you for new account (full-block format).

May 12, 19X2

Mr. Bill Weddleton
Administrative Manager
John Wagner & Associates
One Park Place
Sibling, Ohio 02222

Dear Bill:

Thank you for opening the agency account with New National Bank. John Wagner & Associates and New National have a good deal in common. The new account relationship will help seal our friendship which has developed over the last couple of years.

Feel free to call on me any time you need information or assistance.

With kindest regards,

Roger Nelson
Vice President

jdg

Sample letters 10.5 and 10.6 were written as follow-up letters to new savings and credit customers. Each letter requests some "feedback" from the customer. The bank uses these as quality control letters to make sure its services are giving the customers what they want.

SAMPLE LETTER 10.5. Follow-up. Quality control—borrower (full-block format).

June 2, 19X6

Ms. Jennifer Brown
56 Fidelity Way
Holliston, Vermont 43434

Dear Ms. Brown:

I hope that the processing and closing of your mortgage loan was handled to your satisfaction.

To insure that the bank maintains a high level of service I would appreciate you providing me with some feedback on your experience with New National Bank. Sixty seconds or less is all it takes to complete the enclosed form. Your comments are confidential and will be helpful to me.

Enclosed for your information is a brochure which explains our banking philosophy. I am confident that you will agree with our emphasis on providing our customers with personalized, responsive service and competitive rates paid on savings accounts.

I am also enclosing our latest deposit rate sheet along with a new account application and bank-by-mail envelopes. As you can see from the rate sheet, the bank continues to offer competitive rates, with the added security of FDIC insurance.

I look forward to receiving your feedback on the quality of our service. Please call me if you need additional assistance.

Sincerely,

Loren Gary
President

enc.

SAMPLE LETTER 10.6. Follow-up. Quality control—depositor (full-block format).

July 2, 19X6

Mr. Dan Wallace
2400-17th Street N.W.
Washington, D.C. 20009

Dear Mr. Wallace:

Thank you for opening a savings account with New National Bank.

We are striving to provide you and every customer with excellent service. It would help us to know how successful you think we are. I would appreciate it if you would take the time to complete the enclosed form and return it to me. Your comments will be confidential.

I am also enclosing our brochure, ''A New Breed of Bank,'' and our current deposit rate sheet. Thank you for your time. We appreciate your business.

Sincerely,

Desmond St. Clair
President

ds/mn

Enclosures

Sample letters 10.7 and 10.8 are letters written to express appreciation of a continued business association with a customer. The letter writer in sample letter 10.8 enclosed a yearly tax guide along with his letter. Giving fairly inexpensive, but useful gifts, such as tax guides or mortgage amortization charts, is an effective way to build good customer relations.

SAMPLE LETTER 10.7. Letter expressing appreciation for business (semiblock format).

August 25, 19X0

Mr. Roger Nelson
Vice President
DMI, Inc.
3542 Bethany Road
Crawford, New Jersey 01234

Dear Roger:

I wanted to let you and Dave know how much we at New National Bank appreciate your business and the opportunity to be able to serve you. I hope that this is the beginning of a long and beneficial relationship for both you and New National.

If there is anything I can do for you and DMI, please do not hesitate to give me a call. When you're in the area, make sure to drop in and say hello.

Best regards,

Mike Pondus
Vice President

MP/JG

SAMPLE LETTER 10.8. Letter expressing appreciation for business and enclosing gift (block format).

December 20, 19X2

Ms. Lisa Coleman, Esq.
Aland, Thomas, and Powers
987 Government Avenue
Darlac, Rhode Island 55487

Dear Ms. Coleman:

We at New National Bank hope you will find the enclosed 19X2 Tax Guide a useful and handy reference in your practice. Please accept it with our compliments and best wishes.

New National has appreciated your business throughout the past year. I hope we can continue to develop our good working relationship.

Sample Letter 10.8 continued

Call upon me in the future if I can be of service to you or your clients. I hope the holiday season finds you healthy.

Sincerely,

Melanie O'Rourke
Vice President

jsh

Enclosure

Sample letters 10.9 and 10.10 were written to customers who had closed their accounts at the bank. The former is to a customer who has reopened his account; the latter to one whose account has remained closed. Both letters are aimed toward letting the customer know the bank wants his business, and, if they are doing anything wrong, they would like the customer's suggestions for improvements. Asking for customer input is a good way to make the customer feel that the account is important to the bank.

SAMPLE LETTER 10.9. Letter to customer who recently reopened account (block format).

November 17, 19X2

Mr. Samuel H. White
822 Second Street
Alquippa, Kansas 81601

Dear Mr. White:

I am happy to see that you recently reopened your account at County Savings Bank. I appreciate the renewed confidence that you have shown in County Savings. I assure you we will do our best to merit it.

We at County Savings Bank sincerely desire to be of real service to you. Feel free to call on us any time you need assistance.

Cordially yours,

Dean Wheaton
Assistant Vice President

dw/kj

SAMPLE LETTER 10.10. Letter to holder of closed account (full-block format).

November 15, 19X2

Mr. Gordon Day
3233 - 38th Street N.W.
McLean, Wisconsin 68590

Dear Mr. Day:

I regret that you closed your checking account with County Savings Bank. I hope that this was not due to any displeasing incident, but if it was I would appreciate your writing me about it so it will not happen again.

County Savings Bank appreciates your favoring us with your account and hopes that you may again find it convenient to use our facilities.

If at any time I can be of service to you in any phase of your financial affairs, please call me.

Sincerely yours,

Lester L. Cooper
Assistant Vice President

LLC/JLS

Information to Customers

Sample letters 10.11 through 10.17 are examples of letters written to provide information to customers. Sample letters 10.11 and 10.12 give the customer information on direct deposit services.

SAMPLE LETTER 10.11. Direct deposit services (hanging indented format).

March 20, 19X0

Mrs. Felitia Trust
1984 Baleaux Place
Bethesda, Nebraska 98543

Dear Mrs. Trust:

The safest, most convenient way to put money in the bank is through direct deposit.

Direct deposit may have started with Social Security checks, but millions of people have found out just how easy it is to have their checks sent directly to the bank.

Now you can have any recurring payment sent directly to us for deposit in your free N.O.W., Checking, or Savings Account. No mail to get lost or stolen. No trips to the bank in inclement weather. No worries about depositing checks when you're away from home. It's all done automatically with direct deposit at New National Bank.

To have your Social Security, retirement, or paychecks sent directly to us for deposit, come in and talk to any one of our customer service representatives, or give me a call at 876-3434. You'll quickly find out why so many people are taking advantage of direct deposit.

Cordially,

T. James Stout
Assistant Vice President

TJS:LMR

SAMPLE LETTER 10.12. Direct deposit services (full-block format).

January 29, 19X4

Ms. Beverly Luans
1918 Northern Road
Grand Isle, New Hampshire 30303

Dear Ms. Luans:

With direct deposit, every payday your paycheck is automatically deposited into your New National checking, money market, or savings account. New National credits your account each payday, and you can withdraw your funds the same day.

When you have your paycheck directly deposited into our Low-Fee checking account, you'll pay a service charge of just $1.00 a month plus transaction fees if your balance falls below the required minimum. If you keep a minimum balance in either your checking or companion savings account, your account will be free of monthly service charges and transaction fees.

Every payday, you'll receive your payroll statement confirming that your check has been deposited. Each month, you'll also receive a statement from New National that lists all your checking and savings activity (including your direct deposits).

Ask your employee benefits manager if your company offers direct deposit—and how you can arrange for it. For more information, and to receive the special direct deposit discount available with New National Low-Fee checking, just call our 24-hour Customer Service Hotline, 800-HOTLINE. Or stop by any New National office.

Sincerely,

Max Nilges
Vice President

mn/jls

Sample letter 10.13 was written to give the customer information she needed for a school project. By providing this information and showing his interest in the project, the letter writer showed his commitment to the community.

SAMPLE LETTER 10.13. Letter providing information for school project (semiblock format).

November 2, 19X1

Ms. Sheila A. Harold
County High School
3535 Lathrop Avenue
Williamstown, New Jersey 16536

Dear Ms. Harold:

I am pleased that you have given the County Savings Bank the opportunity to help you meet one of your class objectives. Enclosed is a copy of our Bank Services Card which will give you the information you requested on the services County Savings has to offer.

You will find the enclosed card to be a good reference for your students to use in their study of the banking industry. If I can be of further assistance, do not hesitate to get in touch with me.

Sincerely,

Theodore H. Beaumont
Assistant Vice President

klj

enc.

Sample letter 10.14 provides a customer with information she requested on Individual Retirement Programs. Because the letter gives a good description, it could be an effective sales tool used to attract this customer's business. As a result of writing this customer relations letter, the letter writer not only might have helped to keep his customer's current business by showing how willing he is to help her by providing information, but also might have brought more of her business to the bank.

SAMPLE LETTER 10.14. Letter providing information on retirement programs (full-block format).

February 9, 19X2

Ms. Darlene Behrens
Long & Berrigan
200 Andover Street
Bar Harbor, Michigan 67892

Dear Ms. Behrens:

In response to your letter of January 28, I've listed below the various Individual Retirement Programs we offer to our customers. We do not charge any fees to customers for these accounts.

The New National Bank has three IRA plans. Two are at a fixed rate and one is at a variable rate.

The first is a 2 1/2 year Small Savers Certificate with a fixed rate that is determined when the certificate is initiated. A minimum deposit of $500 is required. Additional deposits are made by new certificates at what may be different rates.

The second is a 6-month Money Market Certificate with a minimum deposit of $10,000. Like the Small Savers Certificate, rates are quoted at the time of deposit and additional deposits require a new certificate at the then current rate.

The third plan is an 18 month variable rate account that changes weekly based on U.S. Treasury Bills. No minimum deposit is required, and additions may be made at any time without extending the maturity date.

Each account has a $2,000 annual contribution limitation. Couples with one income may contribute $2,250. Working couples may contribute $2,000 to separate IRAs. If you make less than $2,000 in taxable income during the year, you may only contribute a sum equal to those earnings.

I hope this information helps you. If I can be of further assistance, please call.

Sincerely,

Philip G. Catton
Vice President

pgc/jld

Sample letter 10.15 informs a customer that his bank does not provide a particular service requested. The letter writer does, however, let the customer know that he is readily available for questions about any other services his bank might be able to provide. The brevity of sample letter 10.15 should reassure the customer of this banker's straightforwardness. He doesn't try to fast talk (or, in this case, "fast write") his way out of not being able to provide services to a customer, but rather is up front with his customer. Honesty and straightforwardness can't hurt when customer service is involved.

SAMPLE LETTER 10.15. Letter informing customer bank does not provide type of service (semiblock format).

March 13, 19X1

Ms. Darcie Eliot
125 Cairo Drive
Pakistan, Indiana 58132

Dear Ms. Eliot:

I am sorry to inform you that County Savings Bank does not participate in the guaranteed student loan program. Please let me know if County Savings can provide you with any other banking service.

Yours truly,

Theodore H. Beaumont
Assistant Vice President

thb/klj

Sample letter 10.16 is a basic cover letter to send along with information or materials requested by the customer.

SAMPLE LETTER 10.16. Letter accompanying information requested (full-block format).

April 2, 19X1

Mr. Jeffrey Lender
45 Tewaker Place
Paducah, Kentucky 39393

Dear Mr. Lender:

We're pleased to provide the information you requested on checking account service charges. If you'd like further information or assistance, please stop by any New National office. Or call our customer service hotline at 800-HOTLINE.

We look forward to continuing to do business with you.

Sincerely,

John Reynolds
Assistant Vice President

jsl

Enclosure

The letter writer of sample letter 10.17 shows his commitment to his customer by going out of his way to introduce the customer to the person who will replace him. The personal nature of the letter accounts for the use of the official style format, which is used mainly for personal correspondence.

SAMPLE LETTER 10.17. Letter introducing new account officer (semiblock format).

November 14, 19X1

Dear Ralph:

I spoke to you last week about my decision to leave New National Bank. Taking over for me at New National will be Joyce McDougal. Joyce is a vice president who has been with the bank for four years, primarily in the Michigan area.

We will be in your area on June 21 and 22. We would like to take some time on one of those two evenings

Sample Letter 10.17 continued

to entertain you and Dave McLarn at dinner and a hockey game. I hope this will give both of you a chance to get to know Joyce.

Ralph, I hand-picked Joyce to replace me knowing she will give Thomson Enterprises the attention it deserves. You will be pleased with my choice.

I look forward to hearing from you soon.

Best regards,

Larz Manneng
Vice President

Mr. Ralph Embry
Thomson Enterprises
111 Prospect Street
Hamilton, California 00012

LM:js

cc: Joyce McDougal

Sample letters 10.18 and 10.19 provide the customer with information on the bank's funds availability policy and on the community reinvestment act. Both letters provide a service to the customer by letting him know where the bank stands on these two important issues.

SAMPLE LETTER 10.18. Funds availability policy (semiblock format).

May 9, 19X6

Mr. William Berrigan
67 Sailboat Lane
Maui, Hawaii 09087

Dear Mr. Berrigan:

When you deposit a check or money order which is drawn on another financial institution, there is a time delay before the check reaches that institution and The County Bank receives payment. Our policy is to give you use of your deposited funds as early as possible. When you accept a check or money order, you assume ultimate responsibility that the item will be honored. Be-

Sample Letter 10.18 continued

cause the item can be returned to us and charged back to your account, you should only accept checks from people you know and have confidence in.

Funds deposited at a County Banking Office or County Automated Teller Machine (ATM) before 3 p.m. any business day or received by the Bank at P.O. Box 3542, Savin Hill, Hawaii 02342 will generally be made available to you the next business day after the date of deposit. If you deposit a check drawn on a financial institution outside of Hawaii, it may be up to three business days before the funds are made available. Even though the funds from a deposited item have been made available to you, it may still be returned to us due to a stop payment overdrawn account, or a closed account. If this happens, the item will be charged back to your account and you will be notified. For new customers, we reserve the right to make funds available subject to final payment.

If you have any questions about The County Bank's funds availability policy, please call me at (713) 555-2323.

Cordially,

Evan Marshall
Director
Customer Service Center

EM/JM

SAMPLE LETTER 10.19. Community Reinvestment Act statement (full-block format).

August 6, 19X6

Mr. Brian Palay
743 Rees Drive
Boonton, New Jersey 07005

Dear Mr. Palay:

The County Bank cares about its community. As one of the oldest chartered businesses in New Jersey, The County Bank has always been committed to serving the communities of which we are an integral part. We have a firm commitment to the needs of our customers and to investment in the state. The County Bank is authorized by law to make a loan in any city or town in New Jersey and, under certain conditions, out of state. Many of our loans, though, tend to be concentrated in Northern New Jersey where we operate full-service banking facilities.

We define our ''community,'' as required by the Community Reinvestment Act, as the cities and towns that comprise Newark, Union, Montclair, North Arlington, Morristown, Boonton, and all other adjacent cities. These are areas where we conduct business in our full-service offices. We have made and will continue to make an attempt to participate in the revitalization efforts of the cities and counties in which we are physically located.

In addition to the many lending programs we are associated with, The County Bank is also actively involved in many of the local merchants' associations and community development organizations in areas where we operate branches and residential mortgage offices. These groups help us to better understand the needs of our ''community'' and enable us to be a more effective corporate citizen.

The County Bank is prepared to extend, subject to our normal underwriting standards and lending policies, the following types of credit:

Residential Loans
Rehabilitation Loans
Commercial and Industrial Mortgage Loans
Consumer Loans
Home Equity Loans
NOW Overdraft Protection
Home Improvement Loans
Automobile Loans

Mr. Brian Palay -2- August 6, 19X6

Passbook Loans
Education Loans
Construction Loans
Commercial Loans

The Federal Community Reinvestment Act requires the Federal Home Loan Bank Board to evaluate our performance in helping to meet the credit needs of this community, and to take this evaluation into account when it decides on certain applications submitted by us.

Your involvement is encouraged. You may send signed written comments about our Community Reinvestment Act Statement of Performance in helping to meet community needs to me at The County Bank, 45 Lorraine Terrace, Boonton, New Jersey 07005, and to the Federal Home Loan Bank Board, 1700 G Street, N.W., Washington, D.C. 20552. Your letter, together with any responses made by us, may be made public.

Thank you for your participation.

Sincerely,

Loren Gary
Senior Vice President

ejc

Sample letter 10.20 informs a customer that his bank has been closed and that the letter writer's bank will take over his accounts.

SAMPLE LETTER 10.20. Notice of bank closing by bank that has taken over accounts (full-block format).

February 3, 19X6

Ms. Andrea Hills
76 Dearborn Place
Andover, Missouri 39393

Dear Ms. Hills:

As of January 28, 1991, all 65 branches of Old National Bank became part of New National Bank. On behalf of all our employees, please accept my warm welcome to New National. We are pleased to have the opportunity to serve you.

On January 28, the Missouri Commissioner of Banks declared Old National Bank insolvent and appointed the Federal Deposit Insurance Corporation (FDIC) as liquidating agent. New National Bank immediately assumed responsibility for all of your Old National Bank deposits from the FDIC. By receipt of this letter you acknowledge that New National Bank is now the holder of your deposits.

Through our agreement with the FDIC, New National Bank also has assumed the administration of Old National Bank's commercial loans, consumer loans, credit lines, and mortgages. We will be sending you more information about the continued operation of your consumer loan account. In the meantime, you should make your loan payments as usual. You may also access your credit line as you have in the past.

Each of your deposit accounts will earn interest at the same rate as it did prior to the closing or Old National Bank for 14 days, through February 12. During this 14-day period, you may withdraw your money without penalty. After February 12, FDIC policy allows us to change rates or other terms of any former Old National Bank account. We will certainly give you prior notice of any changes.

Over the next few months, your Old National Bank accounts will be automatically converted to New National accounts. Meanwhile, you can continue to use your Old National Bank checks and ATM cards as usual.

You will be hearing from us again shortly as we begin to convert your accounts to New National Bank accounts. All of us at New National Bank are committed to providing you the same high quality, personal service you were accustomed to from Old National Bank. If you have any ques-

Sample Letter 10.20 continued

tions, please visit your local branch or call us on the special hotline we have made available just for you: 800-NEWBANK.

Sincerely,

Rebecca Grimes
Senior Vice President

lg

Customer References

Writing a reference for a customer may become necessary, whether it is for a job or for credit approvals. Sample letters 10.21-10.27 are examples of different types of customer references you might have to write. Sample letters 10.21-10.23 are credit references for three different customers. The writers all write of the good business relationship they have had with the customer. Sample letter 10.21 is written for a business which has maintained accounts with the bank; sample letter 10.22 for a customer who has maintained a checking account; and sample letter 10.23 for a customer who has been issued loans.

SAMPLE LETTER 10.21. Credit reference for business customer (block format).

September 16, 19X2

Mr. William C. Robertson
Credit Manager
County Supply Company
7986 Monroe Drive
Lawrence, North Dakota 61163

Dear Mr. Robertson:

Subject: Simon Springs Window Shade Company, Inc.

Simon Springs Window Shade Company, Inc. has maintained accounts with New National Bank since December 19X0. The accounts average in the middle four figures. We have credit outstanding in the moderate five figures which is being handled as agreed.

We are quite familiar with the owners of this company and hold them in very high regard. We would not anticipate your having any difficulty with normal trade credit.

Sample Letter 10.20 continued

Sincerely,

Philip G. Catton
Vice President

pgc/dam

SAMPLE LETTER 10.22. Credit reference for checking account customer (full-block format).

April 12, 19X2

Ms. Roberta C. Williams
Credit Manager
City Supply Corporation
34 Lester Drive
Crawford, New Jersey 01234

SUBJECT: COLIN Z. MURPHY

Mr. Colin Z. Murphy has an open checking account with the County Savings Bank. The account was opened in October 19X5 and has a current balance in the low five figures. The average balance in the account is a mid-four figure. Our relationship has been totally satisfactory.

I have known Mr. Murphy for several years and have found him to be conscientious and responsible in his dealings with the County Savings Bank. I would not anticipate your having any difficulty with normal trade credit with Mr. Murphy.

If I may be of further assistance, please do not hesitate to get in touch with me.

Theodore H. Beaumont
Assistant Vice President

klj

SAMPLE LETTER 10.23. Credit reference for loan customer (full-block format).

June 3, 19X2

Ms. Catherine Fraser
Bimini Mortgage Company
98 Diamond Road, Suite 150
Bethesda, Nevada 93303

SUBJECT: DAVID E. LONG

Dear Ms. Fraser:

New National Bank's records indicate that David Long has been a customer of our bank since 19X4. He has borrowed several times during the intervening years in amounts varying between the low five and high five figures. The loans always have been and are being handled as agreed. Checking account balances during the last year have averaged in the high four figures and are also responsibly handled.

We have enjoyed a close association with Mr. Long and are sure you will find him to be responsible for his normal business commitments. Please call if additional information is needed.

Very truly yours,

Philip G. Catton
Vice President

dam

Sample letters 10.24 and 10.25 are brief letters verifying that a customer's checks will be honored by the bank. Sample letter 10.24 deals with materials to be purchased, and sample letter 10.25 with equipment to be bid on at auction. They are both brief and clearly express the bank's support of the customer.

SAMPLE LETTER 10.24. Letter verifying customer's checks will be honored for materials to be purchased (simplified format).

November 20, 19X0

Mr. David L. Bixton
John Wagner & Associates
One Park Place
Sibling, Ohio 02222

SUBJECT: DMI, INC.

I understand that DMI, Inc. has contracted to purchase approximately $10,250 worth of materials from you. My letter certifies that if the materials are delivered as agreed upon this bank will guarantee payment of this order. This guarantee will remain in effect for 90 days.

PHILIP G. CATTON
VICE PRESIDENT

dam

SAMPLE LETTER 10.25. Letter verifying customer's checks will be honored for equipment bid on (simplified format).

February 8, 19X9

Ms. Jane Armitage
Director
McKean Sales Company, Inc.
P.O. Box 9087
Delaware City, Ohio 81979

SUBJECT: JOSEPH A. MALTED CONTRACTORS, INC.

I understand that the Joseph A. Malted Contractors, Inc. is interested in bidding on some equipment which is going to be auctioned by your firm on February 15. My letter to you certifies that any checks issued by this company drawn on our bank will be honored for payment.

PHILIP G. CATTON
VICE PRESIDENT

dam

Sample letter 10.26 is a personal recommendation for a longstanding customer. The letter writer expresses his support of the customer, both personally and professionally.

SAMPLE LETTER 10.26. Personal recommendation for customer (semiblock format).

August 7, 19X1

Mr. Gerald D. Johanson, Chairman
Department of Management
State College
75 Mascot Place
Aldrienne, Missouri 70160

Dear Mr. Johanson:

Subject: Reference for David W. Carmichael

I have known David Carmichael for approximately four years and have found him to be an individual of the highest integrity. In my dealings with him he has impressed me as honest, sincere, and extremely knowledgeable.

There has been no information that I have found in investigating his credit and general background that would indicate that he is not of the highest moral character. It is my opinion that David can only be considered as a fine, upstanding individual. I feel your organization would benefit from his participation.

If I may be of further assistance, please call me.

Sincerely,

John L. Kraft
Assistant Vice President

jlk/gbc

Sample letter 10.27 is a reference written on behalf of a customer who wishes to sponsor a foreign student. Because the banker knows the customer's financial condition, he can show legitimate support for her capabilities as a host to the student.

SAMPLE LETTER 10.27. Reference written for customer wishing to sponsor foreign student (simplified format).

August 18, 19X2
United States Embassy
Ireland

SUBJECT: LINDA ALLENDER AS SPONSOR FOR LAURA WIMSATT

Please be advised that I am familiar with Ms. Allender both personally and professionally. As her banker, I can assure you that she is totally qualified to provide for Ms. Wimsatt during her graduate studies at the State College.

If I may be of further help in this matter feel free to write to me.

Theodore H. Beaumont
Assistant Vice President

THB:KLJ

Credit Card Matters

Sample letters 10.28-10.30 are letters written to or on behalf of customers desiring credit cards. Sample letter 10.28 is a reference for a customer whom the letter writer knows personally. Because of his knowledge of the customer's background, he is able to express his wholehearted support for the issuing of a credit card to his customer.

SAMPLE LETTER 10.28. Request for customer to receive credit card (semiblock format).

December 26, 19X0

Mr. Wallace R. Charles
State Savings Bank
P.O. Box 268
Toano, Wyoming 08916

Dear Wally:

In reference to our conversation last week, I am requesting that a MasterCharge Card be issued to Mr. Jeffrey Maxwell, 210 South Street, Boston, Massachusetts 02111.

Sample Letter 10.28 continued

Jeffrey is the son of Mr. Lester L. Maxwell, Chairman of the Board of Directors of County Savings Bank. Jeffrey is a recent college graduate and has joined an oil firm in the Toano area. I have known Jeffrey for a number of years and have found him to be a most responsible individual. Please forward all necessary applications directly to him.

Any assistance you can give in this matter will be appreciated. I am looking forward to talking to you in the future.

Best regards,

NEW NATIONAL BANK

Philip G. Catton
Vice President

pgc/dam

Sample letter 10.29 is similar to 10.28 but the customer here had been previously turned down for a credit card. The letter writer goes to bat for his customer by detailing why he believes the customer should be issued a card.

SAMPLE LETTER 10.29. Request for customer, who had previously been turned down, to receive credit card (full-block format).

March 19, 19X0

Mr. William T. Allen
Bank Card Center
P.O. Box 190
Valley Way, South Dakota 08919

Dear Mr. Allen:

Please issue a VISA card to Ms. Susan Culleny. She previously filled out an application which was rejected.

Ms. Culleny is the industrial relations officer for the new Belmont Copper & Zinc Plant which recently opened in our area. She has been instrumental in directing many new employee accounts to our bank. In addition, she has an annual income of $18,500 and is a very responsible person.

Sample Letter 10.29 continued

I recommend a credit limit of $600. The card should be sent to Ms. Culleny at 102 Farqhuar Boulevard, Apt. 3D, Valley Way, South Dakota 08919.

Thank you for your cooperation.

Sincerely,

Theodore H. Beaumont
Assistant Vice President

klj

Sample letter 10.30 is a follow-up letter to a customer who has not heard about the status of her credit card application. The banker shows his commitment to the customer by expressing his regrets for the delay and the action he has taken to speed up the process.

SAMPLE LETTER 10.30. Follow-up letter to customer who hasn't received necessary credit card application (block format).

June 22, 19X2

Rachel Victoria
39 Tidewater Place, Suite 725
Boonton, New Jersey 07005

Dear Ms. Victoria:

Thank you for your recent letter. I regret that you have not heard from our VISA Department yet.

Mr. Ralph Detweiler of the VISA Department assures me that his department will respond to your application for a card before the end of this week. I am mystified by the delay, but hope that the department's response will be timely.

If I can be of any further assistance, please let me know.

Very truly yours,

Philip G. Catton
Vice President

PGC:DAM

Commendation on Customer's Business Record

When a customer has conducted consistently good business with your bank, you can benefit by writing the customer commending him or her. Sample letters 10.31 and 10.32 are examples of this type of letter.

SAMPLE LETTER 10.31. Letter commending customer on her good business relationship to the bank (semiblock format).

November 16, 19X2

Ms. Alana Berg
8678 First Avenue
Kananet, New York 22512

Dear Ms. Berg:

Without any fancy words or formality, we want to give a straightforward ''Thanks!'' and say that we appreciate the clean-cut manner in which you handle your affairs. It is nice to do business with you. This note is just to make sure you know that we place a high value on our relationship.

We at County Savings Bank are trying to do a good job for you and will always welcome your suggestions. If you like our service and the way we do business, we hope that you will recommend us to your friends and acquaintances. If not, we hope that you will tell us why, without pulling any punches.

Please feel free to call upon us whenever we can be of service. We want you to feel that County Savings Bank is always friendly and eager to give you the best in banking.

Yours very truly,

Alan D. Armaunde
President

ada/lss

SAMPLE LETTER 10.32. Letter commending customer on her excellent credit rating (full-block format).

August 9, 19X9

Mrs. Catherine R. Ahern
186 First Street
Hollywood, West Virginia 25647

Dear Mrs. Ahern:

Your credit rating with us is excellent. The satisfactory manner in which you have made the monthly payments on your account has made it a pleasure for us to handle your transaction.

We look forward to your continued patronage and wish to remind you that we will be happy to discuss with you any financial needs you now have or may have in the future. A variety of banking services which will afford a saving to you are at your disposal at County Savings Bank.

Come in and see us or call if we can be of service to you.

Sincerely,

Theodore H. Beaumont
Assistant Vice President

THB:KLJ

Special Services

Sample letter 10.33 informs a customer that the bank is willing to waive account fees for any of its customers older than 65 or younger than 18.

SAMPLE LETTER 10.33. Fee waivers on NOW and savings accounts for young and elderly customers (simplified format).

May 5, 19X4

Mr. Edward Coleman
Bethany College
2 Morlan Hall
Bethany, West Virginia 26032

FREE CHECKING AND SAVINGS ACCOUNTS

Mr. Coleman, County Bank customers who are younger than 18 and older than 65 do not have to pay any service charges whatsoever for NOW and savings accounts. Be sure to fill out the enclosed application form and send it in today for your account.

If you are between 18 and 65, there are no service charges for NOW Accounts if you maintain a minimum balance of $1,000 or if you arrange to have your weekly paycheck or any of your Federal recurring payments deposited directly to your account.

You're never too young or too old to have a NOW or savings account at The County Bank, where you can count on personalized attention and an extra measure of service at any age.

WAYNE DOHERTY
VICE PRESIDENT

mn

Enclosure

To Stockholders

Customer relations are successful when a customer can be convinced to invest in a bank. Sample letter 10.34 is written to a customer about a new branch to be opened. Shares of stock are being offered to this customer because of his good relationship with the bank.

SAMPLE LETTER 10.34. Letter offering stock to customer (semiblock format).

November 11, 19X2

Mr. Richard J. Nelson
997 Arlington Drive
Alewife, Maryland 13108

Dear Mr. Nelson:

County Savings Bank has applied to the state and to the Federal Reserve Bank for authority to open a bank in Alewife. Our application has been approved contingent upon increasing capitalization of 20,000 shares of authorized but unissued common stock.

The site for the bank has already been acquired. It is the former Cartwrite property in the very center of the Alewife community. Present plans call for building a full service, fully insured bank.

The new shares will be available for $18 per share. It is our desire to reserve for county buyers as large a portion as possible of the offering. The board reserves the right to approve purchases. If indicated purchases exceed 20,000, an allocation on a pro-rata basis of approved sales will be made.

If you desire to become a participant in this venture, as we hope you will, please fill out the enclosed form. You can either mail it to us or bring it to our present office.

Whether or not you decide to become a part owner, we earnestly solicit your banking business. We will do everything in our power to provide you with local banking facilities as rapidly as possible.

Sincerely,

Francis Cooke
President

lss

enc.

Sample letter 10.35 is a welcoming letter to a new stockholder. It could be written as a follow-up to those customers responding positively to the offer presented in sample letter 10.34.

SAMPLE LETTER 10.35. Letter welcoming new stockholder (full-block format).

March 9, 19X2

Mr. Thomas Alexander
3471 Angel Drive
Newport, Wisconsin 61583

Dear Mr. Alexander:

It is a pleasure for me to welcome you to the growing list of stockholders in the County Savings Bank.

Since 1889, it has been County Savings Bank's privilege and obligation to serve the community. We are happy to enclose a copy of our current, semiannual Statement of Condition. It shows our strong financial condition and the many banking facilities we offer. It illustrates, through our directorate of business and civic leaders, the position and support we enjoy in the community. We take pride in being a local institution.

I would like to invite you to stop in and meet our officers. They will acquaint you with your bank and the many ways in which it may serve you and your family.

Sincerely,

Francis Cooke
President

FC/LS

encl.

Customer Service Memos

Memoranda 10.36 and 10.37 are memos written on behalf of customers who are applying for credit cards. Memorandum 10.36 expresses enthusiastic support for the customer, while memorandum 10.37 discusses the customer's background without making a final recommendation, because the writer does not know the client. Both memos fall under the category of customer service even though they are not written directly to customers because the banker is providing assistance to them.

MEMORANDUM 10.36 Memorandum requesting a credit card be issued to a customer.

TO: Mrs. Beatrice Simons, VISA Department
FROM: Philip G. Catton, Vice President
DATE: December 9, 19X1
SUBJECT: VISA Card to be issued to Sister Francesca Corina

Please issue a VISA card to Sister Francesca Corina. This woman is a nun of the Order of Sancta Dominica, which operates the Sancta Dominica Hospital in Grand Forks. She has been our good customer for years.

Sister Francesca Corina is the Superior of the Sancta Dominica Convent, and is a person of honorable character. I am certain she will not abuse any credit granted. In her position as head of the convent, this credit is warranted.

My division will accept responsibility for collection, should that unlikely necessity arise.

jkl

MEMORANDUM 10.37. Memorandum reviewing a customer's application for a credit card.

TO: Alan R. Simmons, Assistant Vice President
VISA Department
FROM: Philip G. Catton, Vice President
DATE: June 29, 19X2
SUBJECT: Victoria Berrigan's request for VISA card

Ms. Victoria Berrigan is an attorney who has been practicing by herself since December 19X1. She is affiliated with attorneys Aaron Hamilton and Alexander Burr. Her account number at New National is 1065-401-8, which, as of June 9, had a balance of $512.

Her request is for a VISA card from New National Bank. She said she applied in January 19X1 for a credit card during her third year in law school, and was rejected for lack of credit experience. Ms. Berrigan reported that her only debt is to Old National Bank for a student loan for $9,000.

This memo is being sent to you without any recommendation because I do not know this person at all. She reports having had the account with us for four years and is, I think, deserving of an examination for VISA card credit purposes.

pgc/jkl

cc: Berrigan credit file

Corporate Loans 11

Chapter 11 contains loan letters which bankers wrote to their corporate customers.

Whether it is a loan proposal or an acceleration of debt letter, the letters in this chapter will serve as good models for most of the loan letters you will often have to write to corporate customers. A few of the letters in chapter 11 that could also be used as consumer loan letters are duplicated in chapter 12.

Many of the letters in this chapter, particularly the lengthy standardized ones, would lend themselves particularly well for adaptation on a word processor. See chapter 6 for a discussion of how to make the most effective use of these types of letter.

Proposing, Approving, and Granting Loans

Sample letters 11.1-11.5 are examples of loan proposal letters. When the loan or credit process reaches the stage where a proposal is in order, there are important things to keep in mind. Although every proposal will be a unique offer, most proposals share many common elements.

One of the most important things to remember is to be as clear as possible. Try to figure out what is most important to your customer and spell out those items clearly in your proposal letter. Since by this point in your relationship to your client you both have a good idea of what is to be involved in the prospective loan, there is no need to confuse the issue by including a great deal of technical information already known by the customer.

While writing your loan proposal letter you should be aware of the banks that might be competing with your offer. If your bank can offer a form of financing unavailable at competing banks, these financing services should be highlighted in the proposal letter.

The proposal letter is a sales tool. When all of the details are ironed out and the proposal is accepted, a formal loan closing may follow, but now you are trying, in effect, to close a deal with your customer. Since your customer is already familiar with the components of the loan proposal, you don't want to bore that customer by rehashing what is already known. You want to attract the customer and at the same time be concise.

Sample letter 11.1 is an example of a proposal for revolving credit to a utilities customer; sample letter 11.2 for credit and management services; and sample letter 11.3 for a credit line. All three letters are simple and to the point. They would leave little doubt in the customer's mind about the banker's proposal.

SAMPLE LETTER 11.1. Proposal for revolving credit (full-block format).

November 24, 19X1

Mr. Richard W. Salient
Secretary & Treasurer
County Gas Company
598 Curly Drive
Awkland, Massachusetts 46820

Dear Dick:

I have outlined below the terms under which New National would make a revolving credit available to County Gas or County Resources. Most the parameters were developed from our conversation of last week.

While I believe this proposal fully meets County Gas' needs, I can easily understand that you might have some other ideas. I would be happy to consider any changes you might suggest.

Amount:	$3,500,000
Term:	Revolving until January 1, 19X6 when it converts to a three-year term loan amortizing in equal quarterly payments
Prepayment Penalties:	None
Covenants:	Identical to Falcon Mutual Covenants
Facility Fee: facility	1/2 of 1% of the amount of the
Commitment Fee:	1/2 of 1% of the unused portion of the facility
Interest Rate Options:	1. Prime floating or

Sample Letter 11.1 continued

2. IBOR plus 1 1/4% for 7 day, 14-day, 30-day, 60-day, 90 day, or 6 month periods at fixed rates. No prepayments allowed.
   Borrowings to be in increments of $100,000

Balance Requirement: Checking account to be opened at New National—no minimum balance requirement

I look forward to hearing your reaction to may proposal. If the proposal is satisfactory to you, please let me know so that I can take the few credit approval steps needed to convert the proposal to a commitment.

Sincerely,

Max Nilges
Loan Officer

mn/ll

SAMPLE LETTER 11.2. Proposal for credit and management services (semiblock format).

May 4, 19X2

Ms. Cicely Randall
Vice President—Finance
Bethany Manufacturing, Inc.
Journal Building
Bethany, Texas 20987

Dear Cicely:

As you requested, I have outlined the credit/ cash management proposal that New National feels is appropriate in light of your company's financial needs.

Credit: A $5,000,000 unsecured line of credit priced at 75 basis points above the 90 day Eurodollar Rate (LIBOR) with compensating balances on 5% of the line.

Cicely, it is understood that we would review an increase from $5,000,000 to $7,500,000 if appropriate based on Bethany Manufacturing's financing requirements.

Sample Letter 11.2 continued

Cash Management: We propose that Bethany Manufacturing, Inc. elect New National's fully integrated Cash Management System which includes zero balance depository accounts for the subsidiaries as well as zero balance disbursement accounts. The disbursing accounts are funded by a parent concentration account.

The Cash Control System (CCS) will maintain Bethany Manufacturing's target cash balance at $250,000. On a daily basis, any excess will be invested in overnight repos; any shortfall will activate a loan.

New Cash I Balance Reporting provides current balance information by account and automated calculations on average month-to-date balances for each account. The Internal Monitor provides a daily update on each subsidiary's debits and credits from the zero balance account. It also calculates interest expense and interest income for the subsidiaries based on a rate determined by Bethany Manufacturing.

I hope this brief outline has clarified for you what New National is proposing. I look forward to our meeting on May 13, at which time we can consummate Bethany Manufacturing's and New National's new relationship.

If you have any questions, please call me.

Best regards,

Max Nilges
Loan Officer

llc

SAMPLE LETTER 11.3. Proposal for credit line (block format).

May 10, 19X2

Mr. David McDonnell
Vice President
DMI, Inc.
3542 Bethany Road
Crawford, New Jersey 01234

Dear Dave:

PROPOSED CREDIT LINE

As a follow-up to our recent conversation, I've drawn up a credit proposal that would address a portion of DMI's financing needs. If this proposal is acceptable, we'll begin the formal approval process necessary to convert it to a commitment.

Dave, we would like to propose a $1 million unsecured line of credit that gives DMI tremendous flexibility. The line may be used for:

1. Direct borrowings priced at prime
2. Acceptance financing with a 1% commission rate
3. Fixed rate borrowings priced at LIBOR plus 1%

Five-percent balances would be required on the line.

The proposal outlined here illustrates how we feel about DMI. Using New National Bank will give you flexibility as well as assure DMI of getting current market rates and ideas. Again, if you feel it appropriate, I would like to meet with Tim Smith and you to discuss the DMI, New National relationship.

I hope to hear from you in the near future.

Best regards,

Max Nilges
Loan Officer

js

Enclosure

Sample letter 11.4 is a detailed proposal of a loan which a bank is willing to offer a corporate customer. Because of the length of the proposal, the letter writer has numbered the paragraphs discussing the conditions of the proposal. As a result, he can refer within the letter to the paragraph numbers instead of having to repeat lengthy passages.

SAMPLE LETTER 11.4. Detailed loan proposal to corporate customer (block format).

June 15, 19X2

Mr. Julius T. Marx
Consultant Group Leasing Corporation
98 Haymarket Square, Suite 432
Coopersburg, Wyoming 90139

Dear Mr. Marx:

New National Bank is pleased to enter into the following agreement with Consultant Group Leasing Corporation:

1. We are prepared to lend you a total of up to $500,000 to finance your purchase of computer equipment, furniture, fixtures, office equipment, and leasehold improvements to be rented to the law firm of Robert Walker & Associates. The loan will be on a revolving basis with a maximum line of credit declining over time per the following schedule:

Period	Maximum Line of Credit
This date to September 30, 19X3	$500.000
October 1, 19X3 to September 30, 19X4	$400,000
October 1, 19X4 to September 30, 19X5	$300,000
October 1, 19X5 to September 30, 19X6	$200,000
Ocober 1, 19X6 to September 30, 19X7	$100,000
After September 30, 19X7	$ 0

   Each borrowing will be represented by a note in the form of Exhibit A. Notwithstanding that Exhibit A specifies that the note is payable on demand, we will not make any such demand so long as: 1) your total indebtedness remains below the maximum line of credit; 2) you are in compliance with the remaining terms of this letter; and 3) there is no default in the conditions or covenants discussed in paragraph two. All notes representing borrowings will beprepayable without penalty and will bear interest at our prime rate.

2. As a condition of the borrowings described in paragraph one, the firm of Robert Walker & Associates will provide us with a written guarantee of any loans made. The liability of

Sample Letter 11.4 continued

Robert Walker & Associates under this guarantee, however, will be limited to its partnership assets and will not extend to the assets of its partners.

As a further condition to any loans to you, Robert Walker & Associates will: 1) represent and warrant to us that its net worth as of the date is in excess of its and your combined indebtedness; 2) agree to provide us, on September 30 of each calendar year with additional representations and warranties that its net worth continues to exceed the then total of your and its indebtedness; and 3) agree not to make distributions to its partners over and above their regular drawings while your loans are in default or until such defaults are cured.

3. While you have outstanding loans, you will not pledge, hypothecate, or otherwise encumber any amounts due to you under any lease agreements.

If these arrangements are acceptable to you, will you please return a signed copy of this letter, along with a certificate of a vote of your board of directors, authorizing the loan.

Very truly yours,

John A. Williams
Vice President

jaw:jdb

encl.

The foregoing is accepted and agreed to.

CONSULTANT GROUP LEASING CORPORATION

Date:____________________ By:____________________

Sample letter 11.5 is an example of a proposal made as a follow-up to a phone call. The details of the loan are briefly stated in the letter, but there is enough information included for the customer to be able to decide whether or not to accept the offer.

SAMPLE LETTER 11.5. Loan proposal made as follow-up to phone call (semiblock format).

September 15, 19X2

Mr. Bernard T. Haskell, Mayor
City of Malden
400 Wisconsin Drive
Malden, California 10816

Subject: Malden Solid Waste Disposal System

Dear Mayor Haskell:

Alan Ronalds called me yesterday about the financing need for the solid waste disposal system amounting to approximately $200,000. Mr. Ronalds also informed me that the borrowing would take place in October, with repayment to begin in January 19X3.

Amortization of the borrowing would take place so that the loan would be fully paid by July 19X5. We understand the purpose of the financing to be for the development of a waste disposal site in Malden.

New National Bank would be pleased to provide Industrial Revenue Board financing at 65% of the prime lending rate at Old National Bank or World National Bank of San Francisco. This rate would be adjusted semiannually from the date of the borrowing.

Our commitment offer expires November 1, 19X2. Please let us know if we may be of further assistance in clarifying our proposal.

Sincerely,

Max Nilges
Loan Officer

mn/io

Sample letters 11.6-11.15 are letters written to approve or grant loans. Sample letter 11.6 was written as an approval of a demand line of credit for a customer who wished to set up a medical practice. The terms of the credit are clearly listed in the letter, as are the steps necessary for the customer to take to indicate acceptance of the offer.

SAMPLE LETTER 11.6. Approval of a demand line of credit (full-block format).

April 17, 19X1

Dr. and Mrs. Anthony Flywheel
876 Florrine Road
Skater, Florida 30992

Dear Dr. and Mrs. Flywheel:

We are pleased to advise you that your application for a demand line of credit for $50,000 to establish your medical practice in Hackensack, Georgia has been approved subject to the following terms and conditions:

1. Funds will be advanced for capital expenditures upon presentation of invoices (approximately $20,000).
2. Monthly operating expenses, to a maximum of $5,000 a month, may be drawn on or about the first of each month for a period of six months beginning May 1, 19X1.
3. Interest on the loan will accrue at a rate of 11% a year with the requirement of quarterly interest payments only (based on calendar quarter).
4. Security will consist of a blanket security interest in the assets of your practice and your personal endorsements.
5. It is agreed that on or about May 1, 19X2, the note will be renegotiated establishing a pay-out arrangement that will be mutually acceptable to both you and County Savings Bank.

As evidence of your acceptance, please sign and return to us the original of this letter on or before May 1, 19X1. If your acceptance is not received by the above date, the bank may cancel this commitment.

Very truly yours,

Warren G. Maynard
Assistant Vice President

wgm/apv

Enclosure

Accepted:

____
Date

____________________ ____________________
Signature Signature

Approvals of financing appear in sample letters 11.7 and 11.8.

SAMPLE LETTER 11.7. Approval of financing (semiblock format).

October 14, 19X1

Dr. Wilma Barney
765 Spanky Drive
Alfafa, Idaho 11280

Dear Dr. Barney:

I am pleased to advise you that your application for a term loan to relocate your dental practice to the Buckling Professional Building for $18,000 has been approved subject to the following terms and conditions:

1. Funds will be advanced in a lump sum directly to you.
2. Rate on the term loan will be at prime with the requirement of interest and $18,000 principal curtailments payable quarterly beginning with the fourth quarter of 19X1.
3. Security on the line will consist of your personal guaranty.
4. Term of line will be for two-and-one-half years with expected payout in the first quarter 19X4.

As evidence of your acceptance, please sign and return to us the enclosed copy of this letter no later than October 30, 19X1. If your acceptance is not received by this date, this commitment may be terminated and considered null and void.

County Savings Bank is pleased to be of assistance to you in relocating your dental practice. We look forward to continuing to service your total banking needs.

Sincerely,

Warren G. Maynard
Assistant Vice President

apv

Enclosure

Accepted:

____
Date

____________________ ____________________
Signature Signature

Sample letter 11.8 is written to a customer approving construction financing.

SAMPLE LETTER 11.8. Approval of financing (full-block format).

March 24, 19X2

Richard C. Hamill
County Builders, Inc.
98 Albatross Lane
Petersburg, Arkansas 55123

Dear Rick:

We are pleased to inform you that your application for construction financing for $50,000 for the purpose of constructing a single family dwelling at Lot 9-T, Section 8, Hawkins Trace, Bazonka County, Arkansas, has been approved subject to the following terms and conditions.

1. The construction loan commitment of $50,000 will be advanced on a percentage of completion basis. Although we will conduct inspection prior to each draw request, we will assume no responsibility for workmanship or quality or materials used.
2. Interest on the loan will accrue at a rate of prime plus 1% per annum. In addition, there will be a commitment upon your acceptance of the terms and conditions of this letter.
3. The requirement that you establish a passbook savings account in the minimum amount of 25% of the loan commitment. The account may be used to pay monthly interest payments during the term of the note.
4. Delivery of written evidence that adequate Builders Risk Insurance or hazard insurance to include fire and extended coverage in the minimum amount of $50,000 issued to cover construction and endorsed to reflect County Savings Bank.
5. Title insurance to include coverage against both matters of survey and mechanic liens issued in favor of the bank by an acceptable title insurance company.
6. The requirement of at least three working days' notice prior to each draw.
7. Your personal guaranty.
8. All expenses in connection with this loan will be paid by you.

As evidence of your acceptance, please sign and return to us the enclosed copy of this letter on or before April 9, 19X2. You should also remit your check for $500. If you wish, we will deduct this amount from your first draw. If your acceptance is not received by the above date, the bank may at its option cancel the commitment. Moreover,

Sample Letter 11.8 continued

should you accept our commitment, it will be valid only until October 1, 19X2.

Yours truly,

John Savithson
Vice President

js/nc

enc.

Accepted by:

______________________________ ____________________
Richard C. Hamill Date

Sample letters 11.9 and 11.10 are two examples of approvals of loans for contributions to a partnership. Sample letter 11.10 is more personal in nature than sample letter 11.9. Sample letter 11.9 would be an excellent form letter to use in approving such loans.

SAMPLE LETTER 11.9. Approval of loan for contribution to partnership (block format).

June 2, 19X2

Mr. Melvin W. Howard
Long & Berrigan
200 Andover Street
Bar Harbor, Michigan 67892

Dear Melvin:

This letter confirms our understanding about the $25,000 loan New National Bank has made to you, the proceeds of which are for your required capital contribution to the firm of Long & Berrigan. The following are the terms of this loan:

Principal Amount:	$25,000
Principal Reduction:	$5,000 payable in five annual installments beginning January 15, 19X3
Interest Rate:	Prime plus 1%
Interest Payable:	Monthly

The interest rate will change simultaneous with any change in the prime rate at New National. The principal

Sample letter 11.9 continued

may be prepaid in part or in whole on any interest date without penalty.

The entire balance of the note will become due and payable immediately, at the option of the holder, without notice or demand, upon the occurrence of any of the following events:

a. Failure to pay an installment of principal or of interest on the loan when due.
b. Death or insolvency of the maker.
c. Termination, for any reason, of partnership in the firm of Long & Berrigan.

Any deposits or other sums at any time credited by or due from the holder to the maker, and any securities or other property of the maker at any time in the possession of the holder may at all times be held and treated as collateral for payment of this note and any and all other liabilities of the maker to the holder. The holder may apply or set-off such deposits or other sums against such liabilities or obligations of this note.

The maker also agrees to pay on demand all costs and expenses (including reasonable attorney fees) paid by the holder in enforcing this note on default.

Please sign the enclosed copy of this letter indicating your acceptance of the terms outlined in this letter of understanding.

Sincerely,

Max Nilges
Vice President

mn/lg

enclosure
Agreed and accepted:

________________________ ________________
Signature Date

SAMPLE LETTER 11.10. Approval of loan for contribution to partnership (full-block format).

December 11, 19X1

Mr. Elliot T. Dreyfus
Robertson & Maxwell
One Franklin Plaza, Suite 34
Lewiston, Massachusetts 90876

Dear Elliot:

We have reviewed your personal financial statement dated October 30, 19X1. Based upon our review and barring unforeseen changes in your financial affairs, we have approved in principal your loan request for a maximum of $13,000 for the purpose of funding your partnership capital contribution at Robertson & Maxwell.

This loan will bear interest payable quarterly in arrears at our prime rate plus 1%. Principal will be repayable in five equal annual installments beginning June 1, 19X3.

At the time of takedown in April 19X2, there will be execution of a note evidencing this loan and a letter of understanding between the bank, you, and Robertson & Maxwell. The note will be similar in form to the example I previously sent you.

Congratulations on your election to partnership. We at New National wish you the very best and, as your bankers, ask that you feel free to call on us at any time you need professional advice.

Very truly yours,

Max Nilges
Loan Officer

jdg

Sample letter 11.11 is an example of a loan approval written in a simple and clear style. The first paragraph states the amount of the loan and the nature of the security, while the second paragraph lists the conditions involved.

SAMPLE LETTER 11.11. Loan approval (block format).

June 9, 19X0

Mr. Barry K. Byron
11 Newswatch Place
West Freedom, Pennsylvania 15090

Dear Barry:

As we discussed on June 5, County Savings Bank is pleased to grant you a $750,000 loan secured by construction equipment. The loan will be repayable monthly over five years at a simple interest rate of 5 1/2 points over the Federal Reserve's discount rate. Rate adjustments will be made on the first day of every month.

The loan is subject to the conditions of the enclosed loan agreement. The chief covenants of the agreement are:

1. The customer will maintain no less than $200,000 working capital calculated on the basis of generally accepted accounting principals.
2. The customer will maintain a current ratio of at least 2.3 to 1.
3. The customer will not allow total debt to exceed 1 1/2 times the customer's net worth.

We look forward to servicing this loan after the draw down on July 15. In the meantime, please feel free to call us for any other banking service we can provide.

Kindest regards,

John Savithson
Vice President

lhg

enc.

Sample letter 11.12 is a several-page letter of approval. This example is a good form letter to use in approving a loan for a consumer or corporate customer. It could easily be stored in a word processor to be called up whenever such an approval for a loan was to be made.

SAMPLE LETTER 11.12. Loan approval consisting of several-page list of possible terms and conditions (block format).

November 9, 19X1

Mr. Terrence Henries
134 Leone Drive
Millersville, North Dakota 66632

Dear Mr. Henries:

We are pleased to have approved your application for a $59,600 loan subject to all of the terms and conditions which follow. For simplicity, County Savings Bank will be referred to as ''CSB,'' you as ''Borrower,'' the $59,600 loan as ''Loan,'' and the specific security as ''Security Property.''

After we receive your acceptance of our commitment, we will advise the closing attorney to prepare the loan instruments.

We are pleased to have the opportunity to serve you. If you have questions about this commitment, please call us.

Sincerely,

John Savithson
Vice President

js/nc

encs.: 1. Terms of Loan
2. Requirements and Conditions of Loan

Terms of Loan

Borrower: Mr. Terrence Henries

Amount of Loan: $59,600

Purpose: Residential Construction

Endorsers or Guarantors: None

Security: First deed of trust on land and improvements known as Lot 5-U, Grand Forks, Route 76, Millersville, North Dakota

Amortization: On demand
(The closing attorney is to prepare the deed of trust and deed of trust note to read ''Payable on Demand.'')

Maturity: 6 months from the date of our initial disbursement

Mr. Terrence Henries -2- November 9, 19X1

Extensions: To be negotiated

Interest Rate: 10 1/2% per year, payable monthly

Service Charge: 1% ($596), non-refundable

Payee and Place of Payment: County Savings Bank, Real Estate Finance Department, County Shopping Center, Grand Forks, North Dakota 66630

Trustees: Henry Janeway and Curtiss Leroy, Residents of the City of Millersville

Release Provisions: Not applicable

Closing Attorney: Ms. Nanette Mathis

REQUIREMENTS

Prior to the disbursement of any portion of the loan proceeds, Borrower will have satisfied completely the following documentation requirements and other conditions as listed (only those checked):

______ NOTE AND DEED OF TRUST (CSB Standard Form)
The loan is to be evidenced by a deed of trust note of the Borrower and secured by a first deed of trust on the Security Property, the substance of each of which is subject to approval by CSB. The deed of trust note and deed of trust will be submitted to and reviewed by CSB prior to execution and recording. Upon approval and recording, instead of the original deed of trust which should be forwarded to CSB as soon as available, CSB is to be furnished with a standardized copy with the original recording receipt attached.

______ TITLE INSURANCE
Borrower will furnish to CSB a policy of title insurance issued by a company acceptable to and insuring CSB in the amount of the loan, without exception for possible unfiled mechanics' and materialmens' liens and containing only such title exceptions satisfactory to CSB. Should a binder be issued, the term of this binder will not be less than the term of the loan. The title insurance policy or binder must be submitted to and reviewed

by CSB prior to loan closing. If the original title policy is not available at loan closing, a marked-up binder initialed by the title company will be acceptable, providing the original policy is promptly forwarded to CSB.

_______ HAZARD INSURANCE
Borrower will furnish to CSB a standard fire insurance policy issued by a company acceptable to CSB (together with ''Paid'' premium invoice) in an amount which is the greater of the amount of the loan or 100% of the insurable value of the Security Property, with extended coverage, vandalism and malicious mischief insurance. This policy will contain standard mortgagee loss payable clause in favor of CSB, Real Estate Finance Department.

_______ FLOOD INSURANCE
[ ] Flood insurance is not required.
[ ] Flood insurance is required. Borrower is to provide CSB with a standard flood insurance policy issued under the National Flood Insurance Program naming CSB as loss payee.

_______ BUILDING LOAN AGREEMENT
Borrower will furnish to CSB a building loan agreement, the substance of which is subject to approval by CSB.

_______ CURRENT SURVEY
Borrower will furnish to CSB a current survey showing no encroachments and otherwise acceptable to CSB, prepared and certified by a certified land surveyor, which survey will designate, without limitation, (i) the dimensions of the Security Property, (ii) the dimensions and location of the buildings and other improvements constructed on the property, (iii) the dimensions of the parking areas as well as the total number of on-site parking spaces, (iv) the location of all easements of record affecting the Security Property, specifying the holder of each such easement and the pertinent recordation information, (v) any and all building restriction and/or setback lines, and (vi) means of ingress and egress. Borrower will furnish to CSB within ten (10) days after being requested to do so up-dated surveys of the Security Property acceptable to CSB showing all improvements then constructed on the property, prepared and certified by a certified land surveyor. If the loan is a construction loan,

Mr. Terrence Henries -4- November 9, 19X1

the above required survey is to also be furnished to CSB upon completion of construction and prior to final disbursement of the loan proceeds.

______ SUBDIVISION PLATS
Borrower will furnish to CSB a copy of all subdivision plats recorded or to be recorded of the Security Property which plats must be acceptable to CSB. With regard to all subdivision plats to be recorded, Borrower will furnish evidence acceptable to CSB that all such plats have been approved by all necessary governmental agencies.

______ APPRAISAL
Borrower will furnish to CSB an appraisal made by an appraiser acceptable to CSB and which appraisal must be in an amount not less than $___________ and otherwise acceptable to CSB.

______ AUTHORITY TO BORROW
Borrower will furnish to CSB its Corporate Borrowing Resolution (CSB standard form or other resolution in form and substance acceptable to CSB) and acceptable evidence that Borrower is a corporation in good standing.

OR If the Borrower is a partnership, general or limited, Borrower will furnish to CSB a copy of the partnership agreement and any existing or future amendments thereto, a certified copy of the recorded partnership certificate and such other documents as CSB may require.

______ ASSURANCE OF UTILITY AVAILABILITY
Borrower will furnish evidence acceptable to CSB that all utilities (including drainage both on-site and off-site) necessary for the operation or occupancy of the Security Property are available to the Security Property, that the Security Property is connected thereto, and that all requisite tap-on or connection fees have been paid.

______ PLANS AND SPECIFICATIONs
Borrower will furnish to CSB a complete and final set of working plans and specifications in respect of the Security Property. Borrower will also furnish to CSB evidence acceptable to CSB that all plans and specifications have been approved by all necessary governmental agencies.

Mr. Terrence Henries -5- November 9, 19X1

______ COMPLIANCE WITH GOVERNMENTAL REGULATIONS
Prior to the commencement of construction and the initial loan disbursement, Borrower will furnish evidence acceptable to CSB that the Security Property and the improvements to be constructed thereon comply with all applicable zoning ordinances, building codes and all other applicable local, state, and federal laws, rules, regulations and/or requirements.

______ STARTS AHEAD OF SALES LIMITATION
Units started but unsold under this loan as well as all other loans to Borrower may not exceed __________, including model units.

______ OTHER DOCUMENTS
Borrower will furnish such other instruments, documents, opinions and/or assurances as CSB may require.

DISBURSEMENT PROCEDURE

Upon receipt and approval by CSB of all requisite loan documents, and/or provided and so long as Borrower complies with all obligations imposed upon Borrower in the loan documents and in this commitment:

______ a. We agree to disburse funds as construction progresses and based upon inspections acceptable to CSB. In this regard Borrower must notify CSB a minimum of three business days in advance so that CSB may schedule an inspection of the improvements. Borrower will also simultaneously notify the closing attorney to up-date title to the Security Property through the date the requested loan disbursement is to be made and to give telephone advice to CSB of the results of such up-date. An endorsement to the title policy extending the effective date through the date of CSB's disbursement must promptly be furnished to CSB. CSB reserves the right to require receipt of the title up-date endorsement prior to the requested disbursement of loan proceeds.

______ b. CSB agrees to disburse the loan proceeds in accordance with the General Contractor's Requisition for Payment, which must be approved and certified by the supervising architect or engineer of the work performed. The requisition and certification (it is suggested that American Institute of Architects' standard forms be used)

Mr. Terrence Henries -6- November 9, 19X1

must be in a form acceptable to CSB and all items included under the requisition will be subject to CSB's final approval.

______ c. Property inspections and/or loan disbursements will be limited to one per month.

______ d. Other:

APPROVAL OF LOAN DOCUMENTATION & FEES & EXPENSES
The loan will be made without cost to CSB. Borrower will pay all costs and expenses incurred in connection with this loan whether or not the loan is closed, including, but not limited to, title insurance premiums, surveyor's fees, appraiser's fees and legal fees. All requisite loan documents and related instruments will, at the option of CSB, be submitted to CSB's attorney for review and approval. Borrower will be deemed to have expressly agreed to pay all legal fees incurred by CSB in connection with this review.

REPRESENTATIONS OF BORROWER
The validity of this commitment is subject to the accuracy of all information, representations and materials submitted with, and in support of, Borrower's application for the loan. In the event CSB determines that any information or representations contained in the loan application are not accurate or correct, CSB will have the right to terminate this commitment, whereupon CSB will have no further obligations.

ASSIGNMENT OR MODIFICATION
Neither this commitment nor the loan can be modified or assigned without prior written consent of CSB.

ACCEPTANCE OF THIS COMMITMENT
In order for this commitment to remain effective, the acceptance copy of this commitment must be executed by Borrower and returned to CSB at Grand Forks, North Dakota on or before the expiration of ten (10) days from the date of this letter. Any extension for acceptance must be in writing and signed by CSB.

EXPIRATION OF COMMITMENT
To cause this commitment to remain in effect, the loan must be closed and CSB must disburse loan proceeds prior to ____________________ and any extension of such date must be in writing and signed by CSB.
The terms and conditions of this commitment will survive settlement and any violation of these terms and conditions will constitute default under the note and deed of trust.

Very truly yours,
COUNTY SAVINGS BANK

BY: ____________________

The undersigned accepts the commitment and the terms, and requirements set forth in this agreement.

____

BY: ______________________ DATE: ______________

OTHER POSSIBLE TERMS AND REQUIREMENTS

ASSIGNMENT OF STOCK
CSB will be provided with a pledge of 100% of the capital stock of Borrower as additional collateral for the loan. The pledge must be in form and substance acceptable to CSB and must grant to CSB a perfected first security interest in all of the capital stock of Borrower.

AGREEMENT NOT TO DISPOSE OF PARTNERSHIP INTEREST

CROSS-COLLATERALIZATION
The documents evidencing and/or securing the indebtedness of the Borrower will be drawn in such a manner that the Security Property for this loan will also act as security for all other debt of the Borrower and, further, all collateral taken as security for any other debt of the Borrower will be deemed to secure this loan as well.

CROSS-DEFAULT
The note and deed of trust will contain a provision to the effect that any default thereunder will constitute a default under all other existing loans of the Borrower, and that any default under any one or all of the existing loans will constitute default under this note and deed of trust.

COMMISSIONS
All commissions, brokerage claims or other compensation, if any, due or payable to any person, firm or corporation by reason of the making of the loan will be paid by Borrower and Borrower indemnifies CSB against any claims or liability for the payment of any such commission, brokerage claims or other compensation. This obligation will survive the payment in full of the principal and interest of the loan.

Mr. Terrence Henries -8- November 9, 19X1

EQUITY REQUIREMENTS
Borrower will provide evidence of its ability to satisfy certain equity requirements as determined by CSB in connection with the loan and deposit these in escrow.

ESCROWS
Sufficient escrows for real estate taxes and hazard insurance must be prepaid prior to the commencement of the first monthly mortgage payment so that when added to subsequent monthly escrow collections, the escrow account will be adequate to pay the tax assessment and insurance premiums on month prior to their respective due dates.

GUARANTY
CSB standard form or other agreement in form and substance acceptable to CSB.

FINANCIAL STATEMENTS
Borrower will furnish to CSB a copy of all financial statements including an itemized account of gross annual income and expenditures reflecting in detail the operations of the property. This statement will be prepared in accordance with then current and generally accepted accounting principles by an accountant satisfactory to CSB.

OR For as long as the loan remains outstanding, Borrower, at his expense, agrees to deliver to CSB an income statement, balance sheet and other financial information reasonably required by CSB as soon as available but in no event more than 90 days after the end of each of its fiscal years. Borrower is also responsible for providing CSB with annual personal financial statements of all endorsers and/or guarantors of the loan.

NO ADVERSE CHANGE
No part of the Security Property will be damaged and not repaired to the satisfaction of CSB, nor taken in condemnation or other like proceeding, nor shall any such proceeding be pending. Neither Borrower nor any tenant under any assigned lease, nor any guarantor on the loan, or of any such lease, will be involved in any bankruptcy, reorganization, dissolution, or insolvency proceeding.

NON-ASSUMPTION
The loan is subject to call in full or its terms may be modified in the event of sale or conveyance of the Security Property.

SALES REPORT
Borrower hereby agrees to provide CSB, in writing, a monthly status report indicating the number of units, lots, etc., sold, settled and remaining to be sold. This report should be effective on the last week of each month

and should be submitted to CSB within ten (10) days of the report date.

SOIL REPORT
Borrower will submit a soil engineer's report acceptable to CSB. CSB reserves the right to require certification that grading and foundation construction work were performed in accordance with recommendations contained in the report.

BUILDING PERMITS

CERTIFICATION OF OFF-SITE DRAINAGE AVAILABILITY AND CAPACITY

ENGINEER'S FEASIBILITY REPORT

ENVIRONMENTAL IMPACT REPORTS AND/OR HEALTH CERTIFICATES

EXISTING DEEDS OF TRUST OR PURCHASE MONEY DEEDS OF TRUST
Borrower will provide to CSB certified true copies of any deeds of trust encumbering the Security Property subject to the lien of CSB.

LINE OF CREDIT
This loan is considered a part of your ________________ line of credit and advances on this and all other loans made under this line may not exceed __________ at any one time.

MARKETING FEASIBILITY STUDIES

PERCOLATION REPORTS
Where septic tanks are to be used.

PRO-FORMA CASH FLOW PROJECTIONS

RECISION AGREEMENT

REGULATION Z
Truth in Lending Statement.

RESTRICTION ON ADDITIONAL BORROWINGS

RIGHT OF FIRST REFUSAL FOR ADDITIONAL CONSTRUCTION FINANCING SIGNS
CSB reserves the right to erect signs on the Security Property identifying all participating lenders.

SUBORDINATION AGREEMENTS

CONDOMINIUM DOCUMENTATION (Condominium loans only)
All necessary documents for the establishment of a condominium regime in accordance with the Horizontal Property Law will be submitted to CSB's counsel for approval. Upon approval, the Borrower must properly record these documents evidenced by recorder's receipts, and title policy

Mr. Terrence Henries -10- November 9, 19X1

endorsements. Additionally, the foregoing documents should be submitted to the Title Insurance Company for review and approval and the policy of title insurance should include an affirmative statement that the Horizontal Property regime has been created in accordance with and complies with state law. The policy of title insurance should also insure CSB against any loss or damage due to inadequacies of the condominium documentation.

DISBURSEMENTS

Physical inspection by representatives of CSB and construction advances will be limited to one per month and the first advance will not be made until completion of all foundation work and the concrete slab or platform is in place. Aggregate construction advances will be limited to ninety percent (90%) of the loan amount and no further advances will be made until final completion as determined by CSB.

NOTE: This provision has been designed for use on single family residential loans. It is used primarily for the one shot loan to an individual constructing his personal residence. However, it should be considered for use with small builders and builders that CSB has limited previous experience.

FOR OUT OF STATE TRANSACTIONS

Attorney's Opinion Letter

Borrower will furnish CSB with an attorney's opinion letter setting forth that the Borrowing corporation (partnership) is duly recognized and existing under (State) law and all fees, charges, and taxes required to be paid by it to permit it to operate and own any mortgage real property has been paid, that the instruments used to implement this transaction were signed by duly elected and still qualified officers of the Borrowing corporation (partnership) and are in proper legal form and order and executed so as to be valid, binding and enforceable and are according to their tenor under (State) law that the subject transaction does not constitute ''doing business'' in (State) (even were we to engage in more than one or several transactions of the same general type), that we would have access to the Courts of (State) to qualify to ''do business'' there or to pay any fees or taxes other than normal court costs, that the interest rate and all fees collected herein and in implementing the documents are permissible in (State) and do not constitute usury and that the mortgage or Deed of Trust is being recorded as required and will be effective without re-recording for the term of the note as a first lien on all mortgaged premises.

Sample letters 11.13 and 11.14 are examples of an approval of an unsecured line of credit and an unsecured loan. Both letters state directly in the first paragraph the nature of the loan or credit. The second paragraph details any conditions. The remainder of both letters is left for clearing up minor details, and closing on an encouraging note.

SAMPLE LETTER 11.13. Approval for unsecured line of credit (full-block format).

November 9, 19X2

Ms. Mary Alice Quantum
Vice President
Primetrol, Inc.
9 Kirtsickle Drive
Bolinka, Wisconsin 29908

Dear Ms. Quantum:

County Savings Bank is pleased to offer your company an unsecured line of credit for $500,000 for the calendar year 19X2. The line is based upon Primetrol's financial position remaining the same or improving over the next twelve months. The interpretation of your financial condition will be made by County Savings Bank.

We would appreciate receiving your schedule of anticipated use of this line so that we will be able to have the funds available during those times. We would also appreciate you making arrangements for resting this line at least thirty days during the year.

Edward Johnson, with whom you are familiar and who is familiar with Primetrol, has been assigned as your primary loan officer during the coming year. In Ed's absence, however, please call on any of our officers for assistance.

Your business has been important to us for the past 11 years. We are pleased to continue this relationship.

Cordially,

John Savithson
Vice President

js/li

SAMPLE LETTER 11.14. Approval for unsecured loan (full-block format).

January 20, 19X2

Mr. Kyle L. Crystal
234 Highton Road
Highlands, Louisiana 16130

Dear Kyle:

This letter confirms our understanding about the $25,000 unsecured loan made on January 19, 19X2 to you and Mrs. Crystal as evidenced by a demand note of that date.

You have agreed that upon the closing of the sale of your property at 234 Highton Road, Highlands, Louisiana, a minimum of $15,000 of the proceeds will be applied to principal repayment of this loan. The balance will be repaid upon receipt of your annual partnership distribution from Wisenthal & Horowitz. In any case, final repayment will be made no later than June 30, 19X2.

In accordance with your request, the proceeds of the loan have been deposited in your account #9646-319-8.

I trust this correctly states our arrangement. If so, would you and Mrs. Crystal please sign the enclosed copy of this letter and return it to me.

Best regards,

Max Nilges
Loan Officers

mn/jl

enclosure

Acknowledged and agreed:

____
Kyle L. Crystal

______________________________ ____________________
Marian Z. Crystal Date

Sample letter 11.15 was written to a customer who needed loans for special circumstances. The letter clearly states the amount, terms, and appropriate uses of these "specially arranged" loans. Because the customer was already a good customer of the bank, such an arrangement as approved in sample letter 11.15 could only serve to enhance the relationship.

SAMPLE LETTER 11.15. Approval of loan for special circumstances (semiblock format).

January 12, 19X2

Simon L. Chorde, Esq.
Dickerson & Collins
525 Hamilton Street
Oldby, Vermont 05964

Dear Simon:

This letter should further clarify the basis of the arrangement recently made between New National and your firm for meeting certain firm-related borrowing needs of the partners and, in certain cases, the senior associates. New National has agreed, under certain circumstances, to make loans based on its Small Business Prime Rate.

You have said that some partners may from time to time encounter cash flow difficulties through no fault of their own, but merely as a result of the irregular flow of compensation and distributions from the firm. Therefore, these partners may require loans for prudent and necessary expenditures in anticipation of income from the firm later in its fiscal cycle. Loans of this type would be of a short-term, cash flow nature and could include advances for estimated tax payments, large tuition bills, annual tax or estate planning, or other similar major cash demands.

Two other categories of need for which the bank would be willing to make loans on the same rate basis are:

1. To fund short-term real estate bridge transactions
2. To fund partnership contributions to the firm

In the latter case, the bank would be willing to entertain a three- to five-year repayment schedule.

We have mutually agreed that certain types of loans are specifically exempted from this program. These are loans related to other personal, investment, or business transactions which bear no relationship to problems created by the method of disbursement of income from the firm, including: loans for holding or investing in securities or money market transactions, loans for investment arbitrage, and various term loans such as mortgages, automobile, and boat loans.

Sample Letter 11.15 continued

Of course, as we agreed, the bank will continue to independently judge each credit on its own merits. We both understand that the willingness of the bank to extend this accommodation is predicated upon the extent and nature of Dickerson & Collins' overall relationship with the bank.

We at New National look forward to continuing the development of cordial and mutually beneficial ties between our firms.

Kindest regards,

Max Nilges
Loan Officer

mn/jg

A brief letter to renew a line of credit previously approved is featured in sample letter 11.16. Because the letter writer believed the customer to be a good one, he added that his bank would be delighted to increase the amount of the line. The fact that the loan officer is willing to increase the amount should let his customer know of his commitment to the hospital.

SAMPLE LETTER 11.16. Letter renewing line of credit (block format).

September 28, 19X2

Mr. Alan D. Kelly
Administrator of Fiscal Affairs
General Hospital
100 Harlan Drive
Cambridge, Wisconsin 54321

Dear Alan:

This letter acknowledges that New National Bank recently renewed its annually committed line to General Hospital for $1 million unsecured at prime. We would be delighted to increase this availability, but Sven Heen of your office assures me that this is adequate for 19X2-19X3. If I can be of further assistance, please call.

Regards,

Max Nilges
Loan Officer

Sample letter 11.17 instructs an attorney to prepare the instruments necessary for administering an approved loan.

SAMPLE LETTER 11.17. Letter to attorney instructing him to prepare the instruments for the administering of an approved loan. Instructions incorporated into letter (block format).

April 30, 19X9

Mr. Walter B. Jingle
Christophers, Brandleigh & Smith
P.O. Box 98
Menwagon, Washington 90569

Subject: Credit Proposal to Mr. Oscar Peters
Lot C, Block W, Upper Plantation

Dear Mr. Jingle:

County Savings Bank has agreed to extend credit to Mr. Oscar Peters under the terms and conditions of our construction loan commitment letter dated April 10, 19X9. A copy of this letter is enclosed for your information.

You are to prepare documents for this loan in accordance with these procedures:

1. Examine the title and prepare a preliminary report.
2. Secure a formal title binder for the amount of our loan commitment giving the bank protection against both matters of survey and mechanics' liens.
3. Upon evidence of ours being a first lien, prepare the necessary documents, examples of which are enclosed for your convenience. Our trustees are Brandon Vielsbum of Niton County and you.
4. After closing, deliver the following to County Savings Bank:
   a. the original deed of trust note
   b. confirmed and certified copy of the deed of trust
   c. signed copy of our truth-in-lending disclosure statement (enclosed)
   d. signed copy of your closing statement
   e. original title binder issued in favor of County Savings Bank
   f. recordation receipt from the Clerk of the Court

After the initial closing, funds will be advanced in accordance with the terms and conditions of our commitment

Sample Letter 11.17 continued

letter and upon delivery by you of written evidence that the title has been cleared to the date of the advance and coverage increased to include the amount of all advances to date. Additionally, please note that at the time of the first advance we will require that a foundation survey be delivered to the bank.

We look forward to working with you in this transaction. If you have any questions, please call.

Yours truly,

James W. Simonds
Vice President

JWS/NLC

enclosures

Loan-related Matters

A follow-up letter to a sales call must be clear, simple, and timely. The client's needs, problems, or questions must be addressed in such a way that any doubt or confusion that might have existed is erased.

Sample letters 11.18 and 11.19 are two good examples of follow-up letters. Sample letter 11.18 addresses the misgivings a customer had about going out of state for banking services. The letter writer addresses these concerns by giving examples of other firms in the customer's state which already use the letter writer's bank's services.

SAMPLE LETTER 11.18. Follow-up letter addressing customer's concerns (full-block format).

April 29, 19X2

Mr. Simon R. Carradine
President & General Manager
Rosner Electric Corporation
65 Warren Place
Plattsburgh, New York 04820

Dear Simon:

Thank you again for allowing me to attend your annual meeting on Tuesday. I spoke with David Saunders the day before the meeting and he expressed the concern that some board members have about going outside the state for financing dollars. We already have a number of companies located in your state using our services. The two that you would probably be most interested in are Binksey Gas, and Glintown and Morton Gas.

New National Bank is committed to your state and is very excited about working with Rosner Electric. My recommendation to David was to split the allowable short-term debt between Binksey Trust and New National, in order to fully use our cash management system. I believe that New National's favorable pricing and cash management system combined with my personal desire to work with Rosner Electric act in your favor as a borrower.

I look forward to your favorable response and to beginning a lasting relationship.

Best regards,

Max Nilges
Loan Officer

mn/mt

Sample letter 11.19 follows-up a sales meeting by commenting on the status of a loan proposal discussed. A positive note in the last paragraph assures the customer of this loan officer's best intentions.

SAMPLE LETTER 11.19. Follow-up letter commenting on status of loan proposal (semiblock format).

June 4, 19X2

Mr. John J. Grimes
Warrentown Gas and Electric Light Company
3 Palladin Drive
Warrentown, New Hampshire 20130

Dear Jack:

Thank you for the time you and Tim Daniels spent with me last Thursday. A lot of exciting things seem to be happening at Warrentown, certainly enough to keep you very busy.

I will be drawing up a proposal for the inventory financing within 10 days. I will call you midweek to set

Sample Letter 11.19 continued

a time when we can sit down and discuss New National's proposal. My district head, Steve Fishbein, expressed an interest in being included in that meeting and would also like to meet Tim.

A quick perusal of your statements reveals a strong company, one that I would enjoy doing business with. I believe that we can put together a package that will be very appealing. I'm looking forward to beginning a mutually beneficial relationship.

Regards,

Max Nilges
Loan Officer

mat

Sample letter 11.20 provides an excellent form letter to use when seeking information for credit analysis. The firm's name in the first paragraph is really the only item in the body of the letter which needs to be changed in order to use this letter when seeking information about any customer. As a result, sample letter 11.20 could easily be stored in a word processor for future use.

SAMPLE LETTER 11.20. Letter seeking information for credit analysis (block format).

November 18, 19X2

Mr. Lawrence D. Braden
Parks, Bryan, Alan & Sims
78 Goshband Drive
Arcade, Maine 67102

Dear Mr. Braden:

Long & Berrigan, Inc. has applied to New National Bank for use of our credit facilities and has given you as a reference. We would appreciate your assistance in serving our mutual client by providing us with information about the following aspects of your dealings:

1. How long have you done business with Long & Berrigan?
2. What has been the largest amount of credit outstanding to Long & Berrigan?

Sample Letter 11.20 continued

3. What have been Long & Berrigan's terms of payment?
4. What is the reputation of the company and its management?
5. Are they currently eligible for credit?
6. For how much credit are they currently eligible?

We would also appreciate any other information you may have that would help us reach a proper decision.

Please be assured that we subscribe to the established code of credit interchange ethics. All information you provide will be kept confidential.

We appreciate your response. We will be glad to reciprocate at any time.

Cordially,

Max Nilges
Loan Officer

mn:lk

Sample letter 11.21 provides information on a customer's loan status. The letter is written as a response to an inquiry. A prompt response by the banker assures the customer her business is being handled well.

SAMPLE LETTER 11.21. Letter providing information on loan status (full-block format).

February 17, 19X2

Ms. Allison Driebac
Headmistress
Micklic Preparatory School
Micklic, Idaho 98021

Dear Ms. Driebac:

In response to your letter of February 10, 19X2, we are advising you of the status of your loan. The outstanding principal balance is $9,000, with interest payable quarterly at 1% over Prime. Interest has been paid up to November 1, 19X1. The total amount of interest paid in 19X1 is $3,499.55.

Sample Letter 11.21 continued

The principal amount was originally $45,000. The $9,000 remaining balance is due November 19X2, in accordance with the terms of our agreement.

I trust this information is what you need. If I can be of further assistance, please call me.
Very truly yours,

Max Nilges
Loan Officer

mn/op

Sample letters 11.22-11.26 are requests made to customers so the loan officer can be kept up-to-date on the status of the loan. Sample letter 11.22 requests that an enclosed form be completed and an agreement signed.

SAMPLE LETTER 11.22. Request for forms to be signed (semiblock format).

September 21, 19X2

Harold R. Snikport
8 Usetis Street, Apt. 8
Richmond, Virginia 41123

Dear Harry:

In connection with the $30,000 unsecured loan and the side collateral you sent, please sign the following:

1. Form A which tells us what you are doing
2. The pledge agreement which is self-explanatory
3. The three stock powers relating to the three certificates

As we have discussed, I would be delighted to talk with you about the status of your collateral any time.

Best regards,

Max Nilges
Loan Officer

mn/jb

enclosures

Sample letters 11.23-11.26 request various financial statements affecting the customer. Sample letter 11.23 reminds a customer that a current statement is needed from him.

SAMPLE LETTER 11.23. Reminder that a current statement is needed (semiblock format).

April 22, 19X1

Mr. John Klugerman
P.O. Box 908
Toano, Massachusetts 25620

Dear Jack:

In connection with your present obligation to this bank, a review of our files shows we have not received a current statement from you which was previously requested by Loan Officer Max Nilges. Please complete the enclosed form and return it as soon as possible.

Your cooperation is greatly appreciated.

Regards,

Hamilton L. Coronet
Vice President

hlc:jls

enc.

Sample letter 11.24 points out that an interim statement is missing from a pack of financials the customer recently sent the bank.

SAMPLE LETTER 11.24. Notice that interim statement is missing from package of financials received at bank (block format).

November 20, 19X1

Mr. Joseph Y. Smith
45 Archie Way
Elizabeth, Pennsylvania 11234

Dear Joe:

I recently received the package of financials that you sent to me. The five years of annual reports that I requested are all in order. I am going to need interim statements, however, to complete my analysis. The interims need not be audited; management prepared statements will suffice.

I don't expect any trouble in completing my analysis very shortly after I've received the interims. Thank you for your help in this matter.

Best regards,

Max Nilges
Loan Officer

mn:ll

Sample letter 11.25 requests that the customer complete and return an enclosed statement.

SAMPLE LETTER 11.25. Request for completion and return of a statement (full-block format).

April 2, 19X2

Mr. Rodney S. McDonnell
11 Twilight Drive
South Zone, Massachusetts 63910

Dear Rod:

Please complete the attached Personal Financial Statement and return it to me in the envelope provided. Once I have received this form, we can begin consideration of your loan.

Thank you for your cooperation.

Sample Letter 11.25 continued

Best wishes,

Max Nilges
Loan Officer

llk

Enclosure

Sample letter 11.26 is a request to a customer's landlord for her to fill out a required waiver form.

SAMPLE LETTER 11.26. Request to customer's landlord to fill out waiver form (semiblock format).

December 1, 19X1

Ms. Ellen P. Thrall
908 Visitation Drive
Hawthorne, Massachusetts 09087

Subject: Roland Smedson, Smedson's Coffee Shop

Dear Ms. Thrall:

We have recently advanced funds to Mr. Smedson for the purpose of purchasing additional equipment for his business located on property owned by you. In order for us to perfect our lien, could you sign the enclosed Landlord's Waiver and return it to us as soon as possible. A self-addressed envelope is enclosed for your convenience.

If you have any questions about this loan, please call me.

Sincerely,

Simon L. Thorn
Assistant Vice President

bcm

enclosures

cc: Mr. Roland Smedson

Sample letter 11.27 is a thank you note to a customer who has completed some forms. Such a letter improves the likelihood that the customer's cooperation in supplying material will continue in the future.

SAMPLE LETTER 11.27. Thank you letter to customer who has completed forms (semiblock format).

October 8, 19X2

Ms. Rowena O. Temmurz
Director of Finance
Fernald Woolton & Co.
Jancoken Building, Suite 39
Hinsdale, Oregon 10606

Dear Rowena:

Thank you for filling out and returning the signing and borrowing authorities which we recently sent you. We at New National would be delighted to have you activate the $1 million line at your earliest convenience.

I look forward to hearing from you.

Kindest regards,

Max Nilges
Loan Officer

llg

Sample letter 11.28 is a letter to a customer concerning the terms of repayment of a demand note. A new agreement has been made with the customer. The first paragraph explains what the letter is. The remainder of the letter clearly details the terms of repayment.

SAMPLE LETTER 11.28. Letter to customer about terms of repayment of demand note (full-block format).

February 2, 19X2

Mr. J. Harrison Frit
27 Remont Street
Notwent Township, New Jersey 99591

Dear Harry:

This letter will confirm our understanding about the repayment of the $7,500 loan evidenced by a demand note dated January 28, 19X2.

We understand it is your intention to make three annual reductions of this note no later than February 1, 19X3 through February 1, 19X5 from your annual partnership distribution. This is an acceptable arrangement to New National Bank. Notwithstanding New National's willingness to accept such a repayment schedule, it is understood that the note remains a demand obligation, and all other conditions pertaining to our original proposal remain unchanged.

It is acceptable for $5000 of the proceeds of this note to be used for an additional capital contribution to the firm of Long & Berrigan. The terms of your letter to us dated June 7, 19X9, and accepted by Long & Berrigan, however, are still in effect. Please indicate your concurrence by signing the enclosed copy of this letter and returning it to me.

Best wishes,

Max Nilges
Loan Officer

enclosure

Acknowledged and Accepted:

____
Signature Date

Sample letter 11.29 is written to a customer verifying the amount of and purpose for a loan issued.

SAMPLE LETTER 11.29. Letter to customer verifying amount and purpose of loan (full-block format).

November 30, 19X1

Mr. Myron B. Simonson
County Siltation Department
P.O. Box 89
Alterton, Florida 18191

SUBJECT: CASE #SP-19-25, MT. LARIAT LAND TRUST

Dear Mr. Simonson:

County Savings Bank will honor your request for payment to a maximum of $1700 in connection with the Siltation Agreement for Case #SP-19-25. This letter will remain in effect until revoked by you.

If you have any questions concerning this agreement, please call me.

Yours truly,

Simon L. Thorn
Assistant Vice President

slt/bcm

Collection Letters

Sample letters 11.30-11.32 are three examples of well-written collection letters to a corporate customer. Sample letter 11.30 is an example of a second notice sent to a customer notifying him of past due payment. The letter explains exactly what the customer must do to protect his credit and avoid additional charges.

SAMPLE LETTER 11.30. Second notice of past due payment (full-block format).

March 26, 19X3

Mr. Edward C. Franks
Solar Energy, Inc.
908 Wheat Avenue
Roanoke, Wisconsin 75968

Subject: Account Number: 432-4400-0005-61
Amount of Past Due Payment: $121.23 for
March 5, 19X2
Other Charges Accrued: $6.06
Collateral: 19X9 Toyota Truck

Dear Mr. Franks:

We previously sent you a notice of your past due payment. This payment has not been received nor have you contacted us to explain why it was not forwarded.

We are certain that you would like to protect your credit and avoid additional charges. You can do so by forwarding us the past due amount and charges upon receipt of this letter, and by mailing your remaining payments on time. Payments more than seven days past due are subject to a late charge of 5%.

If for any reason you are unable to forward us the past due amount and charges upon receipt of this letter, please call me.

Sincerely,

NEW NATIONAL BANK

Gene R. Louise
Collection Officer

mat

Sample letter 11.31 is an example of a notice that effectively combines a call for payment with an understanding of the customer's situation. By placing a deadline for getting in touch with the bank, the letter writer lets the customer know his understanding will go just so far before he is forced to take possession of the collateral put up for the loan.

SAMPLE LETTER 11.31. Letter to customer with three past due payments on loan for working capital (full-block format).

July 14, 19X4

Mr. Edward James, President
Vandickledyke Enterprises, Inc.
One South Street
Albertsville, New York 23001

Dear Mr. James:

Your $50,000 loan for working capital has three payments that are past due. They total $6,259.80, including accrued interest and late charges. I have attempted to phone you on several occasions and have left word with your secretary to no avail.

Through our years of experience in dealing with commercial customers and our willingness to work with those in difficulty, we both can and do solve problems for our customers. Will you call me before Wednesday to arrange a visit?

You will benefit from visiting with us in two ways. First, we will work with you through any difficulty you may be having. Second, should we not hear from you we must take possession of the collateral and pay the debt with its liquidation.

I look forward to hearing from you before Wednesday.

Sincerely,

Max Nilges
Vice President

mn/lk

Sample letter 11.32 is an acceleration of debt letter written to a corporate customer. Such letters are usually written either after payments on a loan are long overdue or, as in the case of sample letter 11.37 when circumstances arise that make the bank realize they are no longer in a secure position regarding the loan.

SAMPLE LETTER 11.32. Acceleration of debt letter (semiblock format).

January 7, 19X2

Mr. Lawrence E. Vorloffson
Levinson Equipment Company
1123 West Main Street
Leighton, New Jersey 25981

Dear Mr. Vorloffson:

You have a promissory note to New National Bank for $48,000 which has a maturity date of February 25, 19X2. We are notifying you that we have deemed ourselves insecure under the terms of the note and security agreement. The reason for this action is that the Internal Revenue Service has filed against you a federal tax lien for $36,820, and the Martinson Equipment Company has obtained a judgment of $14,462 against you.

New National Bank is therefore accelerating the maturity of your loan from February 25, 19X2, to January 18, 19X2. Demand is made for payment in full of all principal and interest due on your loan no later than January 18, 19X2.

Please call me as soon as possible about the acceleration of your loan.

Cordially,

Max Nilges
Vice President

MN:PY

Collateral-related Letters

Sample letter 11.33 is sent to a customer whose collateral file is incomplete. This is a form letter in which the writer checks off those items missing from the customer's collateral file. Because it is a form letter, it could easily be stored in a word processor to be called up whenever it was needed.

SAMPLE LETTER 11.33. Form letter sent to customer whose collateral file is incomplete (simplified format).

November 20, 19X4

Mr. Paul Vanice
90 Pauline Drive
Oskosh, Washington 12332

SUBJECT: COLLATERAL FILE, LOAN #14-708-9049

A review of our collateral files indicates that the items checked below are required to complete our files:

Item	Required Action
_____Title	If you have the title, please forward it to us immediately. If you do not, please advise us.
_____Evidence of collision and comprehensive insurance showing County Savings Bank as loss payee.	If you do have insurance, please request your agent to send evidence of coverage to us. If insurance is not held, you have ten days from the date of this letter to comply with this request.

We would appreciate your cooperation in completing your collateral file.

John Savithson
Vice President

lak

Sample letter 11.34 notifies a customer that his vehicle was repossessed because of a default in payments on a loan. He is instructed that his truck will be sold and that any amount still due on the loan will be owed to the bank.

SAMPLE LETTER 11.34. Notice to customer of sale after repossession (block format).

February 26, 19X2

Ms. Zoe Jeffries
Laramy Equipment Company
34 Main Street
Apriori, Utah 38928

Subject: 19X0 Ford F-200 truck
Loan #389-286-03

Dear Ms. Jeffries:

Because of your default in payments on account number 389-286-03, your 19X0 Ford F-200 truck, in which New National Bank has a perfected security interest, was repossessed January 17, 19X2. In accordance with the procedures required by the State Motor Vehicle Act, a repossession certificate of title has been obtained from the Secretary of State for the vehicle.

Following the requirements of the Uniform Commercial Code, we are notifying you that the vehicle will be sold at a private sale on March 7, 19X2 at two o'clock at the main office of New National Bank at 102 University Avenue in Postpriori, Utah.

You remain liable to New National for any amounts still due on Account #389-286-03 after the proceeds of the sale have been applied toward the account. You will be notified of any deficiency due to New National.

Cordially,

NEW NATIONAL BANK

Max Nilges
Vice President

klh

Sample letter 11.35 is a follow-up letter to sample letter 11.34 which notifies the customer of the deficiency on his loan after the repossession and sale of his truck. The letter writer instructs him of the steps he must take to pay the amount still owed to the bank.

SAMPLE LETTER 11.35. Notification to customer of deficiency after repossession sale (full-block format).

March 10, 19X2

Ms. Zoe Jeffries
Laramy Equipment Company
34 Main Street
Apriori, Utah 38928

SUBJECT: 19X0 Ford F-200 truck
Loan #389-286-03

Dear Ms. Jeffries:

As indicated in my letter of February 26, 19X2, your 19X0 Ford truck was sold at a private sale conducted at New National's main office at 102 University Avenue in Postpriori, Utah on March 7, 19X2, at two o'clock.

The results of the sale were as follows:

Price received from truck, being the highest amount bid	$3980.00
Less expenses of sale	–$ 84.40
Net receipts from sale	$3895.60
Amount due on Account #389-286-03	$4440.19
Less net receipts from sale	–$3895.60
Amount of deficiency	$ 544.59

Please contact New National Bank by March 20, 19X2, to make arrangements to pay the deficiency shown. If we do not hear from you by that date, we will initiate appropriate legal action to collect the deficiency.

Sincerely,

Max Nilges
Vice President

klh

Sample letters 11.36-11.38 were written to agents who will assist or have already assisted in the repossession of the customer's collateral. The writer of sample letter 11.36 authorizes an officer of another bank to act as an agent in repossessing a customer's truck. The letter details the terms of the loan and the default.

SAMPLE LETTER 11.36. Letter of authorization to officer of another bank who will act as agent in collection of collateral (block format).

March 5, 19X9

Mr. Franklin Thomson
Old National Bank
P.O. Box 19790
Akron, California 20933

Subject: Richard L. Dykson
502 Alabaster Drive
Akron, California 20933

Dear Mr. Thomson:

Enclosed is our letter of authorization granting you the power to act as our agent in repossessing Mr. Dykson's collateral, a copy of the original contract signed by Mr. Dykson, a copy of the security agreement signed by Mr. Dykson, and a copy of the state title with security interest recorded.

Mr. Dykson's loan is in default from January 21, 19X9. In order for Mr. Dykson to retain possession of his vehicle, it will be necessary for you to collect $9,221.93 plus any collection expenses which may be incurred. This payoff will be good until April 7, 19X9.

Collection expenses of $75 are authorized for any expenses your institution incurs. Expenses exceeding the $75 will require my verbal approval.

If you have any further questions, please call me.

Your assistance is greatly appreciated.

Sincerely,

John Savithson
Assistant Vice President

js/mt

encls.

Sample letter 11.37 instructs a collection agency, acting as the bank's agent, what vehicle should be repossessed and what should be done with the vehicle once it has been repossessed.

SAMPLE LETTER 11.37. Letter of authorization to collection agency to act as agent in collecting collateral (simplified format).

October 31, 19X0

Mr. Alan D. Simpson
Aardon Collection Agency
1790 Sevenson Avenue
Biloxi, New Jersey 66629

REPOSSESSION OF COLLATERAL

This letter authorizes you to act as our agent in taking possession of a 19X9 Jeep Wagoner, ID #9251A9J29444, registered to Barklin T. Farkknand Architects. You are authorized to transport the vehicle from Biloxi, New Jersey, to our offices in Boonton, Pennsylvania.

If you need further information, please call me.

John Savithson
Assistant Vice President

oiu

The letter writer of sample letter 11.38 thanks a bank for their assistance in repossession and informs them that it will no longer be necessary because the loan has been paid in full.

SAMPLE LETTER 11.38. Letter of thanks to bank which assisted in repossession (full-block format).

February 26, 19X0

Mr. Ambrose Kemper
Old National Bank
299 Morrissey Boulevard
Encino, Arkansas 10309

Dear Ambrose:

As I indicated in our conversation today, Mr. Robert Z. Kiztul of Bonbon, Arkansas paid his installment loan off in full by selling his Motor Home to Manchester Car Sales, Inc. As a result, your voluntary repossession assistance will no longer be required.

New National Bank and I appreciate your assistance. If I or New National can return the favor, please call us.

Sample Letter 11.38 continued

```
Sincerely,


Max Nilges
Vice President

mn/dd
```

Corporate Loan Memos

Memorandum 11.39 is a letter to the credit file of a corporate customer written as a follow-up to a sales meeting. The customer's company and needs are described, as are the steps the loan officer believes should be taken to attract this customer's business.

MEMORANDUM 11.39. Memorandum to credit file following-up sales meeting.

```
TO: Credit file
FROM: Max Nilges, Loan Officer
DATE: June 1, 19X2
SUBJECT: Meeting with DMI, Inc.

I spoke with David McDonnell today. He outlined for me
DMI's new facility with Old National Bank. The facility
consists of a $4 1/2 MM line priced at prime with 5% plus
5% balances. This replaces the revolving credit line fa-
cility that expired this past May. I explained to David
that their facility gives them much less flexibility than
the $2MM line that I proposed.

I think I must concentrate more on getting to see
McDonnell's boss, Tim Smith. David seems to be a good yes
man, but the decisions are obviously made above him.


mat
```

Memorandum 11.40 is a memo written to recommend the approval of a loan request. The details of the request are simply laid out so that the recipient of the memo can understand without an unnecessarily large amount of deciphering.

MEMORANDUM 11.40. Memorandum recommending approval of loan.

TO: Commercial Accounts Loan Committee
FROM: Max Nilges, Vice President
DATE: July 23, 19X2
SUBJECT: John Wagner & Associates

On June 23, 19X2, the attached loan request was submitted to the Commercial Accounts Loan Committee for approval for $200,000. The request, as submitted, represented two changes in the way the account had been handled historically. First, the line amount was increased from $100M to $200M. Second, the rate was changed to prime from prime plus 3/4. The approval was also contingent upon the receipt of the personal financial statement of Mr. John Wagner, one of the company's principals.

A commitment letter was forwarded to the firm on June 29, 19X2, and returned to the bank agreeing to the terms of the letter. Subsequently, a request was made of the bank by the principals to release their personal guarantees on the credit.

The balance sheet of the firm does not justify an unsecured line of $200M as can be seen on the latest statement received. The firm has been a longstanding customer of New National Bank, however, with no adverse history.

As a compromise to their request, we have offered to approve credit on an unsecured basis for $150,000 with no personal endorsement priced at prime. The company principals are agreeable to this approach and ask that we forward them a commitment letter.
According to the principals of the company, the firm is billing its clients at an all-time high, and earnings in the company should improve significantly this year.

I recommend approval of this request.

mn/jb

encl.

Memorandum 11.41 was written as a follow-up to a business meeting. The memo writer briefly describes the meeting and the problem he sees in continuing to attract the customer's business. This memo is written to an associate at the bank.

MEMORANDUM 11.41. Memorandum written as follow-up to business meeting.

TO: Preston L. Rettaus, Senior Vice President
FROM: Max Nilges, Vice President
DATE: November 9, 19X1
SUBJECT: General Hospital Account Relationship

General Hospital has recently informed us that they are doing a reassessment of their banking needs and intend to shop the area banks to identify competitive service features and costs. This seems to be an outgrowth of new management, plus competitive calling pressure from other banks offering on-site banking ATM's and purportedly superior cash management products.

General Hospital recognizes that the service they continue to get is prompt, courteous, and accurate. Moreover, they recognize that New National supported the institution in years past when its financial condition was much less healthy than it is today. As a result, we are told that we will be given the final crack at their financing package after other banks have given it their best shot.

Attached is an outline of our present relationship to General Hospital and their request for proposal.

mn/ts

enc.

Consumer Loans 12

Loan officers entertain the challenging task of attracting business to their bank, while at the same time making sure the prospective customer is a good credit risk. The tact and skill necessary to write effective credit and loan letters are talents that become stronger as the loan officer gathers experience in the field. Throughout the loan process—from the original customer inquiry to the first sales call to the loan proposal—skillful letter writing is essential for the maintenance of sound banking relationships. The letters in Chapter 12 focus on consumer loans.

Approving and Granting Loans

Sample letters 12.1-12.6 relate to the approval and granting of loans. Sample letter 12.1 is an approval of a demand line of credit. The conditions and terms are clearly defined in the numbered list in the letter.

SAMPLE LETTER 12.1. Approval of a demand line of credit (full-block format).

April 17, 19X1

Dr. and Mrs. Anthony Flywheel
876 Florrine Road
Skater, Florida 30992

Dear Dr. and Mrs. Flywheel:

We are pleased to advise you that your application for a demand line of credit for $50,000 to establish your medical practice in Hackensack, Georgia has been approved subject to the following terms and conditions:

1. Funds will be advanced for capital expenditures upon presentation of invoices (approximately $20,000).
2. Monthly operating expenses, to a maximum of $5,000 a month, may be drawn on or about the first of each month for a period of six months beginning May 1, 19X1.
3. Interest on the loan will accrue at a rate of 12% a year with the requirement of quarterly interest payments only (based on calendar quarter).
4. Security will consist of a blanket security interest in the assets of your practice and your personal endorsements.
5. It is agreed that on or about May 1, 19X2, the note will be renegotiated establishing a payout arrangement that will be mutually acceptable to both you and County Savings Bank.

As evidence of your acceptance, please sign and return to us the original of this letter on or before May 1, 19X1. If your acceptance is not received by the above date, the bank may cancel this commitment.

Very truly yours,

Warren G. Maynard
Assistant Vice President

wgm/apv

Enclosure

Accepted:

Sample Letter 12.1 continued

____
Date

________________________ ________________________
Signature Signature

Sample letters 12.2 and 12.3 are examples of approvals of a customer's financing. Both letters use numbered lists to clarify the conditions and terms. Sample letter 12.3 shows that no matter how many points are included in the proposal, it can be kept clear by good organization and clarity of thought.

SAMPLE LETTER 12.2 Approval of financing (semiblock format).

October 14, 19X1

Dr. Wilma Barney
765 Spanky Drive
Alfafa, Idaho 11280

Dear Dr. Barney:

I am pleased to advise you that your application for a term loan for $18,000 to relocate your dental practice to the Buckling Professional Building has been approved subject to the following terms and conditions:

1. Funds will be advanced in a lump sum directly to you.
2. Rate on the term loan will be at prime with the requirement of interest and $18,000 principal curtailments payable quarterly beginning with the fourth quarter of 19X1.
3. Security on the line will consist of your personal guaranty.
4. Term of line will be for two-and-one-half years with expected payout in the first quarter 19X4.

As evidence of your acceptance, please sign and return to us the enclosed copy of this letter no later than October 30, 19X1. If your acceptance is not received by this date, this commitment may be terminated and considered null and void.

County Savings Bank is pleased to be of assistance to you in relocating your dental practice. We look forward to continuing to service your total banking needs.

Sample Letter 12.2 continued

Sincerely,

Warren G. Maynard
Assistant Vice President

apv

Enclosure

Accepted:

____
Date

______________________ ______________________
Signature Signature

SAMPLE LETTER 12.3. Approval of financing (full-block format).

March 24, 19X2

Richard C. Hamill
County Builders, Inc.
98 Albatross Lane
Petersburg, Arkansas 55123

Dear Rick:

We are pleased to inform you that your application for construction financing for $50,000 to build a single family dwelling at Lot 9-T, Section 8, Hawkins Trace, Bazonka County, Arkansas, has been approved subject to the following terms and conditions.

1. The construction loan commitment of $50,000 will be advanced on a percentage of completion basis. Although we will conduct inspection prior to each draw request, we will assume no responsibility for workmanship or quality of materials used.
2. Interest on the loan will accrue at a rate of prime plus 1% per annum. In addition, there will be a commitment upon your acceptance of the terms and conditions of this letter.
3. The requirement that you establish a passbook savings account in the minimum amount of 25% of the loan commitment. The account may be used to pay monthly interest payments during the term of the note.

Sample Letter 12.3 continued

4. Delivery of written evidence that adequate Builders Risk Insurance or hazard insurance to include fire and extended coverage in the minimum amount of $50,000 issued to cover construction and endorsed to reflect County Savings Bank.
5. Title insurance to include coverage against both matters of survey and mechanic liens issued in favor of the bank by an acceptable title insurance company.
6. The requirement of at least three working days' notice prior to each draw.
7. Your personal guaranty.
8. All expenses in connection with this loan will be paid by you.

As evidence of your acceptance, please sign and return to us the enclosed copy of this letter on or before April 9, 19X2. You should also remit your check for $500. If you wish, we will deduct this amount from your first draw. If your acceptance is not received by the above date, the bank may at its option cancel the commitment.

Moreover, should you accept our commitment, it will be valid only until October 1, 19X2.

Yours truly,

John Savithson
Vice President

js/nc

enc.

Accepted by:

__________________________ ________________
Richard C. Hamill Date

Two examples of loans for contributions to partnerships are shown in sample letters 12.4 and 12.5. Although two different formats are used for the letters, they both clearly detail the loan. Sample letter 12.4 would lend itself particularly well for use as a form letter that could be stored in a word processor and called up when such a loan was to be granted. The names of the customer and the firm could be changed, and new figures could be plugged in to the appropriate spots.

SAMPLE LETTER 12.4. Approval of loan for contribution to partnership (block format).

June 2, 19X2

Mr. Melvin W. Howard
Long & Berrigan
200 Andover Street
Bar Harbor, Michigan 67892

Dear Melvin:

This letter confirms our understanding about the $25,000 loan New National Bank has made to you, the proceeds of which are for your required capital contribution to the firm of Long & Berrigan. The following are the terms of this loan:

Principal Amount:	$25,000
Principal Reduction:	$5,000 payable in five annual installments beginning January 15, 19X3
Interest Rate:	Prime plus 1%
Interest Payable:	Monthly

The interest rate will change simultaneously with any change in the prime rate at New National. The principal may be prepaid in part or in whole on any interest date without penalty.

The entire balance of the note will become due and payable immediately, at the option of the holder, without notice or demand, upon the occurrence of any of the following events:

a. Failure to pay an installment of principal or of interest on the loan when due.
b. Death or insolvency of the maker.
c. Termination, for any reason, of partnership in the firm of Long & Berrigan.

Any deposits or other sums at any time credited by or due from the holder to the maker, and any securities or other property of the maker at any time in the possession of the holder may at all times be held and treated as collateral for payment of this note and any and all other liabilities of the maker to the holder. The holder may apply or set-off such deposits or other sums against such liabilities or obligations of this note.

Sample Letter 12.4 continued

The maker also agrees to pay on demand all costs and expenses (including reasonable attorney fees) paid by the holder in enforcing this note on default.

Please sign the enclosed copy of this letter indicating your acceptance of the terms outlined in this letter of understanding.

Sincerely,

Max Nilges
Vice President

mn/lg

enclosure

Agreed and accepted:

____________________ ____________________
Signature Date

SAMPLE LETTER 12.5. Approval of loan for contribution to partnership (full-block format).

December 11, 19X1

Mr. Elliot T. Dreyfus
Robertson & Maxwell
One Franklin Plaza, Suite 34
Lewiston, Massachusetts 90876

Dear Elliot:

We have reviewed your personal financial statement dated October 30, 19X1. Based upon our review and barring unforeseen changes in your financial affairs, we have approved in principal your loan request for a maximum of $13,000 for the purpose of funding your partnership capital contribution at Robertson & Maxwell.

This loan will bear interest payable quarterly in arrears at our prime rate plus 1%. Principal will be repayable in five equal annual installments beginning June 1, 19X3.

At the time of takedown in April 19X2, there will be execution of a note evidencing this loan and a letter of understanding between the bank, you, and Robertson &

Sample Letter 12.5 continued

Maxwell. The note will be similar in form to the example I previously sent you.

Congratulations on your election to partnership. We at New National wish you the very best and, as your bankers, ask that you feel free to call on us at any time you need professional advice.

Very truly yours,

Max Nilges
Loan Officer

jdg

Sample letter 12.6 is an example of an approval of an unsecured loan. The letter states directly in the first paragraph the nature of the loan. The second paragraph details any conditions. The remainder of the letter clears up some minor details, and closes on an encouraging note.

For an example of a loan approval which uses a several-page list of possible terms and conditions which the letter writer can check off if appropriate, see sample letter 11.12.

SAMPLE LETTER 12.6. Approval for unsecured loan (full-block format).

January 20, 19X2

Mr. Kyle L. Crystal
234 Highton Road
Highlands, Louisiana 16130

Dear Kyle:

This letter confirms our understanding about the $25,000 unsecured loan made on January 19, 19X2 to you and Mrs. Crystal as evidenced by a demand note of that date.

You have agreed that upon the closing of the sale of your property at 234 Highton Road, Highlands, Louisiana, a minimum of $15,000 of the proceeds will be applied to principal repayment of this loan. The balance will be repaid upon receipt of your annual partnership distribution from Wisenthal & Horowitz. In any case, final repayment will be made no later than June 30, 19X2.

In accordance with your request, the proceeds of the loan have been deposited in your account #9646-319-8.

Sample Letter 12.6 continued

I trust this correctly states our arrangement. If so, would you and Mrs. Crystal please sign the enclosed copy of this letter and return it to me.

Best regards,

Max Nilges
Loan Officer

mn/jl

enclosure

Acknowledged and agreed:

____
Kyle L. Crystal

______________________________ ______________________
Marian Z. Crystal Date

Sample letters 12.7 and 12.8 are two examples of letters to attorneys instructing them to prepare instruments for the administering of an approved loan. Sample letter 12.8 is a brief cover letter attached to a list of detailed instructions.

SAMPLE LETTER 12.7. Letter to attorney instructing him to prepare the instruments for the administering of an approved loan. Instructions attached on separate sheet (semiblock format).

November 9, 19X1

Mr. Brett Kanapaux
90 Quincy Avenue
Cooperton, Illinois 06832

Dear Mr. Kanapaux:

Subject: Loan to Andrea Banks

County Savings Bank has agreed to extend a real estate loan to Ms. Andrea Banks. Please contact the borrower who will be receiving our commitment at the same time you receive this letter. The acceptance of our commitment is required for the granting of this loan.

Please prepare and deliver the instruments necessary for the consummation of our loan in accordance with

Sample Letter 12.7 continued

the attached instructions. It is advisable that copies of the proposed documents be presented to us before closing so that any corrections can be made.

If you have any questions, please call me.

Sincerely,

Teresa Marcello
Vice President

tm:nc

encs.

Sample letter 12.8 details the instructions within the letter itself.

SAMPLE LETTER 12.8. Letter to attorney instructing him to prepare the instruments for the administering of an approved loan. Instructions incorporated into letter (block format).

April 30, 19X9

Mr. Andrew Westura
Christophers, Brandleigh & Smith
P.O. Box 98
Menwagon, Washington 90569

Subject: Credit Proposal to Mr. Oscar Peters
Lot C, Block W, Upper Plantation

Dear Mr. Westura:

County Savings Bank has agreed to extend credit to Mr. Oscar Peters under the terms and conditions of our construction loan commitment letter dated April 10, 19X9. A copy of this letter is enclosed for your information.

You are to prepare documents for this loan in accordance with these procedures:

1. Examine the title and prepare a preliminary report.
2. Secure a formal title binder in the amount of our loan commitment affording the bank protec-

Sample Letter 12.8 continued

tion against both matters of survey and mechanics' liens.

3. Upon evidence of ours being a first lien, prepare the necessary documents, examples of which are enclosed for your convenience. Our trustees are Brandon Vielsbum of Niton County and you.
4. After closing, deliver the following to County Savings Bank:
   a. the original deed of trust note
   b. confirmed and certified copy of the deed of trust
   c. signed copy of our truth-in-lending disclosure statement (enclosed)
   d. signed copy of our closing statement
   e. original title binder issued in favor of County Savings Bank
   f. recordation receipt from the Clerk of the Court

After the initial closing, funds will be advanced in accordance with the terms and conditions of our commitment letter and upon delivery by you of written evidence that the title has been cleared to the date of the advance and coverage increased to include the amount of all advances to date.

Additionally, please note that at the time of the first advance we will require that a foundation survey be delivered to the bank.

We look forward to working with you in this transaction. If you have any questions, please call.

Yours truly,

James W. Simonds
Vice President

JWS/NLC

enclosures

Loan-related Matters

Sample letter 12.9 features a letter explaining the details of a special type of consumer loan the customer has taken from the bank. The letter describes all of the details of the offer, highlighting the benefits of the plan.

SAMPLE LETTER 12.9. Letter explaining the details of special type of consumer loan (simplified format).

November 20, 19X2

Ms. Diane Eisenhower
44 Titonman Place
Liberty Corner, Vermont 56852

YOUR CONSUMER INTEREST LOAN

Thank you for the opportunity to meet your borrowing needs with our Consumer Interest Loan. We have tried to design this loan with you, the customer, in mind.

What is different about the Consumer Interest Loan? It is based on simple interest which can save you money.

The monthly payments can be made on any day of the month you have selected. All amounts paid in excess of the regular monthly payment will reduce the interest and produce a larger reduction of principal, on which future interest is computed.

You will be paying interest for only the exact number of days that the money is outstanding. There are no late charges. There is never an interest refund question, should you wish to pay off the loan before maturity. You will receive a monthly statement which shows the date and distribution of the previous payment to principal and interest plus your new balance.

You can skip a payment by using the enclosed Payment Holiday Coupons. Under this plan you may, if you wish, prior to any monthly payment due date, defer one monthly payment for each period during which five consecutive previous installments have been punctually made. You merely sign and date the Payment Holiday Coupon and mail it to the New National Bank.

You can make payments in any amount at any time over and above the regular payments by using the Optional Payment Coupons which are also enclosed. All such posted amounts will be reflected on your next monthly statement.

Sample Letter 12.9 continued

If you have any questions about Payment Holiday Coupons, Optional Payment Coupons, or any other feature of the Consumer Interest Loan, please call or write me.

Max Nilges
Loan Officer

mst

encls. (2)

Sample letter 12.10 is a follow-up to sample letter 12.9, written after the customer has taken advantage of one of the options of her special consumer interest loan. The two letters are written in a clear, direct style. Making the terms understandable and appealing to a customer helps to enhance a good working relationship.

SAMPLE LETTER 12.10. Follow-up to holder of special consumer interest loan after option has been taken (simplified format).

July 28, 19X3

Ms. Diane Eisenhower
44 Titoman Place
Liberty Corner, Vermont 56852

CONSUMER INTEREST LOAN #51052005

Ms. Eisenhower, New National Bank appreciates the opportunity to serve your needs. Your Payment Holiday Coupon has been processed and your next payment is now due on or before August 19X3.

There are no added charges or penalties for using a Payment Holiday Coupon. Interest does continue to accrue during this period on the remaining balance.

If you have any questions about the Payment Holiday Coupon option or any other feature of your Consumer Interest Loan, please call or write me.

NEW NATIONAL BANK

Max Nilges
Loan Officer

mst

Sample letter 12.11 is a brief letter written to respond to a customer's inquiry about the status of her loan. The letter writer's prompt response with the information requested exhibits his conscientious effort to be of service to his customer.

SAMPLE LETTER 12.11. Letter providing information on loan status (full-block format).

February 17, 19X2

Ms. Melissa Kanapaux
Headmistress
Micklic Preparatory School
Micklic, Idaho 98021

Dear Ms. Kanapaux:

In response to your letter of February 10, 19X2, we are advising you of the status of your loan. The outstanding principal balance is $9,000, with interest payable quarterly at 1% over Large Business Prime. Interest has been paid up to November 1, 19X1. The total amount of interest paid in 19X1 is $3,499.55.

The principal amount was originally $45,000. The $9,000 remaining balance is due November 19X2, in accordance with the terms of our agreement.

I trust this information is what you need. If I can be of further assistance, please call me.

Very truly yours,

Max Nilges
Loan Officer

mn/op

Sample letter 12.12 is a letter written to inform a customer about the status of his student loan.

SAMPLE LETTER 12.12. Notice of status of student loan after sale of loan (full-block format).

September 14, 19X1

Mr. Tony D. Coleman
56 Richardson Avenue
Bethany, Massachusetts 23343

Dear Mr. Coleman:

New National Bank is proud of the support we have been able to give to higher education through our participation in the Stafford Loan program. Our continued participation is enhanced by using the services of The New England Education Loan Marketing Corporation (Nellie Mae), the regional secondary market that purchases education loans.

We recently sold a number of student loans, including yours, to Nellie Mae to provide more funds to make more student loans. Your loan has been transferred from College Loan Service (CLS) to Nellie Mae's servicer, Education Loan Services, Inc. (ELSI). The sale of your loan to Nellie Mae does not change your responsibilities in any way except that you are now obligated to repay your loan to Nellie Mae.

A statement of your account is enclosed. If you made a payment and you still receive a computer-generated delinquency notice, please accept our apologies and ignore this notice. Your account balance will be corrected in the next two weeks, of course, with no notice of delinquency record.

If your next payment is due before you receive your new coupon book from Nellie Mae, simply place your social security number on the front of your check and forward it to the address below. It is important to maintain an uninterrupted schedule of payments to avoid subsequent delinquency notices.

All payments on your loan should be made payable to Nellie Mae and mailed to them care of ELSI, P.O. Box 95, Bethany, Massachusetts 23343.

If you have any questions about your loan, please contact ELSI at 800-RATESUP.

New National appreciates the opportunity to help you finance your higher education. If you are in need of fur-

Sample Letter 12.12 continued

ther student loans or other banking services, we would be pleased to discuss it with you.

Sincerely,

Max Nilges
Vice President

Enclosure

Sample letters 12.13-12.15 are examples of requests made to customers so the letter writer can keep up-to-date on the loan. Sample letter 12.13 is a request for an enclosed form and agreement to be signed.

Sample letters 12.14 and 12.15 request various financial statements concerning the customer. Sample letter 12.14 reminds the customer that he had already been asked for a current statement. Sample letter 12.15 asks the customer to complete and return an enclosed statement.

SAMPLE LETTER 12.13. Request for forms to be signed (semiblock format).

September 21, 19X2

Harold R. Snikport
8 Usetis Street, Apt. 8
Richmond, Virginia 41123

Dear Harry:

In connection with the $30,000 unsecured loan and the side collateral you sent, please sign the following:

1. Form A which tells us what you are doing
2. The pledge agreement which is self-explanatory
3. The three stock powers relating to the three certificates

As we have discussed, I would be delighted to talk with you about the status of your collateral any time.

Best regards,

Max Nilges
Loan Officer

mn/jb

enclosures

SAMPLE LETTER 12.14. Reminder that a current statement is needed (semiblock format).

April 22, 19X1

Mr. John Klugerman
P.O. Box 908
Toano, Massachusetts 25620

Dear Jack:

In connection with your present obligation to this bank, a review of our files shows we have not received a current statement from you which was previously requested by Loan Officer Max Nilges. Please complete the enclosed form and return it as soon as possible.

Your cooperation is greatly appreciated.

Regards,

Hamilton L. Coronet
Vice President

hlc:jls

enc.

SAMPLE LETTER 12.15. Request for completion and return of a statement (full-block format).

April 2, 19X2

Mr. Rodney S. McDonnell
11 Twilight Drive
South Zone, Massachusetts 63910

Dear Rod:

Please complete the attached Personal Financial Statement and return it to me in the envelope provided. Once I have received this form, we can begin consideration of your loan.

Sample Letter 12.15 continued

Thank you for your cooperation.

Best wishes,

Max Nilges
Loan Officer

llk

Enclosure

Sample letter 12.16 is written to a customer with whom a new agreement has been made concerning a demand note. The first paragraph explains what the letter is, while the remainder of the letter clearly details the terms of repayment.

SAMPLE LETTER 12.16. Letter to customer about terms of repayment of demand note (full-block format).

February 2, 19X2

Mr. J. Harrison Frit
27 Remont Street
Notwent Township, New Jersey 99591

Dear Harry:

This letter will confirm our understanding about the repayment of the $7,500 loan evidenced by a demand note dated January 28, 19X2.

We understand it is your intention to make three annual reductions of this note no later than February 1, 19X3 through February 1, 19X5 from your annual partnership distribution. This is an acceptable arrangement to New National Bank. Notwithstanding New National's willingness to accept such a repayment schedule, it is understood that the note remains a demand obligation, and all other conditions pertaining to our original proposal remain unchanged.

It is acceptable for $5000 of the proceeds of this note to be used for an additional capital contribution to the firm of Long & Berrigan. The terms of your letter to us dated June 7, 19X9, and accepted by Long & Berrigan, however, are still in effect.

Sample Letter 12.16 continued

Please indicate your concurrence by signing the enclosed copy of this letter and returning it to me.

Best wishes,

Max Nilges
Loan Officer

enclosure

Acknowledged and Accepted:

____________________________ ____________________
Signature Date

Sample letter 12.17 is written to inform one of the customer's creditors that a loan the customer had taken has been repaid after a court judgment had been made. The letter sketches out the necessary background information and brings the creditor up-to-date in the remaining paragraphs.

SAMPLE LETTER 12.17. Letter to customer's creditor explaining loan has been repaid after court judgment (simplified format).

February 15, 19X8

Mr. Paul W. Hudson
Loan Officer
New Commercial Bank
Avella, Ohio 08791

MR. ALAN P. ANDERSON'S PAYMENT OF INSTALLMENT LOAN #6098

On February 6, 19X3, Mr. Alan P. Anderson obtained credit from County Savings Bank for $250 plus interest (Installment Loan #6098). On September 23, 19X3, County Savings Bank was awarded judgment in the County Civil Court for $260.12 plus costs and judgment interest in consideration of the debtor's default on his note.

Today, we received from Mr. Anderson $328.69 representing the full unpaid balance on his obligation, with accumulated interest totaling $68.57. Therefore, Mr. Anderson's

Sample Letter 12.17 continued

obligation is paid in full and satisfied. We are adjusting our records accordingly.

Simon L. Thorn
Assistant Vice President

slt/mat

Sample letter 12.18 informs a customer that a loan affecting her has been assumed and paid.

SAMPLE LETTER 12.18. Letter to customer explaining loan affecting her has been assumed and paid (block format).

July 21, 19X1

Mrs. Beatrice K. Newman
991 Hampthon Place
Ferlinghetti, Oklahoma 96633

Subject: John C. Newman Installment Loan #0-84731

Dear Mrs. Newman:

Installment loan #0-84731 has been assumed by Murray and Rosemary Caracas. The obligation of Mr. John C. Newman is considered paid and satisfied.

If you have any questions or if I may be of further assistance, please give me a call.

Cordially,

Max Nilges
Loan Officer

mn/jk

Sample letter 12.19 explains the terms of a customer's loan to an agency with which he has dealings.

SAMPLE LETTER 12.19. Letter explaining terms of loan to agency with which customer had dealings (block format).

December 8, 19X1

Mr. Lester R. Saganson
Division of Motor Vehicles
23 Pucaro Place
Santiago, Michigan 39040

Dear Mr. Saganson:

Subject: Loan to Marcus MacIntyre

Please be advised that funds advanced to Mr. MacIntyre were for the cost of restoring a 1957 Chevrolet #CV711675. The total amount was not for purchasing the vehicle.

Please call me if you need more information about Mr. MacIntyre's loan.

Cordially,

Simon L. Thorn
Assistant Vice President

slt/bcm

Under the Fair Credit Reporting Act, a customer has the right to dispute the accuracy of the status or terms of his or her loan. If the customer was correct in disputing something in his or her file, a letter such as sample letter 12.20 can be sent notifying the customer that the item has been dropped from the file.

SAMPLE LETTER 12.20. Letter to customer after disputed items have been deleted from his file (full-block format).

November 20, 19X2

Mr. Oscar Y. Ilde
P.O. Box 976
Coronoton, North Carolina 30031

Dear Mr. Ilde:

We have deleted from our files information you disputed concerning you. We have put a copy of your letter disputing these items in our files.

You have the right to make a written request that we furnish you notice of the deletion or a copy of it to any person specifically designated by you who has received from us a consumer report containing the deleted or disputed information within the preceding two years for employment purposes or within the preceding six months for any other purpose.

If you make such a request, we will, prior to furnishing the notices, advise you of any charges we will make.

Sincerely,

Max Nilges
Loan Officer

mat

Sample letter 12.21 was written from one bank to another explaining the customer's financial circumstances, in hopes that the other bank might see fit to grant the customer a loan. This letter was written as a courtesy to the customer by an officer of a bank that could not grant the necessary loan.

SAMPLE LETTER 12.21. Letter from one bank to another explaining customer's financial circumstances (semiblock format).

August 5, 19X2

Peter F. Lybrandman
Vice President
Old National Bank
De Wolfe, Texas 89201
Subject: Peter and Patricia Neal
907 Colony Crossing Drive
De Wolfe, Texas 89201

Dear Pete:

I have examined the financial information provided by Mr. and Mrs. Neal and have determined that the added burden of paying tuition for their daughter cannot be accomplished. At present their debt ratio is 70%, based on a monthly income of $1,826 and expenses of $1,273.

Mr. and Mrs. Neal are supporting in-laws who live in an apartment attached to their house, in addition to three children at home. The housing for the in-laws is provided free of cost.

I have provided copies of the information given me by Mr. and Mrs. Neal for your review. If I may be of further assistance or if additional information is needed please call me.

Best regards,

John Savithson
Assistant Vice President

hlt

enclosure

Sample letter 12.22 is a good example of a letter written to a customer informing him that his loan request has been refused. Rather than a cold out-and-out denial letter, the bank officer includes an encouraging note to an otherwise negative response. Such a note might help to attract the customer's business in a more mutually beneficial situation.

SAMPLE LETTER 12.22. Letter refusing loan to customer (semiblock format).

November 20, 19X2

Mr. Patrick E. Plimptone
89 Nightstalking Drive, Apt. 4B
Caldoran, Wisconsin 909010

Dear Mr. Plimptone:

The enclosed ''Notice of Credit Denial'' form does two things. First, it tells you why we are not able to make the loan that you requested on October 12, 19X2. Second, it represents the minimum legal requirement for declining a loan request. Because we feel that a form is a little too cold and uncaring, and that the minimum requirements are not enough for New National Bank or, we think, for you, we are writing this letter.

New National Bank is not able to make the loan that you requested. Our decision is based on sound credit principles and established credit policy. It does not signify that we feel you have ''failed'' to qualify, or ''failed'' to do what is right. As a matter of fact, we would like to have your business.

We would like you to call Max Nilges, the loan officer who took your application, and make arrangements to visit him. He will tell you exactly why, at this time, your loan cannot be made, and how you can take steps to qualify for your next application. We think you will benefit by your visit. We know we will.

Cordially,

Alan D. Ferdiande
Vice President

adf/mat

Collection Letters

Sample letters 12.23-12.33 are examples of good collection letters. Sample letters 12.23-12.26 are included here because they show different approaches to collecting past due payments from a customer. Sample letters 12.27-12.33 are a series used to collect overdue payment.

Sample letter 12.23 is a clearly written letter which was used to call a loan. The procedure taken is clearly laid out in the letter, as are future steps to be taken.

SAMPLE LETTER 12.23. Letter calling loan (full-block format).

May 4, 19X3

Mr. Lawrence W. Birdie
185A Savin Mountain Road
Dorchester, Pennsylvania 52120

Dear Mr. Birdie:

Your loan payments are now four months past due. Our correspondence to you will reflect our assumptions that began in your favor.

First, we assumed you had forgotten to make payments and would welcome our reminders. Then we assumed that you had a temporary problem and we were willing to work with you through your difficulty. Next we assumed that we had done something wrong and requested that you contact us to let us know so that we could rectify any mistake we had made.

Finally, with no response or cooperation from you, we have to assume that you will not pay unless forced to. We are therefore taking this first step in what we call the ''enforcement stage.'' We are declaring your loan due and payable in full. We hereby make demand that you pay the principal of your loan, all accrued interest, and late charges in the amount appearing on the enclosed statement within ten days from the date of this letter.

If your payment is not received by that time, we will have no choice but to refer this loan contract to our attorney who will be instructed to pursue all legal remedies available to us in collecting the money owed us.

Sincerely,

Max Nilges
Vice President

lk

enclosure

Sample letter 12.24 is an example of a second notice of a past due payment sent to a customer. The letter explains exactly what the customer must do to protect his credit and avoid additional charges. Emphasizing the importance of protecting a good credit rating is often an effective method of eliciting a positive response from a customer.

SAMPLE LETTER 12.24. Second notice of past due payment (full-block format).

March 26, 19X2

Mr. Edward C. Franks
Solar Energy, Inc.
908 Wheat Avenue
Roanoke, Wisconsin 75968

Subject: Account Number: 432-4400-0005-61
Amount of Past Due Payment: $121.23 for March 5, 19X2
Other Charges Accrued: $6.06
Collateral: 19X9 Toyota Truck

Dear Mr. Franks:

We previously sent you a notice of your past due payment. This payment has not been received nor have you contacted us to explain why it was not forwarded.

We are certain that you would like to protect your credit and avoid additional charges. You can do so by forwarding us the past due amount and charges upon receipt of this letter, and by mailing your remaining payments on time. Payments more than seven days past due are subject to a late charge of 5%.

If for any reason you are unable to forward us the past due amount and charges upon receipt of this letter, please call me.

Sincerely,

NEW NATIONAL BANK

Gene R. Louise
Collection Officer

mat

Sample letters 12.25 and 12.26 are examples of a first and second notice sent to a customer about his overdue payment on an installment loan. These letters are included here because they are examples of briefly written, direct notices which have been effective in acquiring past due payments.

SAMPLE LETTER 12.25. First notice to customer about overdue payment on installment loan (block format).

November 11, 19X3

Mr. Gerald Tiffin
5 Washington Drive
Los Angeles, Kentucky 19929

Dear Mr. Tiffin:

Subject: Installment Loan #56-923-853

Our records show that your installment loan is currently past due for the November 5, 19X3 payment for $240. If this date does not agree with your records or payment was made more than five days ago, please inform me immediately.

If not already remitted, please mail your payment in the enclosed envelope or call me to make other payment arrangements.

Cordially,

Paul Krams
Vice President
Installment Loan Administration

pk/kl

enclosure

SAMPLE LETTER 12.26. Second notice to customer about overdue payment on installment loan. Follow-up to letter in sample letter 12.25 (block format).

November 23, 19X3

Mr. Gerald Tiffin
5 Washington Drive
Los Angeles, Kentucky 19929

Dear Mr. Tiffin:

Subject: Second Notice, Installment Loan #56-923-853

We have recently written to you about payment due on your Installment Loan. Unfortunately our records still reflect that it is past due for the November 5, 19X3 payment for $240.

Sample Letter 12.26 continued

Please give this matter your immediate attention by either mailing $240 in the enclosed envelope or by calling me.

Cordially,

Paul Krams
Vice President
Installment Loan Administration

pk:kl

enclosure

Sample letters 12.27-12.33 are a series of effective collection letters. Sample letters 12.28 and 12.29 are two versions of a second notice on an overdue payment. Sample letter 12.27 is a longer version showing understanding and explaining the necessity of making the payment which is due.

SAMPLE LETTER 12.27. Second notice on an overdue payment (block format).

January 15, 19X3

Ms. Jean Credion
89 Western Avenue
Marbleton, Pennsylvania 40910

SUBJECT:LOAN #5925420

Dear Ms. Credion:

Is something wrong? You should be acting now to preserve your good credit standing, but you have done nothing yet to protect it.

A few days ago we sent you a notice that your loan payment was past due for $400. In spite of this notice, you still have not brought your loan up to date. Consequently, we have frozen those funds you have in your savings to be withdrawn and applied against your past-due payment if you fail to contact us at once and act immediately to reinstate your good credit standing with us.

We can be most understanding if there is a good reason why you have not made your payment up until now. Simply phone me and explain the circumstances. We will make

Sample Letter 12.27 continued

every possible effort to accommodate you if you are encountering financial difficulties, as long as you cooperate with us.

If, however, you fail either to bring your account up to date or to contact us and make some new accommodations, we will have to take funds out of your savings, turn the matter over to our Collection Department, and instruct them to inform the various credit-reporting bureaus of your delinquent status.

Cordially,

Max Nilges
Loan Officer

mn/mt

cc: Evelyn S. Nolan, cosigner

Sample letter 12.28 attempts to achieve the same end with a bit more direct approach.

SAMPLE LETTER 12.28. Second notice of overdue payment. More direct approach than sample letter 12.27 (block format).

January 25, 19X3

Ms. Jean Credion
89 Western Avenue
Marbleton, Pennsylvania 40910

Subject: Loan #5925420

Dear Ms. Credion:

Is something wrong? This is your second notice. We're wondering why we have not heard from you about your overdue payment.

If something's gone wrong, won't you come in immediately and talk it over? Perhaps we can assist you to straighten out the trouble. In any case, it is very important that we hear from you quickly.

Sample Letter 12.28 continued

Protect your credit standing. Telephone us immediately if you cannot make your payment in person or by return mail today.

Cordially,

Max Nilges
Loan Officer

mn/mt

Sample letter 12.29 is a follow-up to a partial payment made after sample letter 12.27 or 12.28 was sent to the customer. A request for complete payment is made in the letter.

Sample letter 12.30 is a follow-up to no response to sample letter 12.27 or 12.28. The account has been turned over to the collection department, and the customer is made aware that more serious measures are to be taken if she does not pay the amount owed.

SAMPLE LETTER 12.29. Follow-up to partial payment made after receiving sample letter 12.27 or 12.28. Calls for remainder of payment (full-block format).

January 31, 19X3

Ms. Jean Credion
89 Western Avenue
Marbleton, Pennsylvania 40910

SUBJECT: LOAN #5925420

Dear Ms. Credion:

You have responded to our request to bring your loan up to date by making a partial payment only. To restore your current account status and to protect your good credit rating, you must pay the entire past due payment balance of $250.

Please pay this immediately.

Sincerely yours,

Max Nilges
Loan Officer

jkl

SAMPLE LETTER 12.30. Follow-up to no response to sample letter 12.27 or 12.28. Account has been turned over to collections department (semiblock format).

February 14, 19X3

Ms. Jean Credion
89 Western Avenue
Marbleton, Pennsylvania 40910

Subject: Loan #5925429

Dear Ms. Credion:

Your loan account has become seriously delinquent. The Loan Department of New National Bank has turned it over to us for collection.

You have already been sent a ''Late Payment Notice,'' followed by a letter requesting payment from our Loan Department. Both of these moderate appeals have remained unanswered by you. We also have attempted to reach you by telephone, but have been unable to reach you.

Because you have been unresponsive to those efforts to bring your account up to date and to preserve your good credit standing with us, today we have taken funds from your savings account and applied them against your loan. We also have notified various consumer credit reporting agencies of your present delinquent status. We now intend to expend every legal recourse available to us in an effort to collect from you the entire amount due on your loan, plus whatever late charges and legal fees may be incurred in so doing. This is being done under the terms of the Promissory Note you signed and accepted when you initiated this loan.

It is still not too late, however, to rectify this situation. You can still make restitution and begin to restore your now inferior credit rating at New National Bank by coming in personally, telephoning us, or using the enclosed reply card to make corrective arrangements. You must, however, respond immediately upon receipt of this letter. If we do not hear from you and some corrective action is not taken immediately by you, we will have to take corrective action against you.

Cordially,

Gene R. Louise
Collection Officer

grl/lkj

enclosure

cc: Evelyn S. Nolan, cosigner

Sample letter 12.31 is also a follow-up to no response to sample letter 12.27 or 12.28. This letter is sent to the cosigner on a loan if there is one. The cosigner is notified of her obligation to repay the loan if the customer defaults. She is encouraged to persuade the customer for whom she has cosigned to pay the past due amounts as soon as possible.

SAMPLE LETTER 12.31. Follow-up to no response to sample letter 12.28 or 12.29. Sent to cosigner explaining her responsibility (block format).

May 5, 19X3

Ms. Evelyn S. Nolan
789 Netheron Drive
Marbleton, Pennsylvania 40910

SUBJECT: DELINQUENT LOAN FOR WHICH YOU ARE LIABLE

Dear Ms. Nolan:

You are the cosigner on a loan made to Ms. Jean Credion, account number 5925420, which is now a delinquent account. The balance is $1250 with a date of last payment of January 30, 19X3. The loan is five months past due and is now subject to legal action. It is in your best interest to discuss this delinquency with the borrower and to persuade the borrower to bring the account up to date or you will be obligated to pay the debt.

Please call me to discuss your obligation as cosigner.

Sincerely,

Gene R. Louise
Collection Officer

grl/lkj

Sample letters 12.32 and 12.33 are final warnings in this series of collection letters. After the customer has failed to respond to the previous letters in the series, either one of these letters is sent. Sample letter 12.32 explains the action to be taken.

SAMPLE LETTER 12.32. Final warning after customer has failed to respond to collection letters (semiblock format).

May 15, 19X3

Ms. Jean Credion
89 Western Avenue
Marbleton, Pennsylvania 40910

Subject: Final Warning

Dear Ms. Credion:

We are instructing our attorney to attach your real estate for nonpayment of your contractual debt. Because you have repeatedly ignored your legally-bound obligations, under both state and federal laws, to repay the money you borrowed against your signature and before witnesses, your loan #5925420 from New National Bank is now delinquent more than five months with a total past amount due of $1250. This matter has become so serious that we have no choice but to seek redress by instituting legal proceedings against you.

We are instructing our attorneys to attach any real estate you may own and force its sale, so we can be reimbursed for the money you owe New National, plus all legal fees and expenses incurred by this action.

This action will be taken in five days on May 20, 19X3, unless you pay the entire amount or make some other acceptable arrangement with me.

If you wish to avoid potential loss of your home or other real estate, call me when you receive this letter to notify me of your intentions.

Cordially,

Gene R. Louise
Collection Officer

grl/lj

Sample letter 12.33 explains the action to be taken under various conditions which might exist. Sample letter 12.33 uses a numbered list to make sure the customer knows exactly what steps are to be taken to collect the money that is overdue the bank.

SAMPLE LETTER 12.33. Final warning after customer has failed to respond to collection letters (full-block format).

May 15, 19X3

Ms. Jean Credion
89 Western Avenue
Marbleton, Pennsylvania 40910

SUBJECT: LOAN #5925420

Dear Ms. Credion:

Your loan is now more than five months delinquent for a past due amount of $1250. We have attempted to contact you a number of times by both mail and telephone to inform you of the consequences of this situation. Apparently you have chosen to ignore our notices and have not responded to our many efforts to help you.

This is your final notice from us. You have a deadline of May 20, 19X3, by which to pay your account in full or to contact us and make some positive arrangement to make restitution. We have been more than lenient in this situation and there will be no more evasions tolerated.

If you choose not to respond to this letter by the above date, the following courses of action can be taken against you:

1. If you own residential property we will instruct our attorneys to place an attachment on your home.
2. If you own any other tangible property of value, we will seek an attachment against that.
3. Your account will be turned over to a professional collection agency.
4. Demand for payment will be made of any cosigners you might have.
5. Both national and local consumer credit bureaus will be notified of your delinquency which may have an adverse effect on your credit standing with both present and future creditors.
6. In addition to the loan balance, you now will be liable for any and all collection fees incurred.

Sample Letter 12.33 continued

This letter and all information is being extended to you as one last courtesy. Please reciprocate and avoid unnecessary litigation by contacting us immediately.

Cordially,

Gene R. Louise
Collection Officer

Collateral-related Letters

Sample letter 12.34 is a form letter sent to a customer whose collateral file is incomplete. The letter could easily be stored in a word processor. The letter writer checks off the items that are needed to complete the file and sends the letter to the customer.

SAMPLE LETTER 12.34. Form letter sent to customer whose collateral file is incomplete (simplified format).

November 20, 19X4

Mr. Paul Vanice
90 Pauline Drive
Oskosh, Washington 12332

SUBJECT: COLLATERAL FILE, LOAN #14-708-9049

A review of our collateral files indicates that the items checked below are required to complete our files:

Item	Required Action
_____Title	If you have the title, please forward it to us immediately. If you do not, please adivse us.
_____Evidence of collision and comprehensive insurance showing County Savings Bank as loss payee.	If you do have insurance, please request your agent to send evidence of coverage to us. If insurance is not held, you have ten days from the date of this letter to comply with this request.

We would appreciate your cooperation in completing your collateral file.

John Savithson
Vice President

lal

Sample letter 12.35 is a notice to a customer that her collateral is to be sold because of a defaulted loan. The customer is told precisely what she must do to avoid this sale's taking place.

SAMPLE LETTER 12.35. Notice to customer that collateral is to be sold because of loan default (semiblock format).

March 12, 19X0

Ms. Belinda Drearson
90 Obscure Road, Apt. 8
Yorktown, Kansas 09832

Subject: Installment Loan #030-0421
19X7 Chevrolet Monte Carlo
ID #028085B785H1

Dear Ms. Drearson:

Because your loan was declared in default, County Savings Bank is exercising its right as the secured party, and offering for sale your automobile.

If you wish to avoid this sale, you must pay off the account in full no later than ten days from the date of this letter. The total amount due, to avoid sale, is $7,339.86. The proceeds of any sale will be applied to the balance of your loan.

Cordially,

John Savithson
Assistant Vice President

js/mt

Sample letter 12.36 notifies a customer that his vehicle was repossessed because of default in payments on a loan, that it will be sold, and that any amount still due on the loan will be due to the bank.

SAMPLE LETTER 12.36. Notice to customer of sale after repossession (block format).

February 26, 19X2

Mr. Jeffrey Leigh
Laramy Equipment Company
34 Main Street
Apriori, Utah 38928

Subject: 19X0 Ford F-200 truck
Loan #389-286-03

Dear Mr. Leigh:

Because of your default in payments on account number 389-286-03, your 19X0 Ford F-200 truck, in which New National Bank has a perfected security interest, was repossessed January 17, 19X2. In accordance with the procedures required by the State Motor Vehicle Act, a repossession certificate of title has been obtained from the Secretary of State for the vehicle.

Following the requirements of the Uniform Commercial Code, we are notifying you that the vehicle will be sold at a private sale on March 7, 19X2 at two o'clock at the main office of New National Bank at 102 University Avenue in Postpriori, Utah.

You remain liable to New National for any amounts still due on Account #389-286-03 after the proceeds of the sale have been applied toward the account. You will be notified of any deficiency due to New National.

Cordially,
NEW NATIONAL BANK

Max Nilges
Vice President

klh

Sample letter 12.37 is a follow-up to sample letter 12.36. It notifies the customer of the deficiency after the repossession of collateral and instructs him what steps he must take to pay the amount still owed the bank.

SAMPLE LETTER 12.37. Notification to customer of deficiency after repossession sale (full-block format).

March 10, 19X2

Mr. Jeffrey Leigh
Laramy Equipment Company
34 Main Street
Apriori, Utah 38928

SUBJECT: 19X0 Ford F-200 truck
Loan #389-286-03

Dear Mr. Leigh:

As indicated in my letter of February 26, 19X2, your 19X0 Ford truck was sold at a private sale conducted at New National's main office at 102 University Avenue in Postpriori, Utah on March 7, 19X2, at two o'clock.

The results of the sale were as follows:

Price received from truck, being the highest amount bid	$3980.00
Less expenses of sale	–$ 84.40
Net receipts of sale	$3895.60
Amount due on Account #389-286-03	$4440.19
Less net receipts from sale	–$3895.00
Amount of delinquency	$ 544.59

Please contact New National Bank by March 20, 19X2, to make arrangements to pay the deficiency shown. If we do not hear from you by that date, we will initiate appropriate legal action to collect the deficiency.

Sincerely,

Max Nilges
Vice President

klh

Sample letters 12.38-12.40 are to agents who will assist or assisted in the repossession of the customer's collateral. Sample letter 12.38 is a letter of authorization to an officer of another bank who will act as an agent to repossess the customer's car. The letter details the terms of the loan and its default.

Sample letter 12.39 is to a collection agency which will act as the agent in repossessing the customer's collateral. The letter carefully instructs the collection agency what car should be repossessed and what should be done with the car once it is repossessed.

Sample letter 12.40 is written to a bank thanking them for their assistance in repossession, but informing them that the defaulted loan has been repaid in full.

SAMPLE LETTER 12.38. Letter of authorization to officer of another bank who will act as agent in collection of collateral (block format).

March 5, 19X9

Mr. Franklin Thomson
Old National Bank
P.O. Box 19790
Akron, California 20933

Subject: Richard L. Dykson
502 Alabaster Drive
Akron, California 20933

Dear Mr. Thomson:

Enclosed is our letter of authorization granting you the power to act as our agent in repossessing Mr. Dykson's collateral, a copy of the original contract signed by Mr. Dykson, a copy of the security agreement signed by Mr. Dykson, and a copy of the state title with security interest recorded.

Mr. Dykson's loan is in default from January 21, 19X9. In order for Mr. Dykson to retain possession of his vehicle, it will be necessary for you to collect $9,221.93 plus any collection expenses which may be incurred. This payoff will be good until April 7, 19X9.

Collection expenses of $75 are authorized for any expenses your institution incurs. Expenses exceeding the $75 will require my verbal approval.

If you have any further questions, please call me. Your assistance is greatly appreciated.

Sincerely,

John Savithson
Assistant Vice President

js/mt

encls.

SAMPLE LETTER 12.39. Letter of authorization to collection agency to act as agent in collecting collateral (simplified format).

October 31, 19X0

Mr. Alan D. Simpson
Aardon Collection Agency
1790 Sevenson Avenue
Biloxi, New Jersey 66629

REPOSSESSION OF COLLATERAL

This letter authorizes you to act as our agent in taking possession of a 19X9 Jeep Wagoner, ID #9251A9J29444, registered to Barklin T. Farkknand Architects. You are authorized to transport the vehicle from Biloxi, New Jersey, to our offices in Boonton, Pennsylvania.

If you need further information, please call me.

John Savithson

Assistant Vice President

oiu

SAMPLE LETTER 12.40. Letter of thanks to bank which assisted in repossession (full-block format).

February 26, 19X0

Mr. Carl Anderson
Old National Bank
299 Morrissey Boulevard
Encino, Arkansas 10309

Dear Carl:

As I indicated in our conversation today, Mr. Robert Z. Kiztul of Bonbon, Arkansas paid his installment loan off in full by selling his motor home to Manchester Car Sales, Inc. As a result, your voluntary repossession assistance will no longer be required.

New National Bank and I appreciate your assistance. If I or New National can return the favor, please call us.

Sincerely,

Sample Letter 12.40 continued

Max Nilges
Vice President

mn/dd

Consumer Loan Memos

Memoranda 12.41 and 12.42 are examples of memos written to be included in a customer's credit file. The important function of a memo to a customer's credit file is to keep the files up to date. Whoever might be doing a credit analysis will find reference to these internal memos useful. In addition, the person who ultimately might have to approve the loan proposal can learn a good deal about prospective customers by reading memos dealing with them.

Memorandum 12.41 gives the details of the bank officer's decision to extend credit to the customer.

MEMORANDUM 12.41. Memorandum to credit file giving details of decision to extend credit to customer.

TO: Credit file
FROM: John Savithson
DATE: October 5, 19X7
SUBJECT: Albert Q. Wermer

Today I extended credit to Mr. Wermer for $3,400, on a 90-day basis. This loan is secured by and for the purchase of a 19X4 Dodge Tradesman van.

Mr. Wermer has an open loan with us at this time (#4-2345-08) which is secured by a 19X5 AMC Pacer. It is his intention to sell the Pacer and apply any net proceeds to the balance of today's debt, which at maturity will be refinanced on an installment basis.

Mr. Wermer's previous installment loan #4-2345-09 has been paid as agreed with no ten-day notices. Mr. Wermer also maintains his personal checking account with County Savings Bank.

js/lk

Memorandum 12.42 was written to the credit file specifying the date and reasons for a release of the customer's collateral.

MEMORANDUM 12.42. Memorandum to credit file about release of collateral.

TO: Credit File
FROM: Max Nilges, Vice President
DATE: November 8, 19X7
SUBJECT: Dr. Henry Lapides

Subsequent to a request from Dr. Lapides and based on his excellent payment record on loan #3-0532-1, I am today releasing the collateral held in connection with that credit (19X8 Volvo).

I have made the appropriate notations on the discount sheet and the note.

mn/kl
encl.

Mortgage Loan Letters 13

Sample letters 13.1-13.21 are examples of letters that were written about mortgage loans. From seeking information on a prospective mortgage loan customer to foreclosing, these letters lend themselves well to being adapted for use with customers other than those who were originally written.

Mortgage Approval Letters

Sample letter 13.1 is one example of a mortgage approval letter. It is included here because it is effectively written and can easily be used for any mortgage loan approval made, by filling in the correct names, numbers, and terms.

SAMPLE LETTER 13.1. Mortgage approval letter (semiblock format).

November 20, 19X2

Mrs. Elizabeth Westura
134 Twosome Road
Alquippan, Wisconsin 15780

Dear Mrs. Westura:

I am pleased to report that your application for a mortgage loan has been approved. The terms are stated below and will be firm for the next 45 days, provided your acceptance is received within two weeks.

Our loan will be secured by a good and sufficient first mortgage on the premises. We reserve the right to withdraw this commitment in the event title or other conditions necessary to make the loan are not satisfactory.

Please complete the enclosed form to indicate your acceptance of our conditions, and to authorize our attorney to proceed with title examination and preparation of loan documents. By your acceptance, you agree to pay for all of New National Bank's fees and costs, including our attorney's fees, whether or not the loan is consummated.

Mortgage Loan Terms

Amount: $80,000 Years: 30

Interest Rate: 9.75% for the first 36 months, then subject to adjustment and adjustable every three years.

Payments: $687.33 Monthly Principal and Interest for the first 36 months, then subject to adjustment.

Taxes: $1,875/year

Please call me if you have any questions.

Sincerely,

Max Nilges
Vice President

encl.

Sample letter 13.2 is a much more formatted approval letter which would lend itself particularly well to being used in a word processing system. All you need do is to key in the appropriate numbers.

SAMPLE LETTER 13.2. Mortgage approval letter (full-block format).

July 19, 19X5

Ms. Annmarie Long
456 Adams Road
Oshkosh, Wisconsin 40404

Dear Ms. Long:

Our Board of Investment has approved your application for the following mortgage:

PROPERTY: 456 & 456A Adams Road, Oshkosh, Wisconsin (Two-Family Dwelling)

BORROWER: Annmarie Long

TYPE OF MORTGAGE: Fixed-rate Conventional

AMOUNT: $30,000.00 TERM: 15 Years RATE: 12.00%

PAYMENTS: $360.05—Monthly, plus 1/12th Taxes

ORIGINATION FEE: $600.00; $225.00 application fee to be collected at closing

FIRE INSURANCE: In amounts and types of coverage satisfactory to the bank.

SMOKE DETECTORS: Required_X_ Not Required____

FLOOD INSURANCE: Required_X_ Not Required____

LEAD PAINT: Waiver or Certificate Required

ATTORNEY: Please contact Bethany Coleman at 555-6767.
This commitment is good for 60 days from the date of this letter.

Very truly yours,

Jennifer Smith
Executive Vice President

Sample letter 13.3 is a standard letter written by a bank's attorneys to a mortgagee notifying her of what must be done before the closing on the mortgage loan can take place. Since this letter is standard, it would be another that is easily adapted to different borrowers. Again, storing these standard letters in a word processing system for repeated use would be a simple and intelligent idea.

SAMPLE LETTER 13.3. Notice of requirements before mortgage closing (full-block format).

July 23, 19X5

Ms. Annmarie Long
456 Adams Road
Oshkosh, Wisconsin 40404

Subject: 456 & 456A Adams Road, Oshkosh, Wisconsin

Dear Ms. Long:

We have received a requested from County Savings Bank to begin legal work for the bank in connection with your mortgage loan on 456 & 456A Adams Road. We are pleased to have the opportunity to work with you.

Before we can schedule a closing on your mortgage loan, however, we must:

(1) perform a title examination at the Registry of Deeds to make sure that title to the property is free of any title problems which could later create difficulties for you or bank;

(2) obtain from Oshkosh a Municipal Lien Certificate which tells us whether or not all outstanding taxes have been paid; and

(3) order and receive from a surveyor a current plot plan showing the lot and the location of the buildings and certifying that they comply with local zoning requirements.

Assuming that no title, lien, or zoning problems are encountered, we should complete our work in approximately 15 working days. During that time the bank will be completing its work and forwarding to us an Authorization to Close. Once our work is complete and we have the Authorization to Close, we will contact you to schedule your closing.

In the meantime, there are several things which you must do before the closing. Please refer to the enclosed separate notice which sets forth these requirements. We can-

Sample Letter 13.3 continued

not close your loan unless the items specified are provided at the time of closing.

Very truly yours,

Bethany Coleman

BC:si

Enclosure

Sample letter 13.4 is a basic notification of a closing date for a mortgage loan. The letter writer lists the time and place of the closing and also refers the mortgagee to an enclosed list of what she must do before she comes to the closing. Among other things, this list would include such things as telling the mortgagee to notify the bank about whether or not she plans to use an attorney, secure a binder or policy from her insurance company to prove coverage, and bring a certified check to cover closing costs.

SAMPLE LETTER 13.4. Notice of closing date (full-block format).

August 14, 19X5

Ms. Annmarie Long
456 Adams Road
Oshkosh, Wisconsin 40404

Subject: 456 & 456A Adams Road, Oshkosh, Wisconsin

Dear Ms. Long:

The closing for the mortgage loan on 456 & 456A Adams Road has been scheduled for 11 a.m., August 19, 19X5. The closing will be held in my office.

In the meantime, there are several things which you must do before the closing. Please refer to the enclosed separate notice which sets forth these requirements. We cannot close your loan unless the items specified are provided at the time of the closing.

I will be touch with you about the amount of money you will need to bring to the closing to cover closing costs.

Very truly yours,

Bethany Coleman

Sample Letter 13.4 continued

bc/si

Enclosure

Sample letter 13.5 is a standard letter that notifies the borrower about the payment schedule for her mortgage loan. Sample letters 13.2 through 13.5 could be used as a series of letters to the same mortgage holder.

SAMPLE LETTER 13.5. Notice of mortgage payment schedule (full-block format).

August 28, 19X5

Ms. Annmarie Long
456 Adams Road
Oshkosh, Wisconsin 40404

Subject: 456 & 456A Adams Road, Oshkosh, Wisconsin

Dear Ms. Long:

Your monthly mortgage payment covering the property at 456 & 456A Adams Street, Oshkosh, will be due on the first day of each month beginning with October 1, 19X5. A statement showing the amount due will be sent to you approximately 10 days prior to the due date.

If you have any questions, please do not hesitate to contact the mortgage department.

Sincerely,

Melvin Krauss
Assistant Treasurer

mk

Sample letter 13.6 is a follow-up letter to a mortgage loan approval which welcomes the new customer and encourages her to take advantage of other bank services available. Such a letter is not only good for the mortgage loan department, but also for fostering sales and good customer relations.

SAMPLE LETTER 13.6. Follow-up sales letter to mortgage loan customer (block format).

November 6, 19X3

Ms. Alice Mary Goodworth
167 Pokukney Drive
Production, Rhode Island 16513

Dear Ms. Goodworth:

I was glad to hear that County Savings Bank has the opportunity to assist in the financing of your home. This is a service we have been performing for thousands of Productionites for more than a century and a half.

For your convenience, I am enclosing a loan memorandum prepared by our Mortgage Department which contains information we believe you will find useful.

If you are not already familiar with the many banking services which we have to offer, we invite you to discuss your needs with any of our officers at any of our seven banking offices.

Sincerely,

James Lewis
President

lss

encl.

Insurance Requirements

Sample letters 13.7-13.9 were written to mortgage loan customers about necessary insurance coverage. Sample letter 13.7 is a reminder of the need for insurance coverage.

SAMPLE LETTER 13.7. Letter reminding mortgage loan customer of need for insurance coverage (semiblock format).

August 16, 19X4

Ms. Gloria R. Clark
908 Carson Street
St. Louis, Vermont 79820

Dear Ms. Clark:

In connection with the closing on your new mortgage, you are required to have a binder, or policy if issued, of insurance in an amount at least equal to the mortgage loan balance.

We recommend, however, that you discuss with your insurance agent or company what amount of insurance is adequate to protect your property's replacement value. We require that your fire insurance policy include extended coverage for windstorm and other hazards and that the County Savings Bank be designated as loss payee under the mortgage clause.

Thank you for giving your attention to the insurance coverage necessary for your new mortgage.

Sincerely,

COUNTY SAVINGS BANK

Bixley Armstrong
Vice President

ba/mn

Sample letter 13.8 is written to a mortgage customer who has not filed the required fire insurance coverage on his property.

SAMPLE LETTER 13.8. Letter notifying mortgage loan customer he has not filed fire insurance coverage on his property (full-block format).

November 11, 19X3

Mr. Burgess Bacall
45 Fenton Boulevard
Bakorum, Illinois 00784

Dear Mr. Bacall:

During a recent review of our investment and commercial mortgage loans, we found no record of fire insurance coverage on your property.

It is County Savings Bank's policy to require fire insurance policies on all investment and commercial properties on which we have a mortgage. Therefore, please forward to us a copy of your current fire insurance policy at your earliest possible convenience.

Your prompt attention to this is greatly appreciated. If you have any questions, please call me.

Cordially,

Bixley Armstrong
Vice President

lh

Sample letter 13.9 is a second notice to the same customer after he failed to respond to the letter in sample letter 13.8.

SAMPLE LETTER 13.9. Second notice to customer about required fire insurance coverage on property. Follow-up to sample letter 13.4 (full-block format).

November 25, 19X3

Mr. Burgess Bacall
45 Fenton Boulevard
Bakorum, Illinois 00784

SUBJECT: SECOND NOTICE ON FIRE INSURANCE COVERAGE

Dear Mr. Bacall:

As a follow-up to our letter dated November 11, 19X3, I again am writing you to tell you we have not yet received a copy of the current fire insurance policy on your property as requested.

It is the bank's policy to require fire insurance policies on all commercial and investment properties on which we hold a mortgage. Therefore, please forward us a copy of your current policy as soon as possible.

Your prompt attention to supplying us with the necessary policy would be greatly appreciated. If you have any questions, please call me.

Cordially,

Bixley Armstrong
Vice President

lh

Operating Statements

Sample letters 13.10-13.12 are a series of letters reminding the mortgage loan customer of his obligation to supply an operating statement on his investment mortgage. The three letters are a first, second, and third notice calling for the operating statement.

SAMPLE LETTER 13.10. First notice for operating statement (semiblock format).

May 25, 19X3

Larry G. Choirlin
Choirlin Investment Properties
98 Sellers Drive, Suite 15A
Peterson, New Jersey 97506

Subject: Operating Statements

Dear Mr. Choirlin:

The County Savings Bank is insured by the Federal Deposit Insurance Corporation. Because we are an FDIC insured bank, we are required to obtain current operating statements on all investment mortgages. Your mortgage also contains a covenant which requires you to furnish us with an annual operating statement.

In order to make the preparation of your statement easier, we have enclosed a standard income and expense form. You may elect to enclose your own signed statement.

If the majority of the building's annual income is derived from one or two major tenants whose leases have been assigned as additional security to the bank of the mortgage loan, then a copy of the lessee's financial statement for its current fiscal year should be enclosed.

We would expect to receive this operating statement within thirty days from the date of this letter. If for any reason you are unable to comply with this request, please call me.

Thank you for your cooperation.

Sincerely,

Bixley Armstrong
Vice President

ba/lh

enc.

SAMPLE LETTER 13.11. Second notice for operating statement (semiblock format).

July 5, 19X3

Larry G. Choirlin
Choirlin Investment Properties
98 Sellers Drive, Suite 15A
Peterson, New Jersey 97506

Subject: Second Notice for Operating Statements

Dear Mr. Choirlin:

Around the end of May, we sent you a letter requesting that you send us a current operating statement on your investment property. We have not yet received your statement.

The County Savings Bank is insured by the Federal Deposit Insurance Corporation. Because we are an FDIC bank, we are required to obtain current operating statements on all income property mortgages. In addition, your mortgage contains a covenant which requires you to furnish us with an annual operating statement. It is therefore a technical default on your mortgage not to provide an annual operating statement.

In order to make the preparation of your statement easier, we have enclosed a standard income and expense form. You may elect to enclose your own signed statement.

If the majority of the building's annual income is derived from one or two major tenants whose leases have been assigned as additional security to the bank on the mortgage loan, then a copy of the lessee's financial statement for its current fiscal year should be enclosed.

We will expect to receive your operating statement within thirty days. If you are unable to comply with this request, please call me.

Cordially,

Bixley Armstrong
Vice President

ba/lh

enc.

SAMPLE LETTER 13.12. Third notice for operating statement (semiblock format).

August 6, 19X3

Larry G. Choirlin
Choirlin Investment Properties
98 Sellers Drive, Suite 15A
Peterson, New Jersey 97506

Subject: Third Notice for Operating Statements

Dear Mr. Choirlin:

County Savings Bank is currently in the process of being audited by state and federal bank examiners. We are required by them to obtain current operating statements on all investment properties.

Inasmuch as this is the third time we have requested such a statement and the furnishing of the statement is a covenant of your mortgage deed, we would appreciate you complying with our request as soon as possible.

A standard income and expense form is enclosed for your convenience.

Sincerely,

Bixley Armstrong
Vice President

lh

enc.

Residential Delinquency Series

Sample letters 13.13-13.16 are a series of letters written for residential delinquency. After three notices were sent, the certified foreclosure in sample letter 13.16 was sent.

SAMPLE LETTER 13.13. First notice of residential delinquency (full-block format).

December 6, 19X4

Mr. Matthew R. Hope
43 Lorraine Terrace
Leaventown, Idaho 20617

Dear Mr. Hope:

We have not yet received your November 19X4 mortgage payment. Because you have always had an excellent payment record with us in the past, we assume that you are having some problem which makes it difficult to make a payment at this time. If so, please phone or visit the bank so we can discuss your difficulty with you.

If this late payment was caused by an oversight, please send both your November and December 19X4 payments by return mail.

Yours truly,

Max Nilges
Vice President

SAMPLE LETTER 13.14. Second notice of residential delinquency (full-block format).

January 5, 19X5

Mr. Matthew R. Hope
43 Lorraine Terrace
Leaventown, Idaho 20617

Dear Mr. Hope:

As you know, your mortgage payments are due for November 19X4 and December 19X4, each for $968. We request that you make the payments due on or before January 31, 19X5.

If you cannot comply with this request, please call me.

Yours truly,

Max Nilges
Vice President

mtf

SAMPLE LETTER 13.15. Third notice of residential delinquency (full-block format).

February 1, 19X5

Mr. Matthew R. Hope
43 Lorraine Terrace
Leaventown, Idaho 20617

Dear Mr. Hope:

As you know, your mortgage is currently due for the November 19X4, December 19X4, and January 19X5 payments. You have neglected to answer our previous correspondence. We now consider your delinquency to be serious.

It is imperative that you make the payments on or before February 15, 19X5. Failure to comply with this request will result in further action.

Yours truly,

Max Nilges
Vice President

mtf

SAMPLE LETTER 13.16. Certified foreclosure letter (full-block format).

February 20, 19X5

Mr. Matthew R. Hope
43 Lorraine Terrace
Leaventown, Idaho 20617
Dear Mr. Hope:

SUBJECT: ACCOUNT #98-09-777-9087

You are notified of our intention to foreclose, under power of sale for breach of condition, the mortgage held by us on the property at 43 Lorraine Terrace in Leaventown, Idaho. You may be liable in case of a deficiency in the proceeds of the foreclosure sale.

You are further notified that we demand that you pay in full the unpaid principal of the note which the mortgage was given to secure, together with all interest accrued to the date of payment.

Yours truly,

Sample Letter 13.16 continued

Max Nilges
President

mtf

We hereby certify on oath that on ______ (date), we mailed by certified mail, postage prepaid, and return receipt requested, the notice of a copy of the above letter to the person listed at the above address, which was the last address of this person known to us at the time of mailing.

Signed and sworn to before me, ______ (date).

______
(Signature of Notary Public)

Verification of Employment

Sample letter 13.17 is a form letter sent to a customer's employer seeking verification of his or her employment record. The letter is straightforward and can be used for any customer by merely substituting names. It would easily be stored in a word processor for use with different customers.

SAMPLE LETTER 13.17. Form letter to mortgage loan customer's employer seeking verification of employment (block format).

November 20, 19X4

Mr. Alan P. Voyageman
Teaman Industries, Inc.
98 Colonel Andrews Place
Sykeston, Alabama 83189

SUBJECT: VERIFICATION OF EMPLOYMENT OF JOHN J. KLEND

Dear Mr. Voyageman:

Mr. Klend has made an application for a residential mortgage loan. Your prompt reply will be appreciated by us and your employee. It will be held in strict confidence.

1. Is applicant now employed by you? ______
   If answer is no, please complete the following:
   a. Date applicant left ______
   b. Reason for leaving ______

Sample Letter 13.17 continued

2. Base salary per hour_______ per week _______
   per month _______ per year________
   Is all or part of compensation in the form of
   Bonus or Commission?______________________________
   Overtime earnings? ________________________________
3. How long in your employ? ______________________
4. Position Held____________________________________
5. Are applicant's services satisfactory? __________
6. Probability of continued employment and other
   remarks ____
   ____
   ____
   ____

Please sign and date the enclosed copy of this letter and return it to me. Thank you for your assistance.

Sincerely,

John Savithson
Assistant Vice President

Acknowledged by:

_________________________ _________________________
Date Signature and Title

Verification of First Mortgage

Sample letter 13.18 is written from a bank taking a second mortgage on a customer's property to the bank which holds the first mortgage. The letter clearly lists the information needed by the bank taking the second mortgage.

SAMPLE LETTER 13.18. Letter from bank taking second mortgage to bank holding first mortgage, seeking financial information (block format).

March 21, 19X4

Mr. Alan P. Pierpont
Loan Officer
Old National Bank
908 Amstay Road
Anderson, Kentucky 97911

SUBJECT: MORTGAGE FOR SEBASTIAN T. POLYMAN

Dear Mr. Pierpont:

We have recently taken a second mortgage on Mr. Polyman's property located at 9056 Downs Road, Anderson, Kentucky, for $16,000 with a projected pay-off date of June 19X7. Because you hold the first mortgage on this property, we would appreciate it if you would:

a. Confirm the current balance on your mortgage
b. Record our lien in your files
c. Notify us promptly of any foreclosure on your part when and if that becomes necessary

Thank you for your cooperation and for your acknowledgment on the attached copy. A postage paid envelope is provided for your convenience.

Sincerely,

Max Nilges
President

mn/sw

encs.

Receipt Acknowledged:

OLD NATIONAL BANK

By:____________________________ Date:_________

Current Balance, First Mortgage $________

Returned Materials

Sample letters 13.19 and 13.20 accompany materials returned to borrowers after mortgage loan closings.

SAMPLE LETTER 13.19. Return of materials after closing (full-block format).

February 7, 19X7

Ms. Beverly Long
23 Train Street
Bolton, West Virginia 23232

Dear Ms. Long:

I've enclosed the following items from your recent mortgage closing:

(a) a check payable to you for $47.99, which represents an overpayment at the closing, and

(b) a copy of the Smoke Detector Indemnity omitted from your closing copies.

Please feel free to call me with any questions you may have.

Very truly yours,

Brian Palay

bp

Enclosures

SAMPLE LETTER 13.20. Return of materials after closing (full-block format).

December 14, 19X9

Ms. Matilda Birmingham
186 Savin Avenue
Seattle, Washington 30303

Subject: 186 Savin Avenue, Seattle

Dear Ms. Birmingham:

In connection with your purchase of the 186 Savin Avenue property in Seattle, I am enclosing All County Title Insurance Company Owner's Policy Number 12-34-5678 to you.

Your original deed will be returned to you from the Registry of Deeds. If you purchased the property which is registered land in any county, however, it will take at least one year to receive your Certifi cate of Title.

We wish you well in your new home.

Sincerely,

Jacqueline T. Ortho
Paralegal

jto
Enclosure

Sample letter 13.21 is a simple cover letter written to accompany materials returned to the borrower after a mortgage is paid off.

SAMPLE LETTER 13.21. Return of materials after canceled mortgage (full-block format).

February 13, 19X7

Mr. Arnold Short
59 Testament Place
Bowdoin, Missouri 40945

Subject: 59 Testament Place, Mortgage #9-8765-43

Dear Mr. Short:

Enclosed is the following material relating to the recent payoff of your mortgage:

1. Canceled mortgage note.
2. Mortgage deed.

Please call me if I can be of any assistance.

Sincerely yours,

Darrell Trevino
Assistant Mortgage Officer

DT

Enclosures

Home Equity Loans

Many of the letters in this chapter on mortgage loans can be adapted to use as letters relating to home equity lines of credit. Sample letters 13.22 and 13.23 are two specific examples of standard home equity loan letters. Sample letter 13.22 is a notice of closing requirements, which is basically a variation of sample letter 13.4. Sample letter 13.23 is a letter explaining how the equity line payments work.

SAMPLE LETTER 13.22. Notice of closing requirements (full-block format).

March 22, 19X2

Mr. & Mrs. Zed Planter
98 Penobscot Road
Bethesda, New Hampshire 30303

Subject: Home Credit Application #3542

Dear Mr. & Mrs. Planter:

Our firm has been retained by New National Bank to represent it in the closing of your Home Credit Loan. If you have not already scheduled a closing with our office, please contact us to do so. The closing will take approximately 10 to 15 minutes and will consist of executing the following instruments which will be prepared by our office: Signature Card; Notice of Right of Recision; Home Credit Note; Home Credit Mortgage; and Disburse Authorization (if other liens are to be satisfied with your Home Credit Loan).

You should bring the following items with you to the closing:

1. Homeowner's insurance policy or binder naming as the loss payee New National Bank, 455 Naragannsett Road, Bethesda, New Hampshire 30303. Please make sure that the amount of your insurance covers the Home Credit Loan and your existing first mortgage, if it is to remain outstanding.

2. Copy of your most recent paid tax bill or last mortgage payment stub indicating that your real estate taxes are paid up to date.

3. Original Owner's Duplicate Certificate of Title from the Land Court if any part of your real estate is Registered Land.

Please note that if any of these documents are not brought to the closing, your transaction will be postponed.

Under the Home Credit Loan program only first and second mortgages may be granted. If you already have an institutional second mortgage, this will be paid off from your Home Credit Loan. If you have any other liens on the property, you must bring the appropriate release to the closing. We will tell you prior to the closing what specific instruments, if any, are required. All parties who hold

Sample Letter 13.22 continued

title to the property to be mortgaged must be present at the closing to sign the Home Credit Agreement and Mortgage.

If you currently have no mortgage on your property and the Home Credit Loan will be a first mortgage, you will be responsible for additional title examination charges incurred by our office in conducting a more extensive title search. If your loan is in this category, please call us immediately since we will not begin our examination of title until we review the charges with you.

Please note that we will not be able to schedule a closing until your signed commitment has been received by the bank. Please review the terms of your Commitment Letter and contact us if you have any questions about the closing.

Sincerely,

W. T. Myron

wtm

SAMPLE LETTER 13.23. Notice of equity line procedure (full-block format).

July 28, 19X8

Mr. Zed Planter
Ms. Arlene Planter
98 Penobscot Road
Bethesda, New Hampshire 30303

Dear Mr. & Mrs. Planter:

Welcome as a New National Bank Home Credit Loan customer. With Home Credit, you have access to your credit line whenever you want. The Home Credit Loan checks enclosed are a simple way for you to draw on your credit line.

Each month you will receive a Home Credit statement which reports the status of your credit line. Your statement will summarize your previous and new balance, the amount of credit currently available to you, your minimum payment, and your payment due date. All of your monthly Home Credit activity, both advances against your line of credit and payments, will appear on your statement.

Sample Letter 13.23 continued

To make your monthly Home Credit payment, tear off the top portion of your statement and mail it with your payment to the address on the reverse side. Payments may be made in person at your New National Bank as well.

If you have any questions about Home Credit or other New National services, please don't hesitate to call me.

Sincerely,

Roy Fase
Vice President

RF

Enclosure

Personnel Letters 14

The personnel department of any bank handles a great deal of correspondence. Effectively written, these letters can help to enhance the reputation of the bank's business practices. Although personnel letters might not be written to prospective or longstanding customers, they can help to assure a bank of hiring the best possible people for positions and maintaining their loyalty.

Offering Positions

Sample letters 14.1-14.3 are letters that were written to offer positions to applicants. Sample letters 14.1 and 14.2 are two versions of a letter offering employment.

SAMPLE LETTER 14.1. Letter offering employment (block format).

May 20, 19X2

Mr. Blair P. Josephs
309 Marshall Street
Montville, Massachusetts 00934

Dear Mr. Josephs:

We at New National Bank are pleased to offer you the position of Area Manager—Assistant Data Processing Officer at the annual salary of $38,000. In addition, you will be paid cash in lieu of profit sharing until you are eligible for the normal profit sharing plan, and receive two weeks' paid vacation in 19X2 if you start on or before May 31, 19X2. New National will also reimburse you for family medical insurance coverage until you are picked up on our plan.

New National hopes you will be able to join its family. I hope this letter will assist you in making your decision. We look forward to hearing from you on or before Monday, May 24, 19X2.

If you have any questions about New National, please call me.

Sincerely,

Tracy R. McCaslin
Assistant Personnel Officer

TRM:LT

enc.

cc: John Taylor
Foster K. Ross

SAMPLE LETTER 14.2. Letter offering employment (full-block format).

November 21, 19X2

Ms. Priscilla Connors
89 Avenue Drive
Mayfield, Georgia 29529

Dear Ms. Connors:

We appreciate your visit with us here at County Savings Bank and would like to make you an offer of employment. Your position would be that of a commercial loan officer in the New England Division with a starting salary of $24,500 a year. This offer is made subject to a satisfactory physical examination and full reference. The general responsibilities of the position were explained to you as well as our expectations for merit performance and mobility within the County Savings System.

I am confident that County Savings Bank can offer you a real opportunity and that you will prove to be an asset to our organization. I would appreciate it if you would let me know of your decision by November 25, 19X2. I have enclosed a package of employment forms for your completion and return.

I hope that you give this offer serious consideration. I look forward to hearing from you about your decision. In the meantime, if you should have any questions, please let me know.

Cordially,

William D. Barbaran

Personnel Director

wdb/fmk

encs.

Sample letter 14.3 is a follow-up to a person who has accepted an offer. All three letters clearly explain the position and salary involved, and the day on which the person is to report to work or notify the bank of the decision about acceptance of the position.

SAMPLE LETTER 14.3. Letter to applicant who has accepted offer (block format).

June 15, 19X2

Ms. Alexandra Grant
228 Lincoln Street
Chester, West Virginia 31091

Dear Alexandra:

We are very pleased that you have accepted the position of Programmer Analyst at the annual salary of $23,500, with one week's paid vacation in 19X2. We hope that this will be a mutually rewarding and long-lasting relationship.

I hope that you can start work on July 1, 19X2 at 8:30 a.m., at which time you can be signed up for our benefits plan and I can orient you to our bank. Once again, it is a pleasure to have you join the New National family.

If you have any questions, please call me.

Sincerely,

Frank K. Ross
Assistant Personnel Officer

fkr:sro

cc: John Taylor
Tracy McCaslin

Rejection Letters

Sample letters 14.4-14.16 are various forms of rejection letters which most banks' personnel departments will find themselves sending out quite frequently. Sample letters 14.4-14.8 were written to applicants who for one reason or another were not hired. Sample letter 14.4 informs the applicant that another applicant has been hired.

SAMPLE LETTER 14.4. Letter informing applicant someone else has been hired (semiblock format).

May 28, 19X2

Mr. Gary L. Vaughan
1283 Bearded Road
Middleton, South Carolina 11071

Dear Gary:

Thank you for the time you took to come in and talk with us about the position of personnel assistant.

We cannot place you now, because we have chosen another candidate whose background, we feel, is more closely suited to our present situation. We will keep your resume in our active file, however, should a more suitable position open.

Thank you again for your interest in New National Bank. Best wishes for success in your career endeavors.

Best regards,

Tracy R. McCaslin
Assistant Personnel Officer

trm/sro

Sample letters 14.5 and 14.6 inform the applicant that there are no openings to match his training and experience.

SAMPLE LETTER 14.5. Letter informing applicant there are no positions matching his training or experience (full-block format).

August 4, 19X2

Mr. Benjamin J. Hartley
707 Gunpowder Road
Belinka, Ohio 49080

Dear Mr. Hartley:

Thank you for your inquiry about employment with New National Bank. We appreciated the opportunity to review your qualifications in reference to our current job openings.

Unfortunately, we do not have a position open at present which would properly use your training and experience. We would like to keep a record of your qualifications in our active file, however, so we may consider you for any appropriate future openings.

Although we are unable to offer you any immediate encouragement, we wish you success in your career endeavors.

Sincerely,

Foster K. Ross
Assistant Personnel Officer

fkr/rhb

SAMPLE LETTER 14.6. Letter informing applicant there are no positions matching his training or experience (block format).

August 2, 19X2

Mr. J. Ralph Bakker
16 Paxle Street, Apt. 4
Americus, Massachusetts 53070

Dear Mr. Bakker:

Thank you for the letter and resume indicating your interest in employment opportunities at New National Bank.

After reviewing your resume, we find we do not have an opening appropriate for a person with your background and qualifications. We will keep it in our active file, however, for future reference.

Sample Letter 14.6 continued

We appreciate your interest in New National Bank and extend our best wishes to you for success in your search for employment opportunities.

Sincerely,

Howard L. Andrews
Employment Administrator

hla/pag

Sample letter 14.7 is similar to sample letters 14.5 and 14.6 except for the emphasis it places on the regret the bank feels for not being able to hire a person with such excellent qualifications.

SAMPLE LETTER 14.7. Letter informing applicant there are no positions matching his training or experience. Places emphasis on regret over not being able to hire applicant (full-block format).

November 22, 19X2

Mr. Clyde D. Sanderson
908 Hinkledine Place
Carriage, Wisconsin 07005

Dear Mr. Sanderson:

Thank you for the interest you have shown in employment opportunities at New National Bank.

We have reviewed your fine background carefully and regret to inform you that we cannot place you at this time. This decision was a difficult one because you obviously have excellent qualifications. We have so few openings, however, that we can accommodate only a small number of those who are interviewed.

We are sorry that we cannot be more encouraging. We wish you the best of luck in finding a suitable position.

Sincerely,

John Taylor
Personnel Director

jt/sr

Sample Letter 14.7 continued

Sample letter 14.8 differs from sample letters 14.5-14.7 because it is more personal and expresses regret over not having met the applicant when she had come into the bank.

SAMPLE LETTER 14.8. Letter informing applicant there are no positions open. Expresses regret over not having met applicant when she was at bank (block format).

July 2, 19X2

Mrs. Andrea R. Lamb
912 Wisconsin Avenue
Nodenburk, Virginia 02091

Dear Andrea:

Your application for employment crossed my desk this morning. By now you got our sad story that we have no openings. Things are a bit slow, but you can be assured that we'll keep your application on file in case things change.

I am particularly sorry I did not see you while you were here. Best wishes for success in your job search.

Kindest regards,

John Taylor
Personnel Director

jt/sr

Sample letters 14.9 and 14.10 are two versions of rejections written to applicants who responded to newspaper advertisements. Both conclude with a personal tone, but are easily used for any newspaper ad rejection that has to be made.

SAMPLE LETTER 14.9. Rejection letter responding to newspaper advertisement applicant (full-block format).

August 17, 19X3

Ms. Lauren K. Blocher
7 Merrimac Trail
Felicia, Oregon 74421

Dear Ms. Blocher:

Thank you for your letter responding to our ad for a loan officer. As you can guess, the response was overwhelming. Although your resume was impressive, we had only one opening.

Even though we were unable to place you in this job, we will keep your resume on file for future reference in the event that a suitable position becomes available.

Thank you for your interest in New National Bank. Best wishes in your search for employment.

Sincerely,

Tracy R. McCaslin
Assistant Personnel Officer

trm/cpb

SAMPLE LETTER 14.10. Rejection letter responding to newspaper advertisement applicant (block format).

September 8, 19X4

Mr. James B. Ackroyd
7 Espen Road
Darrellon, Texas 50012

Dear Mr. Ackroyd:

Thank you for the interest you have shown in New National Bank by your response to our recent advertisement.

In light of the fact that we had only one opening, coupled with an unusually large number of outstanding candidates, I am sorry to report that we are unable to offer you the position as personnel administrator.

Sample Letter 14.10 continued

Thanks again for your interest in New National Bank. Best wishes for success in your search for suitable employment.

Cordially,

Tracy R. McCaslin
Assistant Personnel Officer

Sample letters 14.11-14.13 are rejection letters written to applicants to the bank's training program. Sample letters 14.11 and 14.12 are a long and short version of rejections because of limited or no openings.

SAMPLE LETTER 14.11. Rejection letter for bank's management training program (full-block format).

December 5, 19X4

Ms. Melissa K. Worthington
34 Society Hill Place
Dallas, Montana 00579

Dear Ms. Worthington:

Thank you for the interest you have shown in New National Bank. It has been our pleasure to be associated with you.

We feel that your academic and personal qualifications are excellent, and that you would be an asset to any company. In light of the limited number of openings in our Management Training Program, coupled with a large number of outstanding candidates, I am sorry to report that we are unable to place you in our 19X5 program.

Thanks again for the interest you have shown in New National. Best wishes for success in your search for suitable employment.

Sincerely,

John Taylor
Personnel Director

jt/yu

SAMPLE LETTER 14.12. Rejection letter for bank's management training program. Shorter version of sample letter 14.11 (block format).

November 18, 19X2

Mr. Alexander F. Hayes
89 Bolivia Avenue
Cortland, New Jersey 89306

Dear Mr. Hayes:

Thank you for your letter expressing an interest in our training program.

We have no openings at the moment, and do not anticipate any during 19X3. I will, however, keep your resume in our active file in case anything should develop.

Cordially,

John Taylor
Personnel Director

jt/lj

Sample letter 14.13 notifies the applicant that there will be no training program.

SAMPLE LETTER 14.13. Letter notifying applicant that management training program has been canceled (semiblock format).

December 26, 19X2

Mr. Simon Kemper
15 Douglas Road
Norristown, Idaho 00005

Dear Mr. Kemper:

Thank you for your letter and resume indicating your interest in our management training program.

Although the economy looks brighter, things are s till very tight in the banking industry, and it has just been decided that we will not have a management training program this year at New National Bank.

We are also under constant pressure to reduce staff through attrition wherever possible. At this point, the

Sample Letter 14.13 continued

most we can offer you is to keep your resume at the top of our file and to promise consideration for any openings that might become available during the coming months.

Thanks again for your interest in New National. Best of luck to you in your search for suitable employment.

Cordially,

John Taylor
Personnel Director

jt/yu

Sample letter 14.14 is a rejection letter written to an applicant for summer employment.

SAMPLE LETTER 14.14. Rejection letter to applicant for summer employment (semiblock format).

February 19, 19X4

Mr. Geoffrey Spaulding
67 Smithknee Road
Headton, Maryland 33321

Dear Mr. Spaulding:

Thank you for your inquiry about the possibility of summer employment with County Savings Bank.

While we do not anticipate any summer openings at the present time, we will be glad to keep your name on file, in the event that our situation should change.

Thanks again for your interest.

Sincerely,

Jessica Smith
Vice President
Human Resources

js/mn

Sample letters 14.15 and 14.16 are rejection letters written concerning applicants who were recommended to the bank. Sample letter 14.15 is written to an applicant who was recommended to the bank. A copy of the letter is forwarded to the recommender.

SAMPLE LETTER 14.15. Rejection letter to person recommended to the bank (semiblock format).

May 6, 19X2

Ms. Mary T. Jonsen
P.O. Box 167
State College
Bethany, North Carolina 40181

Dear Ms. Jonsen:

Thank you for your response to our search for an employment administrator. While you were recommended by Ms. Leslie Horvard, and your education and experience appear to be exceptional, the response that we received from the few inquiries that we made was overwhelming. I regret to write you that a candidate was chosen shortly before your letter arrived.

I extend to you our best wishes for success in your career search.

Sincerely,

Robert B. Hammond
Personnel Director

RBH/KLL

cc: Ms. Leslie Horvard

Sample letter 14.16 is written to a recommender explaining that the person recommended cannot be placed. A copy of this letter is forwarded to the person recommended.

SAMPLE LETTER 14.16. Letter to recommender of person who could not be hired (full-block format).

August 23, 19X2

Mr. Robert L. Coleman
Coleman, Velasquez & Schindler
1243 Battery Street, Suite 17
Avella, Tennessee 70191

Dear Bob:

I wanted to take a moment to acknowledge receipt of the resume of Simon Angel.

New National Bank is in the throes of a vigorous staff reduction program, which, it appears, will continue for some months to come. As a result, we have a hiring freeze on. I'm afraid you will find this condition exists at most of the city's banks.

There is some growth in the daycare industry. I'm wondering if Mr. Angel has explored the possibility of an administrative position on the staff of one of these centers. He has impressive qualifications in that field.

I will keep alert to other possible openings in the banking industry, but in view of the current situation I would not want to get Mr. Angel's hopes up.

Best wishes,

John Taylor
Vice President

JT:SR

cc: Tracy R. McCaslin
Simon Angel

Come In and Talk Letters

Sample letters 14.17 and 14.18 were written to applicants with whom the letter writer would like to talk. Sample letter 14.17 is to an applicant who had applied at a time when there were no positions available.

SAMPLE LETTER 14.17. Come in and talk letter to applicant who had applied at a time when no jobs were available (full-block format).

March 9, 19X3

Mr. Norman A. Clark
67 Asteroid Drive
Sandford, Rhode Island 15889

Dear Mr. Clark:

If you are still interested in employment opportunities at County Savings Bank, please telephone me.

I am looking forward to hearing from you soon.

Cordially,

Jessica Smith
Vice President
Human Resources

js/mn

Sample letter 14.18 is to an applicant who had just applied for a position.

SAMPLE LETTER 14.18. Come in and talk letter to applicant who has just applied (block format).

November 20, 19X2

Mr. Jerry Smith
23 Heavywire Drive, Apt. 55
Backton, Maine 11109

Dear Mr. Smith:

Thank you for your letter and resume, and for your interest in the County Savings Bank. I have read your resume with considerable interest and suggest that if you are in the Alewife area, you give my secretary a call to arrange a mutually convenient time for us to get together to discuss your interests and our openings.

I look forward to hearing from you. Thank you again for your interest.

Sample Letter 14.18 continued

Cordially,

John Taylor
Personnel Director

jt/gh

Recommendations

Various types of recommendations can be written. It is important for any recommendation to give the reader the impression that the writer is being sincere and honest in his or her evaluation of the person being recommended. Sample letters 14.19 and 14.20 are two good examples of effective recommendations.

SAMPLE LETTER 14.19. Recommendation (semiblock format).

April 9, 19X2

Mr. Timothy Keach
Personnel Officer
Old National Bank
P.O. Box 3542
Winehead, Georgia 20927

Subject: Victor L. Sakklin

Dear Mr. Keach:

It has been my privilege to know Mr. Sakklin for approximately two years. Until my resignation, I was employed at County Savings Bank as Assistant Vice President for Commercial Loans, which is where I met Mr. Sakklin.

Mr. Sakklin's technical expertise was of great value to me in my task of converting commercial loans to computerized accounting. His conscientious effort and cooperation in delivering timely information in formats desired by user departments was appreciated.

As a department manager, Victor is efficient, innovative, and responsible. He motivates his people with challenge and the opportunity for personal growth.

As an individual, Mr. Sakklin is a dedicated father and husband. Both he and his wife, Sarah, are social, outgoing people.

Sample Letter 14.19 continued

If you find that Mr. Sakklin's career objectives match your position description, I know of no reason you would be disappointed by his employment performance or personal habits. Please let me know if you require further information.

Sincerely,

Hunt L. Brinkley
Vice President

hlb/jls

SAMPLE LETTER 14.20. Recommendation (full-block format).

March 15, 19X2

Mr. Lawrence K. Henrix
Personnel Director
Fishbein, Larence, and Quantamyre
56 State Street, Suite 8A
Eclectic, California 16667

SUBJECT: RECOMMENDATION FOR ANTHONY RINGMAN

Dear Mr. Henrix:

In response to your request I am writing you about Mr. Anthony Ringman who worked for me in the savings department of County Savings Bank. He was not, however, a secretary, but rather a teller. Therefore, I am not qualified to comment on his capabilities as a secretary.
Tony was average as a teller. His personal appearance was above average and he made a good impression. He has a pleasant personality which resulted in his getting along well with his fellow employees.

Tony always seemed enthusiastic about his job in savings. His attitude toward his work and his cooperation were above average.

If I can be of further assistance to you, please let me know.

Sample Letter 14.20 continued

Sincerely,

COUNTY SAVINGS BANK

Lowell W. Rentide
Personnel Officer

lwr/yth

Commendations

Sample letter 14.21 is an example of a commendation letter to an employee. It is a good practice to have a copy of such a commendation sent to the person's personnel file.

SAMPLE LETTER 14.21. Commendation (block format).

November 17, 19X2

Mr. Bradley K. Geyser
Commercial Loan Department
New National Bank
119 Faulkner Drive
Tucker, West Virginia 12265

Dear Brad:

I commend you on your outstanding performance during 19X2. Adding six new relationships with an average gross profit of $125,000 is truly remarkable.

Please plan to join my wife and me at the annual awards dinner slated for February 28, 19X3. I hope that Julie will be able to accompany you.
Please accept my warmest congratulations for a job well done.

Best regards,

Thomas E. Stearns
Chairman

tes/jls

cc: Bradley K. Geyser Personnel File

No Longer With Us Letters

After employees stop working for the bank, customers sometimes will be unaware of their departure. Sample letters 14.22 and 14.23 are two letters that were written to notify the customer that the former employee no longer works for the bank. Sample letter 14.22 informs the customer to whom he should now address certain types of business.

SAMPLE LETTER 14.22. No longer with us letter informing person to whom he should now address his business at the bank (semiblock format).

November 19, 19X0

Mr. Mark Runner, Vice President
State Savings Bank
P.O. Box 1142
Bacon, Alabama 30115

Dear Mr. Runner:

As you may or may not be aware, Ms. Gayle Farran is no longer with County Savings Bank. All future correspondence concerning the prime interest rate should be forwarded to Lester L. Cooper, Assistant Vice President.

Thank you for noting this change.

Sincerely,

Jessica Smith
Vice President
Human Resources

js/ap

Sample letter 14.23 gives a forwarding address for the former employee.

SAMPLE LETTER 14.23. No longer with us letter giving forwarding address for former employee (full-block format).

June 30, 19X1

Ms. Jeanne Long, President
Long Systems, Inc.
215 Granite Avenue
Marblehead, Iowa 04494

Dear Ms. Long:

Alan R. Benjamin, Vice President of Operations, left County Savings Bank four years ago. His name should be removed from any correspondence to County Savings.

Mr. Benjamin can be written to at Old National Bank, Operations Center, Bethany, Iowa 18910.

Sincerely,

Pauline L. Menzinger
Assistant Vice President

plm/mla

Terminations

Most personnel directors will agree that there is really no such thing as a standard dismissal letter. Each termination has unique characteristics, and letters must be tailor-made to each situation. Some things to keep in mind when writing and sending a termination letter are:

1. Termination letters should be sent as registered or certified mail with return receipt requested. This protects the person writing the letter from the complaint that it was never received.
2. The reason for termination should be clearly stated.
3. All termination letters should be brief and, as much as is possible, be written in an understanding tone.

Sample letters 14.24-14.26 are examples of termination letters. Sample letter 14.24 is written as a warning to an employee requesting him to respond with certain information by a specific date.

SAMPLE LETTER 14.24. Letter warning employee of possible termination (block format).

February 1, 19X0

Mr. Jeffrey K. Rospaw
14 Divinity Avenue, Apt. 14
Malden, California 58245

Dear Mr. Rospaw:

We have not heard from you about your absence since Monday, January 28, 19X0. Unless I hear from you before February 8, 19X0, your employment with New National Bank will be terminated.

Company policy states that employees who are unable to report to work must notify their supervisor within the first half hour of the working day. An absence is considered excused only when the employees have notified their supervisor and have obtained approval.

Cordially,

Tracy R. McCaslin
Assistant Personnel Director

trm/wap

Sample letter 14.25 is a follow-up letter notifying the employee of his termination because he did not comply with personnel policies.

SAMPLE LETTER 14.25. Termination letter following-up lack of response to sample letter 14.24 (semiblock format).

February 11, 19X0

Mr. Jeffrey K. Rospaw
14 Divinity Avenue, Apt. 14
Malden, California 58245

Dear Mr. Rospaw:

Your employment with New National Bank has been terminated, effective February 8, 19X0, because of your failure to comply with Personnel Policy #9A, and your failure to respond to my letter of February 1, 19X0.

Sincerely,

Tracy R. McCaslin
Assistant Personnel Director

TRM/SRO

Sample letter 14.26 is a termination letter written to an employee who has broken the bank's absence policy.

SAMPLE LETTER 14.26. Termination letter written to employee who has broken bank policy (full-block format).

May 12, 19X2

Ms. Mary T. Bridges
58 Gillette Place, Apt. 4B
Emmafeld, Nevada 55402

Dear Mary:

On Monday afternoon, May 10, 19X2, you and I had a meeting with Mark Nichols in his office. When the conversation was over, you went back to your area and left the bank without telling anyone where you were going.

According to County Savings Bank's policy on absences, employees who will be absent must notify their superior during the first half hour of each working day.

Sample Letter 14.26 continued

Because we have not heard from you for the last two days, and have been unable to reach you, your employment at County Savings Bank is considered terminated.

Sincerely,

William W. Grimes
Executive Vice President

wwg/vjd

Personnel Memos

Memoranda 14.27-14.29 are three examples of memorandums coming out of the personnel department. Memorandum 14.27 concerns the evaluation of employees.

MEMORANDUM 14.27. Memorandum to employees about evaluation of employees.

TO: All Tellers
FROM: Raoul J. Berrigan
DATE: April 27, 19X2
SUBJECT: Evaluation Criteria

The guidelines by which tellers are evaluated are attached.

You are a professional. For a large portion of our clientele you are the County Savings Bank. In light of this, your employer expects you to do the best possible job you can for your bank.

The area in which you work is not simply for paying and receiving money; it is a customer service center. Therefore, you are to:

1. Put your customers first.
2. Serve them with courtesy, concern, and friendliness.
3. Give them the most efficient service possible.

You are also required to sell County Savings Bank's services to our customers.

In short, you are to display a professional attitude, appearance, and conduct in your position. The guidelines in

Sample Letter 14.27 continued

this memorandum are not requests; they are requirements for all tellers employed by the County Savings Bank.

RJB/JLS

enclosure

Copy to Tracy R. McCaslin, Assistant Personnel Director

Memorandum 14.28 details the bank's fair treatment policy.

MEMORANDUM 14.28. Memorandum to employees about bank's fair treatment policy.

TO: All Employees
FROM: John Taylor, Personnel Director
DATE: November 17, 19X2
SUBJECT: Your Assurance of Fair Treatment

A primary objective of New National Bank is to provide working conditions and policies that assure fair treatment. Our longstanding policy is that consideration for employment, training, and promotion at New National is to be based on qualifications without regard to race, color, religion, sex, age, or national origin. Furthermore, New National takes Affirmative Action to employ qualified handicapped individuals and qualified veterans of the Vietnam War.

If for any reason you feel that this policy is not being carried out, or if you have questions, criticisms, suggestions, or job-related problems, you should talk to your supervisor. Feel free to discuss the problem openly. In all likelihood your supervisor will be able to assist in reaching a prompt solution. If the problem is not resolved, however, see the personnel officer in your department or office. You can arrange a meeting either through your supervisor or directly with the personnel officer.

No one in New National Bank or its affiliates is too busy to listen and give you full consideration.

jt/jd

Memorandum 14.29 outlines the bank's job opportunity program.

MEMORANDUM 14.29. Memorandum to employees outlining bank's job opportunity program.

TO: Staff Members
FROM: Jessica Smith, Vice President–Human Resources
DATE: November 22, 19X2
SUBJECT: Job Opportunity Program

The Job Opportunity Program provides a formal method through which staff members can express their interest in a job vacancy that will be posted on the bulletin boards prior to the Personnel Department's effort to seek applicants from outside the company.

Following are some questions with answers pertinent to the Job Opportunity Program.

WHAT ARE THE REASONS FOR THE JOB OPPORTUNITY PROGRAM?
To inform you of job vacancies occurring within your company and to give you an opportunity to apply for these jobs. This program provides an opportunity for you to take initiative toward your own career development and to enhance your possibilities for advancement.

WHAT JOBS WILL BE POSTED?
All full-time, nonexempt job vacancies except those filled from within the department having the vacancy, or those which can be filled by displaced staff members, such displacement having been caused by organizational, technological, or economic changes.

WHERE WILL JOB VACANCIES BE POSTED?
Job vacancies will be posted for five working days on the bulletin board in the cafeteria. A record of the job postings will be kept in the Personnel Department.

HOW DO I APPLY FOR A POSTED JOB?
Employees interested in applying for a posted position complete a ''Job Opportunity Application'' form (available in the Personnel Department) and submit it to the Personnel Department.

WHAT ARE THE ELIGIBILITY REQUIREMENTS FOR APPLYING FOR A POSTED JOB?
You may apply if you believe you have the necessary skills required for the job, a satisfactory performance record, and meet the following basic eligibility requirements:

a. Nonexempt status.
b. In present job for at least six months.
c. No other job applications outstanding. You may, however, withdraw a pending job application when applying for a new vacancy.
d. Have not turned down an offer made in response to an application within the last thirty days.

DO I NEED PRIOR APPROVAL FROM MY SUPERVISOR BEFORE APPLYING?
No, you do not need prior approval in order to apply. You should, however, feel free to discuss your application for a posted position with your supervisor without fear of prejudice or discrimination.

All applications will be handled on a confidential basis. Your supervisor will be notified by the Personnel Department if you are referred for a departmental interview and again later if you are subsequently selected for a position.

WHAT HAPPENS IF I AM ABSENT DURING THE POSTING PERIOD?
If you do not have the opportunity to apply for a position because you are absent from work during a particular period, you will be given an opportunity to apply when you return to work if a commitment has not already been made to another applicant. When you return to work, you may request from the Personnel Department copies of the Job Vacancy Bulletins that were posted during your absence. If desired, you may submit an application for any one of the jobs not yet filled. Your application will be processed in the usual manner and you will be notified of the outcome. Please understand that you may only submit a late application if you are absent during the entire five day posting period.

WHAT HAPPENS TO MY APPLICATION?
Your application will be reviewed first to determine if you meet the basic eligibility requirements to apply for a position. If you *do not* meet these requirements, you will be notified immediately. If you *are eligible,* your skills, job history, and performance records will be reviewed to evaluate your qualifications for the position. If your records show that you are qualified, you will be called for an initial interview with the Personnel Department and, if appropriate, a subsequent interview will be arranged with the supervisors of the position applied for.

Staff Members -3- November 22, 19X2

WHAT ARE THE CRITERIA USED FOR EVALUATING QUALIFIED CANDIDATES?
Preference for filling vacancies is based upon the following criteria:

1. Pertinent skills and training
2. Performance appraisals
3. Length of service
4. Affirmative Action goals.

CAN I APPLY FOR A JOB AT A LOWER GRADE LEVEL?
Yes, if you feel that the position offers a better opportunity to develop yourself.

WHO MAKES THE FINAL DECISION?
The department with the job vacancy makes the final decision in conjunction with the Personnel Department after interviewing all qualified applicants. If you are chosen for the position you will be notified by phone or in person. At the same time, your immediate supervisor will be notified and requested to establish your transfer date with your new supervisor. The optimum time to effect the transfer is two weeks. This time is subject to change, however, to accommodate needs of our departments involved.

WHAT HAPPENS IF I AM NOT SELECTED FOR THE POSITION?
If you are not selected, you will be notified by the Personnel Department. At this time, a counseling session will be arranged to discuss the reasons for your non-selection, your present job performance, and future career development. This conference should provide a more objective insight into your own qualifications and assist you to better prepare yourself for future developments.

WHAT HAPPENS IF I AM SELECTED, BUT UNABLE TO FULFILL THE JOB REQUIREMENTS?
If you obtain a position under the Job Opportunity Program and are not capable of performing the job satisfactorily with the regular three-month performance validation period, and your former position has not been filled, you will be returned to that position. If your former position has been filled, you will be considered for an equivalent position (if available), or for any lesser position you may qualify to fill. If there are no positions available at the time, you may be temporarily dismissed but you will receive preferential consideration for any future openings for which you qualify.

THE SUCCESS OF THE JOB OPPORTUNITY PROGRAM DEPENDS ON ALL OF US.
Remember that the success of job posting depends on all of us. Through your support and free exchange of ideas, we will be able to make improvements to this program; continue to develop the merit system of internal promotions; and provide more opportunities for career development.

If you have any questions, please call the Personnel Department.

js/lt

For a good discussion of personnel policies and letters and memorandums which might be necessary to write, see C. Eugene Looper's book, *Banker's Guide to Personnel Administration,* published by Bankers Publishing Company / Probus (Chicago, Illinois).

Trusts, Estates, Safe Deposit 15

All trusts and estates have unique characteristics and conditions. Therefore, the contents of trust and estate letters will vary from letter to letter. Because of the legal nature of trusts and estates, legal jargon will often find its way into a trust officer's written vocabulary. It is important for the writer of a trust or estate letter to keep in mind that no matter how legalistic these letters might have to be, the reader still has to understand the letter. It is a good practice to keep the legalistic jargon to a minimum. Use it only where absolutely necessary. Don't try to impress your reader. He or she will have enough legal terms to juggle around in correspondence with attorneys about the trust or estate.

Trusts

Sample letters 15.1-15.17 are examples of various types of letters written concerning trusts. Although the details of some of these examples involve specific cases, the format and tone in which these letters are written will serve as good models on which to base the trust letters you write.

Sample letter 15.1 is an example of a sales letter for a trust. It clearly explains the benefits of a trust and encourages the customer to read enclosed information and to come in and discuss personal needs.

SAMPLE LETTER 15.1. Sales letter for trust services (full-block format).

January 29, 19X6

Mr. Peter C. Cooper
79 Goodwill Place
Aurora, West Virginia 15624

Dear Mr. Cooper:

In the booklet, ''The Living Trust,'' which we are enclosing in reply to your request, you will find emphasized these three points:

1. The trust can be terminated at any time you desire.
2. The trust may be altered whenever you desire to change its provisions.
3. You may direct us to obtain your approval before selling or buying securities. You thus retain control over your investments.

These points answer the principal questions raised by men and women who wish to retain some measure of control over their securities and prefer a trust arrangement that will permit them to amend its provisions to meet future unforeseen conditions.

After reading the booklet, you will perhaps want to discuss with us some of the advantages of a Living Trust in relation to your particular needs. If so, we would welcome the opportunity of talking with you and your attorney to outline some of the immediate and future benefits that such a trust might offer you, your heirs, and your estate.

Sincerely,

Adam R. Berrigan
Senior Vice President

ARB/JLS

encl.

Sample letters 15.2 and 15.3 are appraisal letters. Both examples begin by identifying the trust or trusts being appraised. The second paragraph gives an opinion of the present condition of holdings. The remainder of the letter includes thoughts on or possibilities for future investments.

SAMPLE LETTER 15.2. Appraisal letter of trust (semiblock format).

October 19, 19X2

T-9985
T-9986

Mr. Allen D. Figrand
P.O. Box 704
Rigbyville, Rhode Island 43520

Dear Al:

Enclosed are the September 30 appraisals of the Carla and Carolyn Lombardi Trusts. Both accounts have continued to do well in October with the October 15 value of the Carolyn Lombardi Trust at $2,920,239, and the Carla Lombardi Trust at $879,001.

I am happy with the existing listing of holdings. With the recent strength in energy-related issues, all parts of the portfolio are contributing to appreciation. My aversion to any sales is compounded, of course, by the substantial capital gains already realized.

Given the sharp market advance of the past two months, I am reluctant to commit all of the buying reserves currently invested in the U.S. Treasury 8.875% notes maturing on June 30, 19X4. I have enclosed a report on The Boston Post Dispatch, however, which you may find interesting. In addition to being an operation which is putting its house in order, the Post Dispatch shows strong unit growth potential. In a disinflationary environment, unit growth potential is becoming increasingly important.

Please consider this recommendation as well as the other recommendations we discussed last summer. I look forward to hearing your reactions to my appraisal of the Lombardi Trusts.

Best wishes,

Whitney M. Lowman
Trust Officer

WML/PMN

Enclosures

SAMPLE LETTER 15.3. Appraisal letter of trust (block format).

July 27, 19X2

T-98456

Mr. Oscar K. Rheingman, Esq.
Hope, Marshall & Donaldson
908 Ferton Avenue
Thomson, Vermont 01120

Dear Oscar:

Enclosed are a June 30, 19X2 appraisal of the assets of the Bingham Denton Trust and a summary of investment performance.

The performance summary indicates generally similar capital market results in the second quarter as in the first, with positive total returns for Treasury Bills and the Laura Brothers Bond Index, and negative returns for the S & P 500. Portfolio results continue to reflect weakness in cyclical and energy exposures.

Looking ahead, interest rates remain the critical factor for the stock market, in general, and cyclical stocks, in particular. We expect interest rates to continue to gradually decline over the course of the year, budget deficits notwithstanding. The growth of monetary aggregates has slowed to within the Federal Reserve's range of tolerance giving the Fed greater flexibility in meeting liquidity needs. Perceptions that the Fed has indeed been less restrictive resulted in strong acceptance of the Treasury's fundings of late June and early July and meaningful rate declines since then. Furthermore, the absence of a vigorous economic recovery should preclude a ''crowding out'' confrontation between the corporate sector and the Treasury during the second half.

Although a weak economic recovery should help interest rates, it will do little to improve the earnings outlook for the portfolio's cyclical companies. Nevertheless, I think it would be a mistake to cut back further on these types of issues given the price corrections of the second quarter. Investment changes in the portfolio during the past six months have increased its representation in the favored consumer staple, nondurable, and service groups. I would prefer to hold my ground on the less favored cyclical and energy issues in the portfolio.

Sample Lettter 15.3 continued

As always, I invite your comments and suggestions.

Best regards,

Whitney M. Lowman
Trust Officer

WML/ACM

Enclosures

Sample letters 15.4 and 15.5 are both reviews of the same trust spread out over a several month period. Sample letter 15.4 explains why an increase in the amount of monthly remittances cannot be made. The trust officer promises, however, to review the trust and make an upward adjustment when possible.

SAMPLE LETTER 15.4. Letter explaining why monthly remittances from trust cannot be increased (full-block format).

February 6, 19X9

T-78564
Mrs. Roberta T. Cupleman
87 Utopia Lane
Amerton, Vermont 39120

SUBJECT: WERDIE P. UDALL TRUST

Dear Mrs. Cupleman:

I have reviewed the income generated by the Werdie P. Udall Trust with the hope of increasing the monthly remittances made to you from the current level of $320. Unfortunately, I find that I am unable to do so at the present time.

This does not mean that the income generated has not grown in the last year. As a matter of fact, the per unit income paid by the General Stock Fund increased 14.1% in 19X8, following a 16.5% increase in 19X7. However, when this is considered within the context of the portfolio as a whole, where the gross income is derived 70% from the bond portion of the portfolio and only 30% from the stock portion, the effect of dividend increases is much less perceptible.

I must also add that in making the adjustment last year, I stretched the monthly payment amount to the outside pro-

Sample Lettter 15.4 continued

jected limit. In fact, on several occasions, the income account was overdrawn which is a situation upon which our auditors frown. I can assure you, however, that each December I will plan to review the income and make an upward adjustment whenever possible.

I suggest that we arrange to meet to review the trust and its objectives. I will be pleased to call on you in Amerton. You also have a standing invitation for luncheon here at the Bank. Give my secretary a call to arrange a convenient time.

I look forward to meeting with you.

Sincerely,

(Miss) Roxanne T. Quackenbush
Trust Officer

rtq/jst

Sample letter 15.5 is a follow-up letter completing the promised review and making the upward adjustment.

SAMPLE LETTER 15.5. Follow-up to sample letter 15.4 completing review and increasing monthly remittances (semiblock format).

January 24, 19X0

T-78564

Mrs. Roberta T. Cupleman
87 Utopia Lane
Amerton, Vermont 39120

Subject: Werdie P. Udall Trust

Dear Mrs. Cupleman:

As promised, I have reviewed the estimated income to be generated by the Udall Trust over the next twelve months and have determined the following:

Description	Amount
Estimated annual income	$4,596
Less Trustee's Compensation	–$234 (Est.)
Total	$4,362
Less State Fiduciary Tax	– $10.75%
	$3,893
Divided by twelve	$ 324

Sample Lettter 15.5 continued

I will therefore raise the amount of your monthly payments to $325.

The total annual income of the account has increased 3.1% over the past twelve months, with the portion generated by the General Stock Fund up 8% and that generated by the Taxable Bond Fund up .9%. Obviously, the increase in the equity portion is not as strong as in the past two years and largely reflects a slowing in year-to-year growth of corporate earnings, an event which is typical of this point in the business cycle. It also represents some shifting in the General Stock Fund portfolio to better position it for appreciation, establishing holdings of solid quality stocks which have lower current yields, but from which we expect better dividend growth. You might also note that the asset value of the General Stock Fund has increased in excess of 13% over the same twelve-month period.

I again stress that, with more than half of the account invested in bonds where income growth will be minimal, the growth of the portfolio's overall income will be diluted. As an example, had the growth of the General Stock Fund income been as much as 15%, the overall income of the account would nonetheless have increased only a little more than 5%.

To keep you up to date, I am enclosing the most recent reports of the General Stock Fund and the Taxable Fund, as well as our current Investment Strategy Statement. Should you wish any additional information, I would be glad to provide it.

Perhaps you would like to join me for a luncheon meeting here at the Bank for a more in-depth discussion of the account and its objectives. Simply give me a call and I will be happy to make the necessary arrangements.

Sincerely,

(Miss) Roxanne T. Quackenbush
Trust Officer

RTQ:JST

enc.

Sample letters 15.6-15.9 all deal with various examples of the payment of discretionary income. Sample letter 15.6 is written to a customer who had failed to make a written request for the discretionary funds. Because the trust officer judged the payment to be crucial to the customer, she gathered the details in a phone call and wrote out a proposed budget, requesting the customer to sign and return a copy.

SAMPLE LETTER 15.6. Discretionary income to customer who must complete written request (block format).

February 25, 19X2

Mr. Bernard L. Hills
P.O. Box 67
Farmer, Wisconsin 44230

Subject: Hills Family Trust

Dear Mr. Hills:

I am writing you to confirm the current income needs for you and your family.

In the past, the trustee has notified you annually of the available income cash that you may request. As you must know, however, trustees may disburse income at their discretion in accordance with the terms of the trust. This procedure requires that a formal request from you in writing be received before any funds can be disbursed.

In addition to the undistributed net income of $11,002.08, which you have requested, I have also included the $2,300 for the payment of your fuel oil bill that is currently outstanding. In order to formally request and receipt for these funds, please sign and date the enclosed copy of this letter and return it to me in the envelope provided for your convenience.

On the attached sheet, I have included a paragraph that elaborates some general and specific income needs for you and your family based on our recent phone conversation. Please sign and date your approval of the copy of the attached sheet and return it to me with the signed copy of this letter.

Your cooperation is appreciated. Call me if you have any questions.

Sample Lettter 15.6 continued

Cordially,

Pamela A. Hogan
Trust Officer

pah/sjc

encs.

Sample letter 15.7 is a letter written to a customer presenting him with discretionary income for a specific purpose. The letter writer explains the effect this payment will have on the customer's monthly remittances.

SAMPLE LETTER 15.7. Letter to customer presenting him with discretionary income for specific purpose (full-block format).

July 26, 19X2

Mr. Simon F. Wallace
45 Douglas Road
Far Hills, Pennsylvania 06838

Dear Mr. Wallace:

SUBJECT: BERTRAND A. WALLACE TRUST

Enclosed is our check for $20,000 from the principal of the Bertrand A. Wallace Trust. This check represents $12,500 for the payment of the land mortgage and $7,500 for the final payment on the existing second deed of trust. To acknowledge the safe receipt of this check, please sign, date, and return the enclosed copy of this letter in the envelope provided.

As agreed, we have canceled your monthly remittances, effective immediately. This income will be used to pay down the existing $20,000 loan for the remaining four and one-half years. We have paid the July 15 payment for $300.

Because the remittances have been canceled, an Investment Income Account has been opened. The income earned from your trust will be transferred to the principal of the income account, and will be earning money market rates.

Sample Lettter 15.7 continued

Please do not hesitate to call me if you have any questions.

Sincerely,

Pamela A. Hogan
Trust Officer

pah/ohg

enclosure

Sample letter 15.8 also concerns discretionary income. The letter writer explains, however, that the payment is being made under special circumstances so she can put her financial affairs in order. The letter states the arrangement of the payment but stresses the need for the customer to be more prudent in the future.

SAMPLE LETTER 15.8. Letter administering discretionary income. Requests that customer be more prudent in the future (semiblock format).

August 12, 19X4

Mrs. Allison Q. Rumpole T-564809
546 Havershord Drive
Massapequa, Vermont 38003

Subject: Simone K. Douglass Trust

Dear Mrs. Rumpole:

Today I forwarded to Judge Henderson our check for $30,390.65, which has been drawn from the principal of the trust established for your benefit under your mother's will.

The decision to make this large payment of principal to you has been reached only after long and careful deliberation on your current situation. As trustee of this trust, we feel an obligation to administer the trust in a manner that reflects your mother as expressed in her will. We therefore believe that to assist you in putting your financial affairs in order is in your best interests. We also believe that you have demonstrated a sincere desire to conduct your future financial affairs in a prudent fashion, as evidenced by your retention of Judge Henderson's services as your attorney. Under these circumstances and bearing in mind Dr. Latoni's assessment of your present medical condition, we believe the payment of your outstanding bills for $30,390.65 is appropriate.

Sample Lettter 15.8 continued

In making this payment, however, we cannot emphasize too strongly that this is not to be construed as a precedent which we will readily repeat. I feel sure that you realize that continued use of capital will seriously jeopardize the trust's ability to support you over the years ahead. It is therefore incumbent upon you, with the help of Judge Henderson, to refrain from incurring unnecessary debts and to endeavor to live within your income. We feel confident that you are now committed to such a course of action.

Cordially,

(Mrs.) Leslie T. Waters
Trust Officer

ltw:dar

Copies to: Judge Henderson
Paul Alexander, Esq.
Lindsey Sevareid

Sample letter 15.9 concerns the payment of discretionary income for unforeseen health costs. The trust officer stresses the need for the customer to control her expenses and keep within the parameters of the trust in the future.

SAMPLE LETTER 15.9. Letter administering discretionary income for unforeseen health costs (block format).

November 1, 19X8

T-09345

Mr. George T. Folger
78 Effortless Trail
Denville, Montana 03003

SUBJECT: TRUST OF ESTELLE T. WILLIAMSON

Dear Mr. Folger:

I have shared the information in your letter of October 18, 19X8 with members of our Trust Administration Committee. Although the Committee noted that they had previously seen the reports provided by Dr. Salinder, they are, of course, concerned about Mrs. Williamson's health. Accordingly, I am enclosing a check for $2,829 as reimbursement for amounts paid to Dr. Salinder and the Main Clinic by Mrs. Williamson.

Sample Lettter 15.9 continued

I have not yet received the copies of Mrs. Williamson's federal and state tax returns for the past three years, a revised budget, and a full financial statement which I requested in my letter of October 2. The Committee is not inclined to exercise its discretion for other principal disbursements until it is provided with this information.

We do not think that our request for documentation is unreasonable. We cannot invade trust principal every time Mrs. Williamson's spending exceeds her not inconsiderable income. Although we are primarily concerned with Mrs. Williamson's welfare, we also have an obligation to the remainder interests which are potentially her children's or a charity's. We are concerned that regular invasions of trust principal will both erode its value and its ability to earn income and provide for Mrs. Williamson in the years to come.

Although we are anticipating a revised budget from you or Mrs. Williamson, we are concerned about the monthly expenditures that are attributable to the support of her children on the budget supplied in January 19X8. Especially in the case of her married daughter, who is legally the financial responsibility of her husband, we feel that some disbursements are not necessarily called for by the language in the instrument.

If Mrs. Williamson cannot control her expenditures so that she and her children can live on the $30,000 produced by the trust, it may well be that the children should now be concerned about what they, as adults, can contribute financially to the household if they continue to live there.

We feel that hospitalization or health insurance should be incorporated into the monthly budget of a financially responsible person and should not be treated as a separate item. We will wish to see the revised budget before we approve such an inclusion.

I urge you to provide us with the requested information at your earliest possible convenience.

Sincerely,

(Mrs.) Leslie T. Waters
Trust Officer

itw/dar

enclosure

Sample letters 15.10 and 15.11 are letters written about promissory notes drawn against trusts. Sample letter 15.10 calls a promissory note; sample letter 15.11 notifies a customer of past-due payments.

SAMPLE LETTER 15.10. Letter calling promissory note (full-block format).

August 2, 19X2

Mrs. Milicent Conroy
P.O. Box 678
Taylor, New Jersey 26210

SUBJECT: PROMISSORY NOTE ON LAWRENCE E. THOMASON TRUST

Dear Mrs. Conroy:

As you recall, last year on August 4, 19X1, the Lawrence E. Thomason Trust lent you $20,000. Our records indicate that this loan was secured by a Promissory Note with interest compounded at 6% per year. Therefore, one year's interest calculated at 6% would be $1,200.

The Promissory Note will become due on August 4, 19X2. At your convenience, would you please forward a check for $21,200 for repayment and one year's interest. Please make the check payable to the Lawrence E. Thomason Trust. When we receive the check we will forward the canceled promissory note to you.

Please feel free to call me if you have any questions.

Sincerely,

Lawrence T. Dawson
Trust Administrator

ltd/lcd

SAMPLE LETTER 15.11. Letter notifying customer of past-due payments on promissory note (block format).

December 1, 19X0

Mr. Harold T. Crenshaw
P.O. Box 98
Williamsburg, Massachusetts 86520

Dear Mr. Crenshaw:

Upon reviewing my files, I was troubled to discover that the interest and principal payments on your Promissory Note at 6% date November 15, 19X8, have become quite long overdue.

Projecting through December 10, 19X0, the total payment currently due is $420, which includes $155.47 in principal as well as $264.53 in income. Your last check was received by us on June 2, 19X0.

May I suggest that you make arrangements to meet this obligation on time in the future. Quite possibly, you might sell whatever it is that you bought with the money in order to pay off the debt.

You may return your payment to me in the envelope provided for your convenience.

Sincerely,

Lawrence T. Dawson
Trust Administrator

ltd/lcd

enclosure

Sample letters 15.12 and 15.13 were written to get the customer to fill out a domicile card for tax purposes.

SAMPLE LETTER 15.12. Letter requesting customer to fill out domicile card (semiblock format).

August 27, 19X2

Mrs. Katherine Wagner
98 Tretoned Drive
Chrysalis, Utah 10148

Dear Mrs. Wagner:

Enclosed is the letter to the IRS for your signature. Please sign the letter and return it to me in the envelope provided. On October 15, we will send the letter along with the final check to the IRS office.

Also enclosed is the Statement of Domicile. Please complete this form and return it to me. It will be forwarded to our tax department and, in turn, will be filed with the state tax office. When this process is completed, your quarterly installments for state income tax will be stopped.

We have changed your address for accountings and remittances to your Utah business address. When you obtain a permanent address in Utah, please let me know so we can change our records.

I wish you and Mr. Wagner the best of luck in your move. Please do not hesitate to call me if you have problems or questions.

Sincerely,

Lawrence T. Dawson
Trust Administrator

ltd/lcd

enclosures

SAMPLE LETTER 15.13. Letter requesting customer to fill out domicile card (full-block format).

July 1, 19X2

T-90876

Mr. Bertrand K. Flala
78 Esmerald Place
Loni, Nevada 30280

Dear Mr. Flala:

For tax purposes it is necessary for our records to show you domiciled in one state or another for the twelve months ending September 30, 19X2. In this way, we can prepare the appropriate state income tax information concerning your trust income so that you may then incorporate it in your state tax returns. I am therefore enclosing a domicile card which should be completed and signed by you. The domicile card should indicate where you expect to be a taxpayer for the forseeable future.

It is also necessary for us to know what state or states you considered yourself to be a taxpayer in from October 1, 19X1 through June 30, 19X2. If you would use the enclosed copy of this letter to clarify this situation, I will pass it along to the income tax department.

I send my best wishes and hope that your summer in the Rockies is a splendid one.

Sincerely,

Kate O. Peterson
Senior Trust Officer

KOP:DAR

Enclosures

Sample letter 15.14 is a request on behalf of a customer to a company in which he holds stock. Such a letter fosters good customer relations and provides a service to the customer which he will appreciate.

SAMPLE LETTER 15.14. Letter to company in which customer holds stock (block format).

July 22, 19X2

Mr. Jackie Mustain
Whist, Inc.
98 Primiano Circle
Pennsacola, Ohio 40304

Dear Mr. Mustain:

New National Bank holds three hundred shares of your company stock in our nominee for the benefit of Mr. Armand Bellini. All dividends derived from these shares are forwarded to New National.

Mr. Bellini has requested that the quarterly statements of reports that frequently accompany the dividend checks be sent to him under a separate cover. If it is possible, please send out a separate quarterly report to Mr. Bellini at 44 Pocum Place, Bimini, Idaho 27120.

Thank you for your help.

Sincerely,

Kate O. Peterson
Senior Trust Officer

kop:lcd

cc: Mr. Armand Bellini

Sample letter 15.15 was written to a lawyer who is cotrustee on a customer's trust. The trust officer explains the action she wants to take and requests the cotrustee's signature of approval.

SAMPLE LETTER 15.15. Letter to lawyer who is cotrustee on customer's trust, requesting approval (block format).

August 12, 19X2

Mr. James Plax, Esq.
Evans, Evans & Fultimore
89 Plankton Drive
Loining, Vermont 88097

Subject: Mr. William T. Franklin Trust

Dear Mr. Plax:

We are preparing a discretionary form for approval of amounts paid to Mr. and Mrs. Anderson Quail during the year 19X1. During this time period, $350 a month was remitted from income to Mrs. Anderson Quail and the balance ($32,216) of the net income was remitted to Mr. Quail. In addition, a principal distribution of $3,032.67 was made to Mr. Quail by payment to Whist, Inc.

In view of Mr. Quail's situation and circumstances, it is felt that these payments to him were appropriate. If you, as cotrustee, are in agreement with us, please sign and date the enclosed copy of this letter and return it to me in the envelope provided for your convenience.

Please call me if you have any questions.

Cordially,

Kate O. Peterson
Senior Trust Officer

kop/lcd

Encls.

Sample letter 15.16 is an apology for a mix-up. The trust officer is careful to explain the measures she has taken to correct a recurrent problem affecting the customer.

SAMPLE LETTER 15.16. Letter apologizing for mix-up (semiblock format).

August 4, 19X8

T-0987658

Miss Diane Parker
98 Headley Drive
Lichfield, England

Dear Miss Parker:

I received your letter of July 23 and apologize that once again the transmittal instructions were not properly followed. I spoke again with the head of our International Department—reading the riot act—and have personally seen the proper instructions placed in their remittance file. I have also reinforced the instructions by having the Trust Department's Bookkeeping Group indicate the instructions of their internal transmittal to the International Department.

I feel that I have sufficiently rattled the right cages to prevent this problem from occurring again. Based on past experience, however, that might be too bold a statement to make.

Thank you for your extraordinary patience in what I am sure is a matter of great inconvenience to you. I will mark my calendar for the next remittance to personally supervise its departure from the bank.

If I can be of further assistance, please let me know.

Sincerely,

Kate O. Peterson
Senior Trust Officer

kop/lcd

Sample letter 15.17 is a letter written concerning the final distribution of funds from a trust. The trust officer has written a brief letter describing the items enclosed and the papers the customer is to receive concerning the final distribution.

SAMPLE LETTER 15.17. Letter about the final distribution of funds from a trust (full-block format).

October 8, 19X2

Mr. Harvey H. Gleckman
89 Dinman Road
Fitchburg, Vermont 24711

Subject: Muriel T. Gleckman Trust, Final Distribution of Funds

Dear Mr. Gleckman:

Enclosed is our check for $1,542.13 representing the final distribution to you from your mother's trust.

We were surprised that the tax clearance from the state was received so quickly. We did not expect clearance until March, 19X3.

Currently we are in the process of preparing a final account of the trust. A copy will be sent to you for your files when it is complete.

Please do not hesitate to call me if you have any questions.

Sincerely,

Kate O. Peterson
Senior Trust Officer

kop/lcd

Enclosures

Estates

Sample letters 15.18-15.20 are sales-oriented letters which were written about estates. Sample letter 15.18 informs the customer of the benefits of planning an estate.

SAMPLE LETTER 15.18. Sales letter informing customer of benefits of planning an estate (block format).

January 9, 19X3

Mr. Murray T. Feingold
908 Ellenberry Place
Carlisle, Illinois 48200

Dear Mr. Feingold:

Your Will—when drawn by your attorney and kept up to date by frequent review—may serve as a highway to future financial security for your family. If you leave no Will, however, your spouse and children may find the road beset with difficulties because you have neglected to give serious thought to their financial welfare when you are no longer here to guide them.

If your estate is small, you may think that you do not need a Will. This is a dangerous doctrine. Small property owners must be especially careful to provide in the most effective manner possible for their families. A Will helps to attain this goal. Without a Will, your property passes by state law perhaps to those you do not wish to benefit.

The New National Bank—long experienced in estate work and with a wide knowledge of local problems—has acted as Executor for many small and large estates. A talk with an attorney and one of our trust officers has helped others provide greater security for their families. You, too, are invited to obtain the benefits of our experience.

Cordially,

NEW NATIONAL BANK

Pamela A. Hogan
Trust Officer

pah/lkh

Sample letters 15.19 and 15.20 are two versions of follow-up letters written after a meeting where estates were discussed. Both letters express the appreciation for the meeting and the desire to follow-up with the customer.

SAMPLE LETTER 15.19. Follow-up letter to sales meeting discussing estates (semiblock format).

September 8, 19X2

Mr. Alan J. Newhart
210 North Street
Austin, Oregon 11123

Dear Mr. Newhart:

Thank you for the time you spent with me discussing the trust services of the New National Bank. Now that the Labor Day weekend has passed, I hope that we will have the opportunity to discuss the estate planning requirements of your mother.

I am interested to know if you have completed your survey of other trust services in the area, and whether or not any questions arose from your review of our literature. I would appreciate hearing from you once you have completed your review and evaluation process, either to respond to any questions or to be informed about your final decision.

Thank you again for the opportunity to acquaint you with our capabilities.

Sincerely,

Roscoe P. Pullman
Vice President

rpp/pcp

SAMPLE LETTER 15.20. Follow-up letter to sales meeting discussing estates (full-block format).

May 27, 19X2

Mrs. Joanna Neord
30 Cole Street
Spring Valley, Wisconsin 77901

Dear Mrs. Neord:

It was a pleasure speaking with you about County Savings Bank's investment management service. I'm enclosing a brochure which will provide more information for your consideration. The fee schedule is also enclosed.

As we discussed, you will be working with an experienced portfolio manager who will help you create and maintain a securities portfolio which will always meet your particular investment needs and goals. Our investment officers are professional and pleasant to work with. I am sure you will find our investment management service to be of great benefit to you.

I look forward to speaking with you soon. If you should have any questions in the interim, please call me.

Sincerely,

Lillian D. Ispepson
Trust Officer

ldi/hlc

encl.

Sample letter 15.21 was written to an attorney requesting accountings on a customer's estate.

SAMPLE LETTER 15.21. Letter to attorney requesting accountings on estate (full-block format).

June 11, 19X2

Ms. Nancy Coleman
Farquand, Farquand, Farquand & Smith
One Park Place
Atlantic City, Delaware 80120

Dear Ms. Coleman:

SUBJECT: COLIN P. O'LEARY

Enclosed for filing is the original and one copy of the Third and Final Account of The New National Bank, Executor under the Will of Colin P. O'Leary, along with our check for $175 to cover the filing fees.

We request that you have the First and Final Account of The New National Bank and the Third and Final Account of the Estate allowed by the court. In due course, please advise us of the date of allowance. You may keep the copy of the Accounting for your files.

In order to acknowledge the safe receipt of this check, please sign and date the enclosed copy of this letter and return it to me in the envelope provided for your convenience.

Thank you for your assistance.

Sincerely,

Kate O. Peterson
Senior Trust Officer

kop/lcd

Enclosures

Received by: ____________________ Date: ____________

Sample letter 15.22 is written to the Executrix of an estate requesting her approval on the first and final accountings of the estate.

SAMPLE LETTER 15.22. Letter to executrix requesting approval on first and final accountings of estate (block format).

September 28, 19X2

Ms. Jennifer Barnes
8 Pohdunk Place
West Quantum, Rhode Island 58910

Gwendolyn W. Johnson Estate

Dear Ms. Richards:

As executrix of the Gwendolyn W. Johnson Estate, it is required that you approve the First and Final Accountings of the estate. Please review the Accountings that were sent to you on March 4, 19X2 and, if they meet with your approval, sign the Accountings and return the original and two copies to me. You may keep the third copy for your records.

Please call me if you have any questions.

Sincerely,

Warren W. Snopper
Trust Officer

wws/lcd

Sample letter 15.23 is a request to an attorney for an informal accounting of an estate.

SAMPLE LETTER 15.23. Request to attorney for informal accounting of estate (semiblock format).

November 1, 19X2

T-0983456

Mr. Alan G. Guido
Truman, Gillespie, Smith & Guido
One Foundation Place
Barton, Florida 10140

Subject: Estate of Thomas P. Opener

Dear Mr. Guido:

I have been asked to write you about an Executor's account for the Opener Estate.
While we recognize that the Executor in Florida has no duty to account to the Probate Court, our legal department feels that we have an obligation, as Residuary Trustee, to review the Executor's transactions.

We therefore request that you provide us with an informal accounting which allows us to review the progression of transactions in the estate. I hope that your internal records will allow for such an accounting to be prepared with a minimum of inconvenience.

Your cooperation, as in all our dealings in the past, is greatly appreciated.

Cordially,

Warren W. Snopper
Trust Officer

lcd

Sample letter 15.24 is a brief letter confirming the details of an appointment for an appraisal which is to be made of the estate.

SAMPLE LETTER 15.24. Letter confirming appointment for appraisal of estate (block format).

March 26, 19X2

Mr. Parker T. Stevenson
President
Estate Appraisal, Inc.
67 Warsaw Court
Brooklyn, Ohio 61120

Dear Mr. Stevenson:

Subject: Appraisal of Cooper T. Serum Estate

This letter confirms our appointment with you for appraisal work on Thursday, April 8, at ten o'clock. The Serums' address is 22 Old Bethany Road, Brooklyn.

For your records, you should note that New National Bank is the sole Executor of the estate.

If you have any questions, please call me.

Cordially,

Valera D. Jespers
Assistant Trust Officer

lcd

Sample letter 15.25 was written to reimburse a customer for the costs incurred during the settling of his father's estate, and to inform him of the procedure to be taken with the property left in the estate.

SAMPLE LETTER 15.25. Letter reimbursing customer for cost incurred in settling of estate (full-block format).

September 28, 19X2

Mr. Howard R. Jacobs
5 Tretaman Road
Billerica, New York 02501

SUBJECT: OSCAR JACOBS ESTATE AGENCY FIDUCIARY ACCOUNT

Dear Howard:

Enclosed is our check for $441.96 representing payment for the various household and transportation expenses incurred in connection with your father's estate. To acknowledge the safe receipt of this check, please sign and date the enclosed copy of this letter and return it to me in the envelope provided.

Catherine Lowery of our Trust Department confirmed the sale of the painting with Mrs. Harriet Justus of the Lewis Gallery in New York City. The approximate price for the illustration in the catalogue is $75. The painting will be insured for $10 per thousand on the sale price. The auction will be on Tuesday, December 2.

If you have any questions, please call me.

Best regards,

Warren W. Snopper
Trust Officer

wws/pat

enclosure

Received by:____________________ Date: __________

Sample letter 15.26 clearly outlines the effect the provisions of a deceased woman's will will have on a person who had been receiving monthly remittances from a trust set up in the now deceased woman's name.

SAMPLE LETTER 15.26. Letter informing recipient of remittances from trust fund about the provisions that have been made for her organization in the estate (full-block format).

September 20, 19X2

T-68309

Ms. Andrea J. Tuttle, Director
Hoskins Halfway House
45 Blossom Ridge
Togetherness, California 64523

Dear Ms. Tuttle:

We have recently been informed of the death of Margaret T. Higgins, the annuitant by whose life the duration of the Higgins Trust in its present form is measured.

In accordance with the terms of Mrs. Higgins' will, the trustees are now to divide the trust into five equal shares, one for each of the five named charities. One-fifth of the trust is therefore to be distributed to the Hoskins Halfway House to establish a Memorial Fund in the name of Estelle P. Haskell (Mrs. Higgins' sister). The House is then instructed to add one-half of the income earned by this fund to principal each year, with the other one-half of the income available for you to use for the general purposes of the House.

We have therefore asked outside counsel for the trust to review the legal issues surrounding this distribution. As soon as counsel has provided us with an opinion as to proper procedures, we will be in touch with you.

Now that the trust is in the process of distribution, Mr. Warren W. Snopper, Trust Officer, will have primary responsibility for the account, although I will continue to be available for consultation. You should direct any inquiries to his attention at New National.

I realize that the disruption in income which will occur while the plan for distribution is worked out may cause some hardship, but I can assure you that we will do everything we can to keep the delay to a minimum. It might also be wise for you to revise your budget and financial planning as soon as possible to reflect what is a cut of 50% in the income available to you from this source.

Sample Lettter 15.26 continued

Thank you for the cooperation you have shown me over the course of our association.

Sincerely,

Kate O. Peterson
Senior Trust Officer

lcd

Sample letter 15.27 was written to cash in a travelers check a woman held at the time of her death. This letter is a good model to use when a letter has to be written to collect various funds for the estate account.

SAMPLE LETTER 15.27. Letter written to cash in travelers check (block format).

August 12, 19X2

Mr. Alan P. Quantimyre
American Express Company
Travelers Check Refund
67 Rockefeller Road
Oshkosh, Montana 40001

Attention: Redemption Unit

Dear Mr. Quantimyre:

Subject: Gladys E. Thomson Estate Agency
Fiduciary Account

Gladys E. Thomson, late of 98 Maxwell Drive, Oshkosh, Montana, died on July 1, 19X2. At the time of her death, she held one American Express Travelers Check.

Enclosed is Travelers Check #45345 for $20. Also enclosed for your records is a copy of Mrs. Thomson's death certificate and Mr. Peter Thomson's certificate of appointment as temporary executor of her estate.

Please redeem the enclosed Travelers Check and send to me a check made payable to the Gladys E. Thomson Estate Agency Fiduciary Account. So that I will know you have received the enclosed check and documents, please sign, date, and return the enclosed copy of this letter to me in the envelope provided.

Sample Lettter 15.27 continued

Thank you for your assistance.

Cordially,

Gregory T. Koch, Jr.
Trust Officer

GTK/JKL

encs.

Received by: ____________________ Date: ____________

Sample letter 15.28 is written to a bank instructing it to close out a deceased customer's accounts and send the proceeds to be deposited in an estate account.

SAMPLE LETTER 15.28. Letter instructing bank to close accounts and send money to estate account (semiblock format).

October 27, 19X2

T-9056742

Raoul J. Berrigan
County Savings Bank
76 Vineyard Avenue
Wellesley, Oregon 08720

Subject: Alan T. Denverson
NOW Account and Savings Account #5-5067-678

Dear Mr. Berrigan:

New National Bank has been appointed conservator of the property of Mr. Alan T. Denverson. Enclosed is a certified copy of our appointment.

Please use this letter as your authority to close Mr. Denverson's accounts at County Savings Bank. Send a check for the balances payable to the Alan T. Denverson Conservatorship to my attention at:

New National Bank
P.O. Box 704
Hingham, Oregon 10120

If you have any questions or require additional documentation, please let me know. Would you also please

Sample Lettter 15.28 continued

see that the final statement produced for this account is sent to my attention.

Cordially,

Gregory T. Koch, Jr.
Trust Officer

jkl

encl.

Sample letter 15.29 was written to an attorney instructing her to prepare a petition for probate.

SAMPLE LETTER 15.29. Letter to attorney instructing her to petition for probate (full-block format).

July 21, 19X2

Louise T. Harlan
Donohue, Baker & Lazamatan
908 Government Street, Suite 9
Sewickley, Kansas 02081

SUBJECT: ESTATE OF MELISSA T. CHIPPER

Dear Ms. Harlan:

Enclosed for filing in the County Probate Court is the original Will of Melissa T. Chipper, date October 8, 1972. Mrs. Chipper, late of Sewickley, Kansas, died on July 1, 19X2. To acknowledge receipt of this Will, please sign and date the enclosed copy of this letter and return it to us in the envelope provided.

Mrs. Chipper is survived by her son, Mr. Victor K. Chipper, of 76 MacIntyre Drive, Belinka, Kansas 02501, and her daughter, Mrs. Maxine D. Mobley, of Doubley Road, Sewickley, Kansas 02081. We estimate that Mrs. Chipper's probate estate will amount to approximately $200,000 in personal property and $300,000 in real estate.

Please prepare a petition for probate for the signature of Mr. Victor K. Chipper, as the named surviving co-execu-

Sample Lettter 15.29 continued

tor. In addition, would you also prepare the fiduciary bond, without sureties, for Mr. Chipper's signature.

Thank you for your assistance.

Cordially,

Gregory T. Koch, Jr.
Trust Officer

GTK:JKL

Encs.

Sample letter 15.30 was written to inform an attorney that necessary clearances have not been received and the procedure to be taken as result.

SAMPLE LETTER 15.30. Letter informing attorney necessary clearances have not been received (block format).

June 25, 19X2

Mr. James V. Lewis, Atty.
78 Rosner Place
Baltimore, Arkansas 02233

Wallace W. Cleaver Estate

Dear Mr. Lewis:

In response to your recent letter, please take note that we have not received the state or federal clearances for the Cleaver Estate. New National Bank's tax department has told me that we can anticipate an audit on both the Wallace W. Cleaver Estate and the Barbara K. Cleaver Estate. The reason for the audit is due, I believe, to the closeness of the Cleaver deaths.

With this in mind, I recommend that we wait to distribute the real estate until clearances are received. New National Bank, as Executor, could file an affidavit with the court to release the property. This procedure, however, could be costly to the Estate. If Miss Cleaver is considering the sale of the land in West Baltimore, then we should proceed with the filing of the affidavit.

Sample Lettter 15.30 continued

I would appreciate it if you would advise me whether or not there is an urgency for the release of the West Baltimore property prior to receiving the proper clearances.

Sincerely,

Gregory T. Koch, Jr.
Trust Officer

gtk/jkl

Sample letter 15.31 was written to a bankruptcy court listing all bankruptcy estate accounts opened by trustees appointed by the court. This letter is a simple one to use as a model if you remember to include:

1. The date of the report
2. The name of the appropriate bankruptcy judge and court
3. The account number
4. The name of the bankruptcy company or individual
5. The name and description of the trustee
6. The case number
7. The current balance of the account
8. The balance not insured by FDIC
9. The total balance not insured by FDIC

SAMPLE LETTER 15.31. Letter to bankruptcy court listing all bankruptcy estate accounts opened by trustees appointed by the court (semiblock format).

September 30, 19X4

The Honorable Patrice Connelly
U.S. Bankruptcy Judge
U.S. District Court
United States Court House
Cae, Massachusetts 57140

Dear Judge Connelly:

This report shows the balance on deposit in each bankruptcy estate account opened or taken over by authority of your court.

Sample Lettter 15.31 continued

Account Number	Account	Current Balance	Balance Not Insured by FDIC
2-5139-60	Joan Selin as trustee for the bankruptcy estate of DMI, Inc., Case #222-47	$42,000	$2,000
5-6098-60	Jim Lewis as receiver for the bankruptcy estate of Cullen Enterprises, Inc., Case #308-47	$15,000	$ 0
		Total	$2,000

If we at County Savings Bank can be of further assistance, please let me know.

Sincerely,

Virginia T. Collins
Vice President

vtc/jls

Safe Deposit

Sample letter 15.32 is a sales letter written about safe deposit boxes available at a bank. The letter describes the benefits of the boxes, and lists the annual costs.

SAMPLE LETTER 15.32. Sales letter for safe deposit boxes (simplified format).

November 23, 19X2

Mr. William G. Petty
14 Weetning Place
Detroit, Wisconsin 00510

SAFE DEPOSIT BOXES

Mr. Petty, County Savings Bank has safe deposit boxes in a variety of sizes at most of our offices. These boxes are perfect for protecting personal valuables, legal documents such as wills, deeds, or stock certificates, and jewelry. The vault in which the boxes are housed exceeds

Sample Lettter 15.32 continued

the requirements of the Federal Bank Protection Act of 1968 to assure customers that their valuables will receive the greatest possible protection. Rooms are available for reviewing the contents of the boxes in utmost privacy.

Investing in a safe deposit box is probably, dollar for dollar, the best investment you can make in terms of protecting your personal property. Join the growing number of people who recognize the importance of having a numbered safe deposit box. To reserve your box, please call or stop in at our nearest office.

Listed below are the box sizes available, and the annual costs for these boxes.

Size	Annual Rental Fee
2″ x 5″	$ 15.00
3″ x 5″	$ 20.00
5″ x 5″	$ 30.00
3″ x 10″	$ 38.00
5″ x 10″	$ 60.00
10″ x 10″	$120.00

If I can give you any other information or help you in the selection of a safe deposit box, please let me know.

COUNTY SAVINGS BANK

Carl D. Simonson
Assistant Vice President

cds/jus

Sample letter 15.33-15.35 are examples of letters written to customers whose payments are overdue on safe deposit boxes. Sample letter 15.33 is a second notice to the customer informing him that the contents of his safe deposit box will be sold if he does not pay the amount overdue. By replacing the names, dates, times, and amounts in sample letter 15.33, you could use this letter as a form letter for notifying customers of the sale of safe deposit contents to take place after past due payments are not made.

SAMPLE LETTER 15.33. Letter to customer notifying him of sale of safe deposit box items after payments have not been made (block format).

June 5, 19X3

Mr. Thomas P. Pound
7856 Escrow Lane
Bamboo, Rhode Island 22011

Dear Mr. Pound:

On June 1, 19X1, you were notified by postpaid, securely sealed, and registered letter, that the contents removed from your safe deposit box would be held in safekeeping in the vaults of New National Bank's main office for a period of at least two years, at the end of which time the contents may be sold and from any proceeds the Bank would deduct for itself any amounts then due the Bank for unpaid rentals, cost of safekeeping, incurred expenses, and interest.

Safe Deposit Box #704, located at New National's main office

Leased to Thomas P. Pound

Box opened on June 1, 19X3

You are now notified by postpaid, securely sealed, and registered letter that two years have elapsed since the opening of the safe deposit box and the mailing of a notice to you, and that the amounts set out, plus interest are now due the Bank:

1. Unpaid rentals to the time of opening of box	$600.00	
2. Safekeeping costs since opening of box	$125.00	
3. Cost of locksmith to open box	$ 50.00	
4. Costs of notary service	$ 50.00	
5. Cost of mailing	$ 17.00	
6. Other costs	$______	
7. Tax	$ 30.00	
	$872.00	Total

Unless all amounts and any further charges that might accrue, plus legal interest to all are paid on or before 1 p.m., local time, on July 15, 19X3, New National Bank will sell, not less than sixty days after the time of mailing this notice, all the property and articles of

Sample Lettter 15.33 continued

value at public auction at our main branch, and will deduct from the proceeds of the sale all amounts then due the Bank.

The balance, if any, from the proceeds of the sale will be deposited in an account with New National Bank.

The actions taken by New National Bank are under the provisions of existing statutes of the state.

Sincerely,

NEW NATIONAL BANK

Sebastian T. Bellaire
Executive Vice President

stb/hjk

Sample letters 15.34 and 15.35 are letters that were written to a safe deposit customer after he failed to make overdue payments. The former notifies him of his past due payments and the time he has to make payment before his safe deposit box will be forcibly opened.

SAMPLE LETTER 15.34. Notification to safe deposit box customer of past due payments and time he has before his box will be forcibly opened (semiblock format).

February 8, 19X2

Mr. Earl K. Loster
P.O. Box 987
Persian, New Jersey 02987

Dear Mr. Loster:

Our records indicate that the rents on the following Safe Deposit Box have remained unpaid for two years.

1. Box #892. Annual rent of $360 (plus 10% Federal Excise Tax for all periods prior to July 1, 1965).
2. Leased to Earl K. Loster.
3. Leased on January 5, 19X9.
4. Date rent was last paid was January 31, 19X0.
5. Amount of rent due this date is $720 plus a tax of $36.

Sample Lettter 15.34 continued

Therefore, under the provisions of the existing statutes of the state, you are notified by this postpaid, securely sealed, and registered letter, that if the amount of rents now due, with interest at the legal rate and the amount of tax where applicable, is not paid within sixty days from the date of this letter, New National Bank will cause the Safe Deposit Box to be forcibly opened by a locksmith. The contents will be inventoried and placed in a sealed package. The package will be placed in one of the general safes or boxes of the Bank.

Nothing will be deemed a waiver by the Bank of any of its rights, powers, or privileges given by law or contract. This notice will also serve as any notice required under any existing contracts of lease.
Please give the overdue rents on your Safe Deposit Box your immediate attention.

Cordially,

Sebastian T. Bellaire
Executive Vice President

hjk

Sample letter 15.35 is a follow-up after no response from the customer, explaining that the box has been opened, the contents placed in general safekeeping, and the time left before sale of these items to collect overdue payments will take place.

SAMPLE LETTER 15.35. Follow-up to sample letter 15.34 after no response, explaining box has been opened, contents placed in general safekeeping, and time left before sale of contents will take place (full-block format).

April 9, 19X2

Mr. Earl K. Loster
P.O. Box 987
Persian, New Jersey 02987

Dear Mr. Loster:

On February 8, 19X2, you were notified by postpaid, securely sealed, and registered mail, that the following Safe Deposit Box, located at our Main Branch, would be forcibly opened because of two years unpaid rent.

1. Box #892. Annual rent of $360 (plus 10% Federal Excise Tax for all periods prior to July 1, 1965).
2. Leased to Earl K. Loster.
3. Leased on January 5, 19X9.
4. Date rent was last paid was January 31, 19X0.
5. Amount of rents due this date is $720 plus a tax of $36.

In compliance with existing state statutes, you are notified that the Safe Deposit Box was opened on April 8, 19X2. We enclose, with this postpaid, securely sealed, and registered letter, a certificate prepared and sworn to by a Notary Public which describes all contents removed from the Safe Deposit Box. These contents have been placed in a sealed package, upon which the Notary Public has distinctly marked the name of the lessee in whose name the Safe Deposit Box stood on our records.

You are also notified that the contents of the Safe Deposit Box have been placed, at your expense, in general safekeeping in the vaults of our main branch, and will be kept there for a period of not less than two years unless removed by you before then. You may, at any time before the expiration of two years from the date of this letter, obtain delivery of the contents of the box by paying all rentals, the cost of opening the box, the fees of the Notary Public, and all other charges accrued, together with the legal interest. If the contents are not claimed and costs and charges paid, the Bank may take action to sell the contents in the manner prescribed by the state, and recover for itself all amounts due us for unpaid rental, subsequent costs of safekeeping, and incurred expenses, together with legal interest.

Sample Lettter 15.35 continued

We will place any balance remaining to your credit in a demand deposit account of New National Bank.

Sincerely,

Sebastian T. Bellaire
Executive Vice President

STB/HJK

Enclosure

Sample letters 15.34 and 15.35 also lend themselves well for use as form letters if the names, dates, times, and amounts are changed.

Trust & Estates Memos

Memorandum 15.36 is a memorandum written to the accounting officer of the bank requesting him to gather all account connections and interest earned at the bank for the completion of an estate tax return.

MEMORANDUM 15.36. Memorandum to accounting officer requesting account connections and interest earned for the completion of an estate tax return.

TO: Alan R. Patrickson
Senior Accounting Officer
Operational Accounting
FROM: Robert A. Rosky
Trust Administrator
DATE: September 7, 19X2
SUBJECT: Grace P. Michener Estate—Agency Account

Grace P. Michener died on July 1, 19X2. Please obtain all account connections with New National Bank and the date of death values. We will also need the interest that the various accounts have earned from January 1 through July 1, 19X2, for the estate tax return.

If you have any questions or comments, please call me.

rar/yut

Social & Personal Letters 16

Effective letters should be written whether or not you are writing specifically about bank business. If you are offering a dinner invitation, correcting a vendor on an error, or expressing condolences on the death of a friend, your letter should be prepared with the same precision and clarity as were the letters in the previous chapters of part two of this book.

The examples of letters here were written by bankers on various occasions which might not have related directly to a loan closing or a foreclosure on a mortgage. The letters in this chapter will serve as good guides for you to use when writing letters on similar occasions.

Congratulations

Various types of congratulations letters can be written. Sample letter 16.1 was written to congratulate an associate on a new position. Such letters serve to maintain good relationships with business associates and customers.

SAMPLE LETTER 16.1. Congratulations on new position (block format).

April 26, 19X2

Mr. Scott Ralston
President
Countryside Savings Bank
P.O. Box 1130
Heart, Arkansas 76787

Dear Scott:

I had the pleasure of learning that you recently became the president of Countryside Savings Bank. Congratulations on your new position.

I hope I will have a chance to stop in and see you next time I'm in Heart. In the meantime, good luck with your new responsibilities.

Sincerely,

Douglass R. Tixxon
Executive Vice President

drt/smd

Thank You Letters

Sample letters 16.2-16.4 are three examples of effectively written thank you letters. They assure the people that their kindness is appreciated and that the letter writer thinks enough of them to respond. Sample letter 16.2 is for a business meeting.

SAMPLE LETTER 16.2. Thank you letter for business meeting (semiblock format).

May 6, 19X2

Ms. Lauren Palay
Marshall and Smith
90 Baxter Place
Mattapan, Kansas 66130

Dear Lauren:

Thanks to you and your colleagues for coming over to give our officers the talk on positioning for eventual workout situations. I have had positive comments about the discussion which, although hitting only the high points, was creatively presented and provided a sound basis for reflection when structuring a deal.

In addition to learning a great deal, I think we've also filled an acquaintanceship gap between our people and yours. Thank you again for your help.

Best regards,

Lawrence P. Anderson
Vice President

lld

Sample letter 16.3 is a thank you letter for a letter received.

SAMPLE LETTER 16.3. Thank you letter for a letter received (full-block format).

September 6, 19X2

Dr. Bertrand R. Sogel
98 Bugley Drive
Ferton, Vermont 90610

Dear Bert:

Thank you for your letter and kind thoughts. I'm embarrassed that it has taken so long to reply. It hardly seems possible that I left County Savings eight years ago, and its holding company, Countibank, four years ago.

Penny, our three sons, and I moved to San Diego in 19X8. We still get to Ferton for social events and occasional

Sample Lettter 16.3 continued

meetings. Perhaps next time we are in town we can meet for dinner.

Thank you again for your good wishes. Please give my best wishes to your family.

Best wishes,

Max Nilges
Loan Officer

lwg

Sample letter 16.4 is a thank you letter for a letter received following a meeting.

SAMPLE LETTER 16.4. Thank you letter for a letter received following a meeting (block format).

September 16, 19X2

Mr. Oscar G. Jones
Vice President
Hoskings Equipment, Inc.
876 Anderson Way
Newton, Pennsylvania 22001

Dear Oscar:

Thank you for your letter following our breakfast meeting with you, Carl Thorney, and Sara Simonson. I look forward to your visit in the next few months.
In the meantime, I wish you and your family well.

Best regards,

Simone T. Chinet
Personnel Administrator

Invitations

Sample letter 16.5 was written as an invitation to a customer to have dinner. The letter is clearly written in a personal tone. The use of the official style format indicates the personal nature of the letter.

SAMPLE LETTER 16.5. Invitation for dinner (official style format).

December 1, 19X1

Dear Ralph:

Mark E. Mathews, the president of our bank, joins with me in inviting you to cocktails and dinner at six o'clock on the evening of Thursday, December 10, 19X1, at the Palay Restaurant, 79 July Street, Hamilton, California.

While the evening will be principally social, I do expect that Mark will have some informal remarks after dinner on a topical aspect of the economy. We anticipate about thirty good friends of the bank joining us for the evening.

I hope you will be able to attend and look forward to seeing you that evening.

Regards,

Joanne Tufts

Mr. Ralph Embry
Thomson Enterprises
111 Propsect Street
Hamilton, California 00012

JT:js

Condolences

A condolence letter is a difficult one to write. The recipient, however, will usually be very appreciative of the warmth and compassion shown by such a letter. Sample letter 16.6 is one example of a well-written condolence letter.

SAMPLE LETTER 16.6. Condolence letter (full-block format).

March 30, 19X2

Carla Moore
Stanley, Broker & Smith
One Park Street
Quality, North Dakota 02137

Dear Carla:

I was sorry to learn of the death of your father. I hope you will accept warm condolences from your friends at New National Bank.

If I or anyone else can be of help to you, please let us know. I look forward to meeting with you as soon as you get back into the swing of things.

Best wishes,

Joanne Tufts
Vice President

JT/JS

Requests for Information

Sample letters 16.7-16.9 are examples of letters written requesting information. Sample letter 16.7 is for information on seminars offered, while sample letter 16.8 is for a reprint of an article. Sample letter 16.9 is a follow-up letter requesting more information about a possible purchase her bank will make.

SAMPLE LETTER 16.7. Letter requesting information on seminars offered (block format).

March 9, 19X2

Timothy P. Marshall
Dean
School of Business
State University
Ausley, Montana 21787

Dear Mr. Marshall:

Please advise me of any seminars you might have which focus on training top officers of banks in bank management.

Thank you for your assistance.

Sincerely,

Julia K. Giffin
Assistant Vice President

jkg/jls

SAMPLE LETTER 16.8. Letter requesting reprint of article (semiblock format).

April 14, 19X1

Mr. James B. Dreyfus
Editor
Informational Bank Notes
65 Cinnamon Place
Lattice, Kentucky 90660

Dear Mr. Dreyfus:

I would like to receive a reprint of the article you published on Money Market Funds, on pages 9 through 11 of your April 19X1 issue. Please send the reprint to me at: 789 Ramapo Street, Aliceton, Kentucky 90661.

Thank you for your assistance.

Sincerely,

Julia K. Giffin
Assistant Vice President

JKG/jls

SAMPLE LETTER 16.9. Letter concerning purchase of premium gift for customers (full-block format).

October 25, 19X7

Personal

Ms. Jan Spiro
Financial Books, Inc.
4228 16th St., NW
Boston, MA 02110

Dear Ms. Spiro:

Thank you for the complimentary copy of 301 Great Management Ideas by Sara Noble. Both I and my assistant have read the book and agree that it would make a wonderful premium gift to our small business customers or prospective customers.

We would be willing to purchase at least 250 copies of the book on two conditions. First, we would like to take you up on the suggestion you made on the phone to me that we could have a personalized message printed on a blank page bound in with the book. We would supply the letter on our letterhead.

Second, we would like to negotiate a 50% discount off of the cover price. We believe this is a fair arrangement since we will be purchasing a significant number of copies of the trade paperback edition prior to your first press run.

Give me a call and let me know if this arrangement sounds viable to you. We, of course, will provide you with the exact number we need as well as our letter to be printed and a check for the cost of this endeavor.

Sincerely,

Rebecca Grimes, President
The County Bank

rg/js

Letters to Vendors

Sample letters 16.10-16.12 are examples of letters written to vendors for a variety of reasons. Sample letter 16.10 was written to a check company to change the business arrangement that had existed.

SAMPLE LETTER 16.10. Letter to vendor requesting change in services (full-block format).

June 10, 19X1

Ms. Jessica E. Divane
Check Printing Company, Inc.
P.O. Box 1010
Warren, Wisconsin 23284

Dear Ms. Divane:

Please increase our mark-up from 10% to 15% on all of our check orders. This change should take effect as soon as possible. I would appreciate it if you would forward me enough catalog inserts to reflect the pricing change in the cost of checks to our customers.

Thank you for your assistance.

Cordially,

Timothy T. Bixerdiddle
Director of Operations

ttb/doo

Sample letter 16.11 is a clear, brief letter written to discontinue a vendor's services.

SAMPLE LETTER 16.11. Letter to vendor discontinuing services (semiblock format).

August 17, 19X1

Mrs. Doris P. Winkler
Copier Corporation
55526 Pepper Street
Feldston, Missouri 67084

Dear Ms. Winkler:

Please do not renew our contract, which expired August 15, 19X1, for the use of a Copier 760 copying machine.

The machine is located at our main branch in Feldston. We would like the machine removed at your earliest possible convenience.

Sincerely,

Lester L. Cooper
Assistant Vice President

DPW/smr

Sample letter 16.12 is about as angry in tone as any of the letters in this book get. It was written as a follow-up to a complaint from a vendor that his services were not paid for. The letter writer mentions the cancelled check and encloses a copy and expresses his distress that the letter from the vendor threatened his bank before they had all the facts straight. Note that although this is an angry letter, the writer does not get threatening or accusatory. He merely states the facts firmly and asks that corrections in his bank's accounts be made.

SAMPLE LETTER 16.12. Letter to vendor clearing up his error (semiblock format).

October 31, 19X1

Mr. John B. Nerton
Customer Service Department
Royckle Business Products, Inc.
108 North Street
Alleyway, Illinois 60619

Dear Mr. Nerton:

Enclosed is a photostatic copy of our expense check #51988 (front & back) that was used for payment of your invoice #95680. Please note that your company endorsed this check and that it was processed by your bank on September 29, 19X1.

I think it would be wise for your company to investigate the policies and procedures used in processing payments on your accounts receivables. It seems to me that you should correct your problems prior to sending past due notices threatening to turn your customers over to Dun & Bradstreet commercial collection division.

I hope the enclosed photostatic copy of our expense check #51988 will help clear up your processing error and place our account in a paid-in-full status.

Sincerely,

Ferdinand B. Bosley
Assistant Vice President

fbb/aff

enclosure

Miscellaneous

Sample letter 16.13 is a well-written letter expressing reaction to legislation. The letter writer clearly outlines his position by using a numbered list. This technique is usually helpful in clarifying a series of points when they are included in a letter.

SAMPLE LETTER 16.13. Letter expressing reaction to legislation (semiblock format).

August 13, 19X2

Mr. John Butterworth
Modern Banking Association
New National Bank Building
One Collins Square
Curtis, Pennsylvania 10726

Subject: House Bill 2505

Dear Mr. Butterworth:

I am writing in response to the Modern Banking Association (MBA) Alert date July 27, 19X2, requesting to add to the recommendations MBA will offer the Department of Agriculture to rectify the situation created by the passage of House Bill 2505. In my opinion, this bill has done more to jeopardize grain dealers' and warehousemens' secured creditors; it has circumvented the Uniform Commercial Code in such a way that no external parties can be certain of their positions.

My suggestion to rectify this situation is a three-step process.

1. Rescind House Bill 2505.

2. Enact new legislation to eliminate that class of farm producers who formerly stored grain on open account without warehouse receipts. This can be accomplished by a bill providing for the following:

   a. Any grain dealer or warehouseman accepting delivery of grain should be given thirty days to either make payment for delivered grain or tender a valid warehouse receipt.
   b. Failure to comply with the above provisions should be a criminal offense.
   c. Increase in the required bond of licensed grain dealers and warehousemen from the present structure to 25% of the aggregate dollar amount paid to producers the previous year for grain dealers and $1 per bushel storage capacity for warehousemen, with no provision for a maximum bond in either case.

These provisions will allow banks to continue to finance grain dealers and warehousemen and allow produc-

Sample Lettter 16.13 continued

ers a valid ownership claim in any grain on hand in the event of a business failure.

We appreciate MBA's concern in this Bill and will continue to work for a more equitable and workable structure of the law relating to creditors of grain dealers and warehousemen.

Sincerely,

Wendell T. Wright
Commercial Banking Officer

wtw/jab

cc: Governor James Lewis
Representative Lawrence Turnbill
Representative David L. Palay
Senator Harold B. Oscarson

Sample letter 16.14 is a letter to a customer describing a public service in which the bank is involved. Such a letter does wonders for building good customer relations.

SAMPLE LETTER 16.14. Letter describing bank's involvement in public service project (full-block format).

February 28, 19X2

Mr. Joshua K. Bradbury
435 Sweetboy Drive
Anderson, Wisconsin 32551

Dear Mr. Bradbury:

Enclosed is a small booklet describing our Community Foundation. The Community Foundation, of which the New National Bank is trustee, is one of the pioneers in this modern plan for the promotion of efficient public giving.

The Community Foundation offers a wise means of making permanent gifts to philanthropic, educational, and religious organizations in the County. It was conceived for the purpose of giving complete protection and economical administration to these bequests to the end that they may be forever operative in effective channels.

I feel sure this booklet will prove interesting to you and many of your clients who seek your opinion about plans for charitable giving. You will find that the Commu-

Sample Lettter 16.14 continued

nity Foundation plan offers a great ease and flexibility, surrounded by many safeguards.

I'd be glad to send you more information if you are interested in this worthwhile project.

Sincerely,

Maxwell Leigh Nilges
President

mln/jls

enclosure

Sample letters 16.15 and 16.16 were written to the chief of police requesting a police officer be present at a grand opening of a new branch of the bank. Sample letter 16.15 requests the officer's services.

SAMPLE LETTER 16.15. Letter requesting police at opening of new branch (block format).

November 25, 19X0

Chief Jonas Belinex
Leighton Police Department
75 Lathrop Avenue
Leighton, New Jersey 07704

Dear Chief Belinex:

Could a uniformed police officer be provided for the grand opening of our new branch office located at 78 Alana Street in Leighton? The grand opening date and time are scheduled for December 13, 19X0 between the hours of 9:00 a.m. and 3:00 p.m.

Please let me know of the availability of an officer and the usual compensation for services. I would appreciate it if you would respond to my request as soon as possible.

Thank you for your assistance.

Cordially,

Maxwell Leigh Nilges
President

mln/gbc

Sample letter 16.16 is a follow-up letter which includes thanks and payment for the officer's services. Although in the case of the letter written in sample letter 16.16, the check was returned because the police department furnished the service gratis, the letter effectively showed the bank's appreciation. The money was instead given to a charity designated by the police department.

SAMPLE LETTER 16.16. Letter thanking police for service and offering payment for services (semiblock format).

December 26, 19X0

Chief Jonas Belinex
Leighton Police Department
75 Lathrop Avenue
Leighton, New Jersey 07704

Subject: Security Officer for Grand Opening

Dear Chief Belinex:

Enclosed is our check #2465 for $49 which represents compensation for Officer Denton's services at the grand opening of our new branch in Leighton on December 13, 19X0.

We appreciate the help and cooperation your department has given us. If I may be of assistance to you or your department, please do not hesitate to call me.

Sincerely,

Maxwell Leigh Nilges
President

mls:gbc

enc.

Sample letter 16.17 is an example of a letter which might have to be written from time to time. It was written on behalf of a customer who had had some money accidentally burned. The letter requests the cash department of the bank to make a determination of the value and issue a check to the customer. In some banks sample letter 16.17 could be written as a memorandum from one department to another.

SAMPLE LETTER 16.17. Letter to cash department of bank on behalf of customer whose money was burned (block format).

March 23, 19X1

Mr. Simon R. Gilbert
Cash Department
County Savings Bank
P.O. Box 122656
Criminy, West Virginia 16232

Dear Mr. Gilbert:

Enclosed is the remaining portion of the burned money we discussed. Please determine the total value and issue a check to:

Brian Palay
210 South Street
Boston, Massachusetts 02111

Thank you very much for your assistance.

Sincerely,

COUNTY SAVINGS BANK—LEIGHTON BRANCH

Alice T. Nicholson
Branch Manager

atn/gbc

enclosure

cc: Brian Palay

PART III
THE APPENDICES

Words to Watch

I

The words listed in this appendix are often used incorrectly in correspondence.

acknowledge with thanks or **acknowledge receipt of** Using the words "thank you" is a more direct way of expressing gratitude after receiving something.

affect vs. **effect** When used as verbs, affect means "to influence," effect means "to accomplish." Both words can also be used as nouns. Affect, as a noun, is usually only used in psychological context. When the construction calls for a noun, and you are not using the word in a psychological sense, you will almost always use effect.

aforesaid Write "named" or "mentioned earlier."

after the conclusion of Write "after."

all right Always written as two words.

allude vs. **elude** You allude to a piece of literature. You elude someone chasing you.

a lot Always written as two words.

alternative Means the choice between two possibilities. In constructions such as "no other alternative," the word "other" is unnecessary.

amounting to or **in the amount of** Write "for" or "of" or "totalling."

and/or Avoid the use of and/or unless it is absolutely necessary as a legal term. It destroys the flow of a sentence and can cause confusion or ambiguity.

anybody An indefinite pronoun meaning "any person." Should be written as one word, as should "somebody," "nobody," and "everybody." If you are writing about a body that was looked for but not found, you could write, "The investigators did not find any body." Such usage would be rare in banking.

anyone Best written as one word unless meaning, "any one of them," as in the sentence: "He didn't like any one of them."

as of even date herewith Unclear. Merely give the date.

as per copy Instead of writing, "We wrote you last Friday as per copy enclosed," it is clearer to write, "We have enclosed a copy," or "Enclosed you will find a copy...."

as requested It is a little more personal to write "as you requested," "as you described," or "as you mentioned."

as soon as possible Give a specific date when possible.

as to Write "about."

as to whether Write "whether."

as yet Write "yet."

at Do not use after the word, "where."

attached hereto Forget the hereto, write "attached."

at the present time or **at this time** or **at this writing** Write "now" whenever possible, instead of these words.

attorney vs. **lawyer** A lawyer who has a client is an attorney.

bad or **badly** The adjective "bad" is used after verbs of the sense—smell, sound, feel, look, taste. For example: "He looks bad" or "It tastes bad." Badly indicates manner. For example: "He was hurt badly in the accident."

beside vs. **besides** Beside means at the side of. Besides means in addition to or other than. Sometimes the use of besides can result in an ambiguous sentence, such as: "Something besides the defaulted loan caused us to sever business ties." It would be best to clarify by writing, "in addition to the defaulted loan," or "other than the defaulted loan."

between vs. **among** Where the number exceeds two, use among for both persons and things. Between is a preposition which takes the objective pronoun (see chapter six for a complete discussion of objective pronouns).

bimonthly Every two months.

biweekly Every two weeks. (Sometimes bimonthly is used to mean "twice a month" and biweekly to mean, "twice a week." The preferred usages, however, are the ones given here.)

both alike Both is superfluous. Write "alike."

by means of Write "by."

calling for Often used needlessly. In a sentence such as, "A proposal calling for seventy shares," the word "calling" can be omitted.

communication Avoid using to mean a letter, telegram, or conversation. Use the specific reference. See section on jargon in chapter six.

contact Use more specific words, like "talked to," "wrote," or "called."

data vs. **datum** The plural form, data, is generally used, and it takes a plural verb. The singular reference is datum.

different from vs. **different than** Things differ *from* one another. Write "different from."

direct vs. **directly** Direct is both an adjective and an adverb. "The man was sent direct (or directly) to Chicago." The sentence, "The officer made a direct trip to Chicago," takes the adjective "direct." Directly is always an adverb, as in the sentence, "We send directly to a beneficiary if there is no intermediary."

disinterested Means impartial. Do not confuse with the word, "uninterested."

due to the fact that Write "because."

early convenience Encourages delay. Be more specific.

enclosed herewith Forget the herewith, write "enclosed."

enclosed please find Write "enclosed is."

etc. Don't use unless the omitted context is understood. Because the meaning of *et cetera* is "and so forth," you would never write "and etc." or "etc. etc."

equally as well Write "equally well."

farther vs. **further** Farther refers to distance. Further refers to discourse or to something additional. The distinction between these two words is blurred by many writers who also use further to refer to distance. Eventually, this usage may become acceptable.

hopefully An adverb meaning "with hope" or "in a hopeful manner." It is used incorrectly by many writers to mean "I hope."

however Best used in the middle of a sentence. When however is used at the beginning of a sentence, it usually means "to whatever extent."

i.e. vs. **e.g.** I.e. is an abbreviation for *id est,* which means "that is" and is set off by commas in a sentence. E.g. is an abbreviation for *exempli grata* which means "for example" and is set off by commas in a sentence.

in position Implies "at attention," or "standing around." Write "prepared," "ready," "willing," or "available."

in receipt of Write "we (I) have received," or "we (I) have."

in reference to or **in regard to** or **in reply to** Write "concerning," "proposing," "inquiring about," or "suggesting."

in which you enclosed Write "with which you enclosed." Information is given *in* a letter. You receive an enclosure *with* a letter.

irregardless Not a word. The proper word is "regardless."

its vs. **it's** "Its" shows possession. "It's" is a contraction for "it is."

like vs. **as** Like is a preposition which introduces a prepositional phrase and is used to compare things: "He looks like his mother." As is usually used as a conjunction and introduces a subordinate clause (Clauses have a subject and a verb.): "He acts as his mother did."

matter Too general a term. Use the specific word: "problem," "request," "subject," "question," or whatever you may be writing about.

most Don't substitute for almost. Write "almost everyone," instead of "most everyone."

myself, ourselves, himself, herself, yourself (pronouns ending in -self) Avoid using as the subject in a sentence. Write "Max and I are approving the loan," instead of "Max and myself ...". Pronouns ending in -self are used for reference and emphasis in a sentence. In the sentence, "I approved the loan myself," myself emphasizes I.

neither, nor and **either, or** These correlatives should be kept together.

party vs. **person** Use party as a legal reference. Person should be used in ordinary reference.

people vs. **persons** Use people when referring to large groups; persons for small groups.

per Use of per is acceptable in an economic context, such as "twenty shares per dollar." Although it has been said to avoid mixing Latin and English, and "per" is Latin, if the construction is made less awkward by using per, use it. Avoid writing "per your letter" or "per my last letter," however, because this fills your writing with technical jargon.

please be advised that Avoid this wordy construction.

presently The preferred definition for presently is "in a little while" or "soon." To be clear, when you mean currently, use the word "currently."

previous experience Write, "Our experience with this person," instead of "Our previous experience."

principal vs. **principle** Principle refers to basic truths. Principal, as an adjective, means "leading" or "chief." As a noun, principal means either a person in charge or, in finance, capital.

shall vs. **will** The rule that "shall" is the future indicative of to be in the first person and "will" in the second and third person, and that to express determination the forms are reversed, is no longer followed by most people in the United States. "Shall" sounds too lofty to many people's ears and is avoided. Most educated people use will instead of shall in their writing.

taking this opportunity Instead of writing, "We are taking this opportunity to thank you," write, "We thank you."

than vs. **then** Than is used for comparison. Then is used to indicate time.

that vs. **which** A simple rule is to use the pronoun "which" if the clause it modifies can be separated from the rest of the sentence with commas. Otherwise use "that."

thereafter Too lofty. Use "after that" when possible.

this will acknowledge receipt of your letter An answer to a person's letter will let him or her know it was received.

transpire Means "to become known." Used incorrectly to mean "occur" or "happen."

try and vs. **try to** Write "try to."

under date of Write "on," "dated," or "of."

under separate cover Write, "we are sending separately," or "you will receive."

unique There are no degrees of uniqueness. "Very unique," "most unique," or "extremely unique" are incorrect.

utilize Inflated language for "use."

via means "by way of" (geographically), and is properly used as a railroad, airline, or steamship term. Write "by express," or "by parcel post."

we ask you to kindly Write "please."

we wish to thank you Write "thank you."

Punctuation

apostrophe (')

The apostrophe indicates omission; possession; and sometimes the plural of certain letters, nouns, numbers, and abbreviations.

1. The possessive pronouns—its, hers, his, ours, yours, theirs—do not use an apostrophe.
2. The possessive of singular nouns that end in "s" is formed by adding an apostrophe: Miss Jones' loan.
3. The possessive of plural nouns ending in "s" is formed by adding an apostrophe: ten days' trial.
4. Joint possession is indicated by adding an apostrophe and an "s" to the last noun only: Seglin and McDonnell's check. To indicate separate possession, add the apostrophe and an "s" to each noun: Seglin's and McDonnell's checks.
5. Add an "s" with no apostrophe to form the plurals of letters, nouns, numbers, and abbreviations, if it is possible to do so without causing confusion: several YWCAs and YMHAs; the 1960s; in fours and fives.
6. Add an apostrophe and an "s" to form the plurals of lowercase letters used as nouns, abbreviations using periods, and capital letters that would be less confusing as a plural if an apostrophe and an "s" were added: C.P.A.'s; a's and b's; I's, A's, U's.

colon (:)
The colon is used to warn the reader that something is to follow that will complete what was promised in the preceding words.

The colon is used:

1. after the salutation of a letter
2. to indicate that pertinent information follows
3. preceding a formal or extended quotation

The words "as follows" and "the following" should be eliminated if possible in your letters. If it is necessary to use either phrase, it should be followed by a colon.

After such expression as "for instance" or "for example," a colon may be used when the example is tabulated or consists of more than one sentence.

A colon is always placed outside of quotation marks.

comma (,)
Use the comma:

1. to separate distinct, independent statements in a compound sentence.
2. to separate a series of words or phrases having equal value and not connected by conjunctions. In a series, do not omit the comma before the word "and."
3. to separate a series of adjectives or adverbs that are equal in value and are not connected by conjunctions.
4. to set off a long dependent clause preceding its principal clause (see section on ambiguity in chapter three).
5. to precede nonrestrictive relative clauses introduced by "who," "which," and similar pronouns. The pronoun "that" is frequently used in a restrictive sense and does not require a comma preceding it.
6. to set apart a parenthetical expression. Do not isolate by parenthetical commas a phrase essential to the meaning of the sentence.
7. to separate the year in a complete date from the continuation of the sentence: June 14, 1981, was his graduation.
8. to separate the name of the state, following mention of the city located within its borders, from the rest of the sentence.
9. when the thought is broken by a connective, such as "however," "obviously," "namely."
10. to avoid a confused reading of the sentence.

Do not use a comma at the end of a subject when that subject is formed by a series of words.

dash (—)
The dash indicates an abrupt change in thought. Dashes are generally preferable to parenthesis. Use dashes to:

1. set off expressions foreign to the sentence.
2. set off explanations and repetitions.

elipses (...)
When letters or words are omitted in a quotation, use an elipses (three periods on the typewriter, ". . .") to indicate the omission. If the omission ends on a period, use an elipses, plus a period (four periods on the typewriter, ". . . .").

exclamation point (!)
An exclamation point should not be overused or it will lose its effectiveness. It should be used:

1. to indicate surprise.
2. to indicate a strong command.
3. to indicate sarcasm.
4. to follow a strong interjection, such as "Ouch!" or "Hurray!"

hyphenation (-)
Avoid hyphenation. Excessive use of the hyphen tends to weaken the meaning of a letter and does not add to its appearance. Consult a dictionary on the proper hyphenation of words.

1. Insert a hyphen in compound adjectives preceding a noun: absent-minded loan officer.
2. Insert a hyphen in compound numerals: twenty-one through ninety-nine.
3. Avoid using a hyphen at the end of the first line or the last full line of a paragraph.

parenthesis (())
Parenthesis may be used:

1. to set apart explanatory detail that can be omitted without changing the grammatical structure of a sentence.
2. to enclose a word or clause that is independent of the sentence in which it is inserted.
   Punctuation should be placed outside of parenthesis unless it is a part of the parenthetical expression.

period (.)
In addition to the traditional uses of the period, use one after a question of courtesy, which is really a request, and when a reply or action is expected.

question mark (?)
Use after every direct question. After a question of courtesy and when a reply or action is expected, use a period.

quotation marks (" ")
Any material quoted within a sentence or a paragraph should be set off with quotation marks.

Use single quotation marks to enclose a quotation within a quotation.

Titles of books, magazines, and plays are underscored. Titles of poems, articles, television programs, or chapters in a book are enclosed in quotation marks.

Lengthy quotations should be set off by indentation—blocking—in which case quotation marks are unnecessary.

If quotation marks are used and the text is continued into two or more paragraphs, use quotation marks at the beginning of each paragraph, but at the end of only the last paragraph of the quotation.

With the exception of the colon, punctuation should be placed inside the quotation marks.

semicolon (;)
The semicolon is used:

1. to separate the clauses of a compound sentence when the conjunction is omitted.
2. between the clauses of a compound sentence that are joined by one of the conjunctive adverbs: accordingly, also, besides, consequently, further, hence, furthermore, however, moreover, nevertheless, otherwise, still, then, thus, yet, therefore.
3. to separate units in a series when they are long and complicated or are internally punctuated.
4. between clauses of a compound sentence that are connected by a conjunction when those clauses are somewhat long, or when a more decided pause is desirable.

word division
Avoid:

1. dividing a one-syllable word.
2. dividing a word of four letters.
3. dividing a word on the first or last syllable unless that syllable has three or more letters.
4. dividing proper names, abbreviations, figures, addresses, or dates.
5. dividing a word before a syllable containing a vowel that is not pronounced.
6. separating the initials or the first name from the surname.
7. separating qualifying letters or signs from the figures to which they belong.

Always divide a compound word on its own hyphen.

Abbreviations

III

Two-letter State Abbreviations

AL	Alabama
AK	Alaska
AZ	Arizona
AR	Arkansas
CA	California
CZ	Canal Zone
CO	Colorado
CT	Connecticut
DE	Delaware
DC	District of Columbia
FL	Florida
GA	Georgia
GU	Guam
HI	Hawaii
ID	Idaho
IL	Illinois
IN	Indiana
IA	Iowa
KS	Kansas
KY	Kentucky
LA	Louisiana
ME	Maine
MD	Maryland
MA	Massachusetts
MI	Michigan
MN	Minnesota
MS	Mississippi
MO	Missouri

MT	Montana	RI	Rhode Island
NE	Nebraska	SC	South Carolina
NV	Nevada	SD	South Dakota
NH	New Hampshire	TN	Tennessee
NJ	New Jersey	TX	Texas
NM	New Mexico	UT	Utah
NY	New York	VT	Vermont
NC	North Carolina	VA	Virgtinia
ND	North Dakota	VI	Virgin Islands
OH	Ohio	WA	Washington
OK	Oklahoma	WV	West Virginia
OR	Oregon	WI	Wisconsin
PA	Pennsylvania	WY	Wyoming
PR	Puerto Rico		

Common Abbreviations

word	abbreviation
Accountant	ACCT
Administrator	ADMIN
Administrators	ADMINS
Affiliate	AFF
Affiliated Company	ACO
Agency	AGCY
Also known as	AKA
Ambassador	AMB
Annex	ANX
Annuitant	ANT
Apartment	APT
Archbishop	ABP
Associate	ASSOC
Association	ASSN
Attorney	ATTY
Authorized Officer	ATO
Auxiliary	AUX
Avenue	AVE
Beneficiary	BENEF
Beneficiaries	BENEFS
Bend	BND
Board of Directors	DIR
Boulevard	BLVD
Branch	BR
Branch Manager	BRM
Brother	BRO
Brothers	BROS
Building	BLDG
Bureau	BUR
Business	BUS
Bypass	BYP
Causeway	CSWY
Center	CTR
Certified Employee Benefits Specialist	CEBS
Certified Financial Manager	CFM
Certified Financial Planner	CFP
Certified Life Underwriter	CLU
Certified Management Consultant	CMC
Certified Public Accountant	CPA

word	abbreviation	word	abbreviation
Chartered Financial Analyst	CFA	Drive	DR
		East	E
Chartered Financial Consultant	ChFC	Electric	ELEC
		Endorser	END
Chartered Property and Casualty Underwriter	CPCU	Ensign	ENS
		Equipment	EQUIP
		Escrow account	ESC
Circle	CIR	Establishment	ESTAB
Comaker	COM	Estate	EST
Cosigner	COS	Executor	EXEC
Colonel	COL	Executors	EXECS
Commission	COMMN	Expressway	EXPY
Committee	CTE	Extended / Extension	EXT
Common-tenancy	CTN	Father	FTHR
Commonwealth	COMM	Federal	FED
Company	CO	Fifth	V
Construction	CONST	Finance	FIN
Consultant	CONS	First-name	F-N
Corporation	CORP	Floor	FLR
Court	CT	Foundation	FNDTN
Cove	CV	Fourth	IV
Creek	CRK	Freeway	FWY
Crescent	CRES	Fund	FND
Custodial	CUST	Gardens	GDNS
Custodian	CUSTOD	Garage	GRGE
Custodians	CUSTODS	Gateway	GTWY
Dealer	DLR	Government	GOVT
Department	DEPT	Group	GRP
Deputy	DPY	Grove	GR
Development	DVLPMNT	Guarantor	GTR
Director	DIR	Guardian	GDN
Distributor	DISTRIB	Guild	GLD
Division	DIV	Heights	HTS
Doctor	DR	Highway	HWY
Doctor of Dental Sciences	DDS	Honorable	HON
		Hospital	HOSP
Doctor of Divinity	DD	Household account	HSA
Doctor of Medicine	MD	Husband	HUS
Doctor of Philosophy	PHD	Incorporated I	NC
Doing business as	DBA	Indirect liability	ILB
Dominion	DOM	Industries	INDS

word	abbreviation	word	abbreviation
Institute	INST	Place P	L
Insurance	INS	Plaza	PLZ
In-trust-for	ITF	Post office	PO
Joint	JNT	Power-of-attorney	POA
Joint venture	JNV	Primary	PRI
Judge	JDGE	Products	PRODS
Junction	JCT	Professor	PROF
Junior	JR	Profit-sharing	PRS
Laboratory	LAB	Property account	PRO-A
Lake	LK	Realtor	RLTR
Lakes	LKS	Redevelopment	REDVLPM
Landing	LNDG	Registered Health	
Lane	LN	Underwriter	RHU
League	LGE	Registered Nurse	RN
Legal	LEG	Rental account	REN
Legal Name	LEGN	Reserve account	RES
Legal title	LGT	Restaurant	REST
Limited	LTD	Retired	RETD
Manager	MGR	Reverend	REV
Master	MST	Ridge	RDG
Manor	MNR	River	RV
Manufacturing	MFG	Road	RD
Market	MRKT	Roadway	RDWY
Meadows	MDWS	Room	RM
Minor	MIN	Route	RT
Minors	MINS	Rural	R
Miss	MISS/MS	School	SCH
Mister	MR	Science	SCI
Mrs	MRS/MS	Second	II
Nontitle party	NTP	Secondary	SEC
North	N	Secretary SECT	
Northeast	NE	Senior	SR
Northwest	NW	Senior Vice President	SVP
Not Sufficient Funds	NSF	Service	SV
Organization	ORGN	Signatory	STR
Park	PK	Signer commercial	
Parkway	PKY	account	SGN
Participant	PTP	Sister	SR
Partner	PTR	Society	SOC
Payroll account	PAYACCT	South	S
Pharmacy	PHAR	Southeast	SE

word	abbreviation	word	abbreviation
Special account	SPEC	Trustee	TTEE
Square	SQ	Trustees	TTEES
Station	STA	Trust account	TRA
Store	STR T	urnpike	TPKE
Street	ST	Union	UN
Subdivision	SUBDIV	United	UTD
Subsidiary	SUB	Vice President	VP
Tax account	TAX	View	VW
Terrace	TER	Village	VLG
Third	III	Warrant Officer	WO
Trading as	T/A	West	W
Trail	TRL	Wholesale	WHSLE
Treasurer	TREAS	Wife	WIF
Trucking	TR		

Grammar Hotline Directory

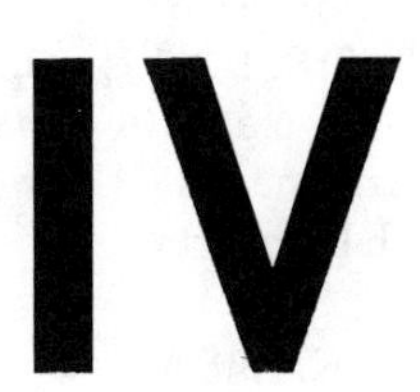

United States and Canada

Because these services are staffed by colleges and universities, many close or have reduced hours during college breaks. You can use any of the services listed in this directory by calling the hotline and asking your grammar question. The universities or colleges sponsoring the hotlines, the contact people, and the phone numbers are all provided for your convenience. The zip codes following the city locations of each hotline are given in case you wish to ask your question in writing. Address your correspondence to the director of the hotline whose name is given at the end of the entry.

ALABAMA

Auburn 36849
(205) 844-5749—Writing Center Hotline
Monday through Wednesday, 9 a.m. to noon and 1 p.m. to 4 p.m.; Friday, 8 a.m. to noon
Auburn University

Lex Williford

Jacksonville 36265
(205) 782-5409—Grammar Hotline
Monday through Friday, 8 a.m. to 4:30 p.m.
Jacksonville State University
Carol Cauthen and Clyde Cox

Tuscaloosa 35487
(205) 348-5049—Grammar Hotline
Monday through Thursday, 8:30 a.m. to 4 p.m.; Tuesday and Wednesday, 6 p.m. to 9 p.m.; Friday 8:30 a.m. to 1 p.m.
University of Alabama
Carol Howell

ARIZONA

Tempe 85287
(602) 921-3616 (residence)—Grammar Hotline
Daily 6 a.m. to 10 p.m.
Arizona State University
J.J. Lamberts

ARKANSAS

Little Rock 72204
(501) 569-3162—The Writer's Hotline
Monday through Friday, 8 a.m. to noon
University of Arkansas at Little Rock
Marilynn Keys

CALIFORNIA

Moorpark 93021
(805) 529-2321—National Grammar Hotline
Monday through Friday, 8 a.m. to noon, September through June
Moorpark College
Michael Strumpf

Sacramento 95823
(916) 688-7444—English Helpline
Monday through Friday, 9 a.m. to 11:45 a.m., fall and spring semesters; 24-hour answering machine
Cosumnes River College
Billie Miller Cooper

COLORADO

Pueblo 81001
(719) 549-2787—USC Grammar Hotline
Monday through Friday, 9:30 a.m. to 3:30 p.m.
University of Southern Colorado
Margaret Senatore and Ralph Dille

DELAWARE

Newark 19716
(302) 451-1890—Grammar Hotline
Monday through Thursday, 9 a.m. to noon, 1 p.m. to 5 p.m., and 6 p.m. to 9 p.m.; Friday, 9 a.m. to noon and 1 p.m. to 5 p.m.
University of Delaware
Margaret P. Hassert

FLORIDA

Coral Gables 33124
(305) 284-2956—Grammar Hotline
Monday through Friday, 8:30 a.m. to 5 p.m.; Monday and Thursday, to 8:30 p.m.
University of Miami
Charlotte Perlin

Pensacola 32514
(904) 474-2129—Writing Lab and Grammar Hotline
Monday through Thursday 9 a.m. to 5 p.m.; occasional evening hours
University of West Florida
Mamie Webb Hixon

GEORGIA

Atlanta 30303
(404) 651-2906—Writing Center
Monday through Friday, 8:30 a.m. to 5 p.m.; evening hours vary
Georgia State University
Patricia Graves

Rome 30162
(404) 295-6312—Grammar Hotline
Monday through Friday, 8:30 a.m. to 5 p.m.
Floyd College
Philip Dillard

ILLINOIS

Charleston 61920
(217) 581-5929—Grammar Hotline
Monday through Friday, 10 a.m. to 3 p.m.
Eastern Illinois University
Linda S. Coleman

Des Plaines 60016
(708) 635-1948—The Write Line
Monday through Friday, 9:30 a.m. to 3 p.m.
Oakton Community College
Richard Francis Tracz

Normal 61761
(309) 438-2345—Grammar Hotline
Monday through Friday, 8 a.m. to 4:30 p.m.
Illinois State University
Janice Neuleib

Oglesby 61761
(815) 224-2720—Grammarline
Monday through Friday, 8 a.m. to 4 p.m.
Illinois Valley Community College
Robert Howard and Robert Mueller

Palatine 60067
(708) 397-3000, ext. 2389—Grammar "Right" Line
24-hour answering machine; calls returned Monday through Friday, 9 a.m. to 1 p.m.
Friday, 9 a.m. to 1 p.m.
William Rainey Harper College
Doris Howden and Nimi Tobaa

River Grove 60171
(708) 456-0300, ext. 254—Grammarphone
Monday through Thursday, 8 a.m. to 8 p.m.; Friday, 8 a.m. to 3 p.m.; Saturday, 9 a.m. to 1 p.m.
Triton College
Natalie Nemeth

INDIANA

Indianapolis 46202
(317) 274-3000—IUPUI Writing Center Hotline
Monday through Thursday, 9 a.m. to 5 p.m.; Friday and Saturday, 9 a.m. to 2 p.m.
Indiana University-Purdue University at Indianapolis,
University Writing Center
Barbara Cambridge

Muncie 47306
(317) 285-8387—Grammar Crisis Line
Monday through Thursday, 9 a.m. to 8 p.m.; Friday, 9 a.m. to 5 p.m., September through May; Monday through Friday, 11 a.m. to 2 p.m., May through August
Ball State University, The Writing Center
Paul W. Ranieri

West Lafayette 47907
(317) 494-3723—Grammar Hotline
Monday through Friday, 9:30 a.m. to 4 p.m.; closed May, August, and mid-December to mid-January
Purdue University
Muriel Harris

KANSAS

Emporia 66801
(316) 343-5380—Writer's Hotline
Monday through Thursday, noon to 4 p.m.; Wednesday and Thursday, 7 p.m. to 10 p.m.; answering machine
Emporia State University

see **KANSAS CITY, MISSOURI**

LOUISIANA

Lafayette 70504
(318) 231-5224—Grammar Hotline
Monday through Thursday, 8 a.m. to 4 p.m.; Friday, 8 a.m. to 3 p.m.
University of Southwestern Louisiana
James McDonald

MARYLAND

Baltimore 21228
(301) 455-2585—Writer's Hotline
Monday through Friday, 10 a.m. to noon, September through May
University of Maryland Baltimore County
Barbara Cooper

Frostburg 21532
(301) 689-4327—Grammarphone™
Monday through Friday, 10 a.m. to noon
Frostburg State University English Department
Glynn Baugher

MASSACHUSETTS

Lynn 01901
(617) 593-7284—Grammar Hotline
Monday through Friday, 8:30 a.m. to 4 p.m.
North Shore Community College
Marilyn Dorfman

Boston 02115
(617) 437-2512—Grammar Hotline
Monday through Friday, 8:30 a.m. to 4:30 p.m.
Northeastern University English Department
Stuart Peterfreund

MICHIGAN

Flint 48503
(313) 762-0229—Grammar Hotline
Monday through Thursday, 8:30 a.m. to 3:30 p.m.; Friday, 8:30 a.m. to 12:30 p.m.; Tuesday and Wednesday, 5:30 p.m. to 8:30 p.m.
C.S. Mott Community College
Leatha Terwilliger

Kalamazoo 49008
(616) 387-4442—Writer's Hotline
Monday through Friday, 1 p.m. to 4 p.m.
Western Michigan University
Siham A. Fares

Lansing 48901
(517) 483-1040—Writer's Hotline
Monday through Friday, 9 a.m. to 4 p.m.
Lansing Community College
George R. Bramer

MISSOURI

Joplin 64801
(417) 624-0171—Grammar Hotline
Monday through Friday, 8:30 a.m. to 4:30 p.m.
Missouri Southern State College
Dale W. Simpson

Kansas City 64110
(816) 235-2244—Writer's Hotline
Monday through Friday, 9 a.m. to 4 p.m.

University of Missouri-Kansas City
Judy McCormick, David Foster, and Karen Doerr

NEW JERSEY

Jersey City 07305
(201) 547-3337 or 3338—Grammar Hotline
Monday through Friday, 9 a.m. to 4:30 p.m.; summer Monday through Thursday, 8 a.m. to 5 p.m.
Jersey City State College
Harlan Hamilton

NEW YORK

Jamaica 11451
(718) 739-7483—Rewrite
Monday through Friday, 1 p.m. to 4 p.m.
York College of the City University of New York
Joan Baum and Alan Cooper

NORTH CAROLINA

Fayetteville 28311
(919) 488-7110—Grammar Hotline
Monday through Friday, 9 a.m. to 4 p.m.
Methodist College
Robert Christian, Sue L. Kimball, and James X. Ward

Greenville 27858
(919) 757-6728 or 6399—Grammar Hotline
Monday through Thursday, 8 a.m. to 4 p.m.; Friday, 8 a.m. to 3 p.m.; Tuesday and Thursday, 6 p.m. to 9 p.m.
East Carolina University
Jo Allen

OHIO

Cincinnati 45236
(513) 745-5731—Dial-A-Grammar
Tapes requests—returns calls
Raymond Walters College
Phyllis A. Sherwood

Cincinnati 45221
(513) 556-1702—Writer's Remedies
Monday, Wednesday, and Friday, 9 a.m. to 10 a.m. and noon to 2 p.m.; Tuesday and Thursday, 11 a.m. to noon University College, University of Cincinnati
Jay A. Yarmove

Cincinnati 45223
(513) 569-1736 or 1737—Writing Center Hotline
Monday through Thursday, 8 a.m. to 8 p.m.; Friday, 8 a.m. to 4 p.m.; Saturday, 9 a.m. to 1 p.m.
Cincinnati Technical College
John Battistone and Catherine Rahmes

Cleveland 44122
(216) 987-2050—Grammar Hotline
Monday through Friday, 1 p.m. to 3 p.m.; Sunday through Thursday, 7 p.m. to 10 p.m.; 24-hour answering machine
Cuyahoga Community College
Margaret Taylor, Norman Prange, and Susan Marsick

Dayton 45435
(513) 873-2158—Writer's Hotline
Monday through Friday, 9 a.m. to 4 p.m.
Wright State University
Maura Taaffe

Delaware 43015
(614) 368-3925—Writing Resource Center
Monday through Friday, 9 a.m. to noon and 1 p.m. to 4 p.m., September through April; answers both written and telephoned questions
Ohio Wesleyan University
Ulle Lewes and Barbara Pinkele

OKLAHOMA

Bethany 73008
(405) 491-6328—Grammar Hotline
Monday through Friday, 9 a.m. to 4 p.m.; June, July, and August, call (405) 354-1739
Southern Nazarene University
Jim Wilcox

Chickasha 73018
(405) 224-8622
Monday through Friday, 9 a.m. to 5 p.m.; Saturday, 9 a.m. to noon
Mrs. Underwood, retired teacher and editor, offers this service through her home telephone.
Virginia Lee Underwood

PENNSYLVANIA

Allentown 18104
(215) 437-4471—Academic Support Center
Monday through Friday, 10 a.m. to 3 p.m., September through May
Cedar Crest College

Glen Mills 19342
(215) 399-1130—Burger Associates
Monday through Friday, 9 a.m. to 5 p.m.
Mr. Burger, formerly a teacher of writing and journalism at several colleges, offers this service through his office, which conducts courses in effective writing.
Robert S. Burger

Lincoln 19352
(215) 932-8300, ext. 460—Grammar Hotline
Monday through Friday, 9 a.m. to 5 p.m., September through May
Lincoln University
Carolyn L. Simpson

SOUTH CAROLINA

Charleston 29409
(803) 792-3194—Writer's Hotline
Monday through Friday, 8 a.m. to 4 p.m.; Sunday through Thursday, 7 p.m. to 10 p.m.
The Citadel Writing Center
Angela W. Williams

Columbia 29208
(803) 777-7020—Writer's Hotline
Monday through Thursday, 8:30 a.m. to 5 p.m.; Friday, 8:30 a.m. to 4 p.m.
University of South Carolina Writing Center
Nancy Butterworth and Suzanne Moore

Spartanburg 29301
(803) 596-9613—Writer's Hotline
Monday through Thursday, 1 p.m. to 6 p.m.; Wednesday, 7:30 a.m. to 9 p.m.
Converse College Writing Center
Bonnie Auslander

TEXAS

Amarillo 79178
(806) 374-4726—Grammarphone
Monday through Thursday, 8 a.m. to 9 p.m.; Friday, 8 a.m. to 3 p.m.; Sunday, 2 p.m. to 6 p.m.
Amarillo College
Patricia Maddox and Carl Fowler

Houston 77002
(713) 221-8670—University of Houston Downtown Grammar Line
Monday through Thursday, 9 a.m. to 4 p.m.; Friday, 9 a.m. to 1 p.m.; summer hours: Monday through Thursday, 10:30 a.m. to 4 p.m.
University of Houston-Downtown
Linda Coblentz

San Antonio 78284
(512) 733-2503—Dial-a-Tutor
Monday through Thursday, 8 a.m. to 9 p.m.; Friday, 8 a.m. to 4 p.m.
San Antonio College Learning Lab
Irma Luna and Jane Focht-Hansen

VIRGINIA

Sterling 22170
(703) 450-2511—Writing Center
Monday through Thursday, 10 a.m. to 2 p.m.
Northern Virginia Community College
Loudoun Campus

Virginia Beach 23456
(804) 427-7170—Grammar Hotline
Monday through Friday 10 a.m. to noon; afternoon and evening hours vary
Tidewater Community College
Donna Reiss

WEST VIRGINIA

Montgomery 25136
(304) 442-3137—Writer's Hotline
Monday through Thursday, 9:30 a.m. to 4 p.m.; 24-hour answering machine
West Virginia Institute of Technology
Eva Kay Cardea

WISCONSIN

Green Bay 54307
(414) 498-5427—Grammar Hotline
Monday through Thursday, 8:30 a.m. to 8 p.m.; Friday, 8:30 a.m. to 4 p.m.; summer hours: Friday, 8:30 a.m. to noon
Northeast Wisconsin Technical College
Rose Marie Mastricola and Joanne Rathburn

Platteville 53818
(608) 342-1615—Grammar Hotline
Monday through Thursday, 9 a.m. to 4 p.m.; Friday, 9 a.m. to noon
University of Wisconsin-Platteville
Sheri Lindquist

CANADA

Edmonton, Alberta T5J2P2
(403) 441-4699—Grammar Hotline
Monday through Thursday, 9 a.m. to 11 a.m. and 1 p.m. to 3 p.m.
Grant MacEwan Community College
Lois Drew

Fredericton, New Brunswick E3B5A3
(506) 459-3631 (residence) or (506) 453-4666 (university)—Grammar Hotline
Variable hours
University of New Brunswick
A.M. Kinloch

Bibliography

The books and publications listed in the annotated bibliography are separated into two categories. The first category lists books and publications dealing specifically with letter writing. The second category lists books dealing with grammar and usage.

Under each listing, a brief description is given of the entry. Asterisks indicate books I consider to be especially helpful additions to any banker's reference shelf.

Letter Writing

Buckley, Earle A. *Let's Write Better Letters,* Vol. I, Nos. 1-24 (1961-1963).

Each of Mr. Buckley's newsletters gives practical advice to letter writers. He does not pretend to be an expert grammarian or scholar. He is a businessman who has written a no-nonsense approach to writing more effective letters. Although they are out of print, Buckley's newsletters can probably be found in the files of many banks.

**The Merriam-Webster Handbook of Effective Business Correspondence.* New York: Wallaby, 1979.

Merriam-Webster's handbook is the best reference on general business letter writing I have seen. Every secretary should have a copy nearby ready for reference. The handbook allows quick reference on a myriad of points and problems.

Morrison, Robert H., and Trudy Sundberg. *Bank Correspondence Handbook.* Boston: Bankers Publishing Company, 1964.

Out of print and difficult to find, this book gives some helpful, common sense tips on writing clear, effective letters. The examples of letters in the book are out of date, but the section on the fundamentals of letter writing is useful for any banker.

*Seglin, Jeffrey L. *The AMA Handbook of Business Letters.* New York: AMACOM, 1989.

More than 270 model business letters for every general business occasion, plus tips on writing, grammar, and usage. Also available in disk format for IBM-compatible and Macintosh from Nova Development Corp. under the title *American Handbook of Business Letters* (Calabasas, California, 800-950-6682).

Shurter, Robert L. *Effective Letters in Business.* Second Edition. New York: McGraw-Hill, 1954.

Shurter's is one of the better general books on business letter writing. His style is clear, and he addresses most issues of letter writing from language to format. The examples in his book would probably not be very helpful to most bankers, but the first five chapters of *Effective Letters in Business* include sensible and helpful tips for the letter writer.

U.S. Postal Zip Code Directory. Canton, Massachusetts: Arrow Publishing Company, Inc. 1020 Turnpike Street 02021, 1974.

An inexpensive, useful addition to any secretary's bookshelf.

Grammar and Usage

*Bernstein, Theodore M. *The Careful Writer: A Modern Guide to English Usage.* New York: Atheneum, 1977.

One of the best books on usage around. Set up in dictionary format, Bernstein's book explains and clarifies language usage. *The Careful Writer* is more exhaustive than Strunk and White, and is a good reference book for all writers to have on their shelf.

The Chicago Manual of Style. Thirteenth Edition. Chicago: The University of Chicago Press, 1982.

An excellent reference on punctuation, spelling, abbreviations, footnotes, bibliographies, and more. *The Chicago Manual* is the bible of the publishing industry, but it can also be useful for anyone who writes.

Corbett, Edward P. J. *The Little English Handbook.* New York: John Wiley & Sons, 1973.

One of the best of the shorter handbooks on grammar and style available. Corbett's book is arranged in a helpful format that makes it a valuable reference for all writers.

**Grammar Hotline Directory.* Virginia Beach, Virginia, 1991.

Tidewater Community College publishes an annual update to the listings in the grammar hotline directory featured in appendix IV. For a free copy of this update, send a stamped, self-addressed envelope to *Grammar Hotline Directory,* Writing Center, Tidewater Community College, 1700 College Crescent, Virginia Beach, VA 23456.

Glorfeld, Louis E., David A. Lauerman, and Norman C. Stageberg. *A Concise Guide for Writers.* Third Edition. New York: Holt, Rinehart, and Winston, 1974.

Although *A Concise Guide* was written for students to help them overcome problems when writing compositions, it is useful as a simple grammar reference for most writers. The book is broken down into sections focusing on common flaws in writing and how to easily correct these flaws.

Miller, Casey, and Kate Swift. *The Handbook of Nonsexist Writing.* New York: Barnes and Noble Books, 1980.

For any writer seriously concerned with sexism in language, Miller and Swift's book is a helpful reference. Although some of their suggestions are, out of necessity, unorthodox, the book is one of the best on this topic available.

*Sabin, William A. *The Gregg Reference Manual, Sixth Edition.* New York: McGraw-Hill, 1985.

A wonderful reference that covers everything from punctuation, grammar, and usage to dictation, letters, and bibliography formats.

*Strunk, William, Jr., and E. B. White. *The Elements of Style.* Third Edition. New York: Macmillan, 1979.

Strunk and White is a good reference on usage and writing. It may not be as exhaustive as Bernstein's *The Careful Writer,* but it can be a saving grace when you are having problems with your writing.

*Warriner, John E., and Francis Griffith. *English Grammar and Composition.* Revised Edition. New York: Harcourt, Brace & World, 1965.

Warriner's is probably the handiest reference book on grammar around. Although it is a textbook, a copy can usually be found at a used bookstore. Warriner's should be on your reference shelf.

Zinsser, William. *On Writing Well.* New York: Harper & Row, 1976.

Although Zinsser's book is not helpful as a reference, it is useful, enjoyable reading for anyone interested in writing better.

Zinsser, William. *Writing with a Word Processor.* New York: Harper & Row, 1983.
For those of you who have a phobia about using a word processor, read this book. It is surprisingly nontechnical. Zinsser's whimsical look at the world of word processing is informative and entertaining. It's a quick read and wonderfully puts the mystique of word processors in perspective.

About the Author

Jeffrey L. Seglin is senior editor of *Inc.* magazine. A graduate of Harvard University and Bethany College, he has written an extensive array of books and articles on banking, marketing, and small business issues. He was consulting editor for WGBH-TV's 13-week personal finance series, *On the Money*. His articles on financial matters have appeared in *Inc., Venture, Adweek's Marketing Week, Boston* magazine, and *USA Today*. Seglin has worked on marketing projects for organizations including Shawmut Bank, Digital Computer, and The New England. He is the author of *Financing Your Small Business, The McGraw-Hill 36-Hour Marketing Course, The AMA Handbook of Business Letters*, and other books. He lives in Boston.

THE BANKER'S HANDBOOK OF LETTERS AND LETTER WRITING SOFTWARE

SAVE TIME & MONEY!!!

Welcome to *The Banker's Handbook of Letters and Letter Writing Software*! With instant letters for every banking situation, you're sure to find the right letter to be persuasive and effective and to generate desired results.

The disk consists of the actual letters in the book in ASCII format so they can be used by any word processing package.

It will save you time because you can load the letters into your word processing package and easily modify them for your own use.

The disk is available at $55 and readers can choose between two sizes:

5-1/4" or 3-1/2"

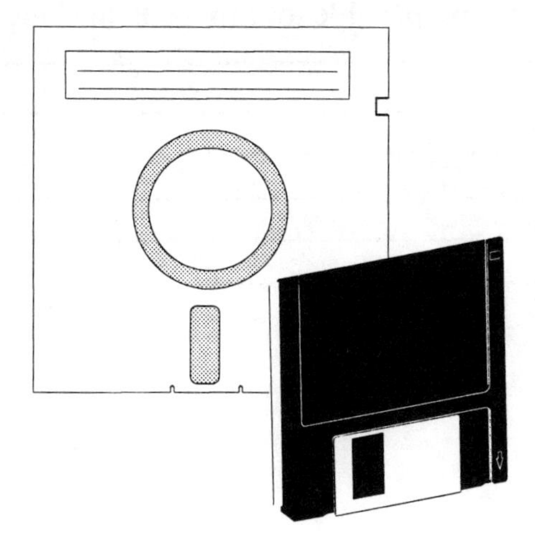

Please enter my order for ___ disk(s) for ***The Banker's Handbook of Letters and Letter Writing Software.***

(Check One)

___ 5-1/4" (Order No. L341) ___ 3-1/2" (Order No. L342)

Call: 1-800-PROBUS-1

Mail Orders to:

PROBUS PUBLISHING COMPANY
1925 N. Clybourn Avenue, Ste. 401
Chicago, IL 60614

Fax:

312/868-6250

Card Number ____________________________ Exp. Date ____________
(Mastercard/Visa/American Express Accepted)

Signature ____

Make checks payable to: Probus Publishing Company

Name ____
Firm ____
Title ____
Address ____
City, State & Zip ______________________________________
Phone ____